Joan Bingham

Noted wine authority Herbert Baus is the author of a nationally distributed wine newsletter. His favorite wines include California wine, French burgundy, and German moselle.

How to Wine Your Way to Good Health

WINE INSTITUTE LIBRARY

How to WINE Your Way to Good Health

Herbert M. Baus

Foreword by Harold C. Torbert, M.D.

Mason & Lipscomb PUBLISHERS   NEW YORK

To Sir Winston Churchill—
man of the twentieth century

ACKNOWLEDGMENTS

The author wishes to thank the people who assisted him with this book. Massive research help was extended by Harry Serlis, President of the Wine Institute; San Francisco's wine and alcoholism authority Milton Silverman, Ph.D.; wine writer and medical expert Salvatore Pablo Lucia, M.D., Professor Emeritus of the University of California School of Medicine and Medical Research Director of the Wine Advisory Board; Leon D. Adams, wine consultant and author; Evelyn Morris and Mlle. Laurence Goud de Beaupuis, who helped me with my research in France; Dr. Everhard Ludemann of Nurburgring, who organized my research in Germany; and Bart Sheridan, an editor of *Medical Economics,* who contributed ideas, insights, medical research, and editorial help.

Special help came from vintners Robert Mondavi, Karl Wente, Joe Concannon, Jimmy Nichelini, Brother Timothy, Sam Sebastiani, Steve Riboli, Louis Martini, and Peter Friedman; wine consultant Lou Gomberg; wine publicists Ted Berland, Roy Taylor, Margrit Biever, Dean Jennings, and Gregg Reynolds; Napa Valley sheriff Earl Randol; researcher Ed Canapery; and librarians Joan Ingalls, Kay Chadwick, and Louisa Cagwin.

For their help in France I thank M. Patrick Lechesne; M. Charles Quittanson; M. Goud de Beaupuis of Savigny de Beaune; M. Bertrand Mure; Dr. Brun Despagne; M. J. M. Courteau, Bordeaux's wine and health sage Dr. J. M. Eylaud; and Bordeaux's wine entrepreneur and author Ed Kressmann. Special thanks for their hospitality to the Chevaliers des Tastevins of Clos de Vougeot.

For their help in Germany I thank Dr. Edith Kayser, Fritz Dahl, Bernard Breuer, Dr. H. Sambale, and Ida Larkin of the American Red Cross, who drove us throughout the Rhine and Mosel wine country and was our hostess while in Germany.

Special help was extended by personal friends, including Robert T. Hartmann, Harold Keen, J. Howard McCallum, Michael Parker, Charles O'Brien, John Knox, Pete Sandford, Mike Mazzei, Frank Cullen, and William F. Taylor.

Books, articles, publications, reprints, and interviews by the hundreds were marshaled and analyzed in the process of creating this book. Special mention and commendation is due four authors: Dr. Salvatore P. Lucia of San Francisco, Dr. Morris E. Chafetz of Boston, Dr. J. M. Eylaud of Bordeaux, and Dr. Heinrich Kliewe of Mainz.

My deepest thanks also to my editor, Peter V. Ritner; my publisher, Tom Lipscomb; my literary associate, C. M. Vandeburg; my translators, Birgit Huneck and Franklin Attoun; my typist, Elsie Cromwell and Joanne Landry; and my chief critic, consultant, and inspiration, Helene W. Baus.

HERBERT M. BAUS

Foreword

When I first heard the title *How to Wine Your Way to Good Health,* my conservatism, as a physician, regarding all therapeutic claims made the title seem a doubtful one to me. However, as one trained by his father since childhood in the proper—that is, the moderate—use of alcohol, and as the owner of a wine cellar for nearly forty years, I was interested. I met Herbert Baus and agreed to read his manuscript. I am glad that I did!

Writing with the enthusiasm of a man twice convinced, Mr. Baus has produced a book which no one without a long acquaintance with wine would have written. The fact that the author is convinced by a good deal of evidence that his new regimen has saved his life, as well as increased his pleasure in it, adds zeal to the enthusiasm brought to the subject.

Mr. Baus's book is a sensible and well-documented plea for moderation, not only in the use of alcohol but also in most other aspects of life. At the same time the book provides a persuasive insight into the pleasures, personal and social, which the intelligent use of wine can bring to every human being for whom its consumption is not contraindicated.

The author's own opinions are buttressed with as thorough a review of the written material on the subject as I have ever read. Extensive quotations indicate that he is familiar with nearly everything that has been printed on the medicinal uses and the joys of wine drinking. Wise physicians throughout the ages have used wine to warm the old, to soothe the distraught, and to help ease the pain of many diseases.

Although the blight of Prohibition put this traditional and pleasant medicine in eclipse for a generation, an increasing number of hospitals and physicians are finding in wine the same uses which have retained it in the list of useful remedies for thirty centuries.

All of the study and work on the part of the author would

have been in vain, if he had not presented his findings with intelligence and a lightness of touch which clothes his scholarship with appealing humor. But the humor and lightness of this book do not make it shallow. It is a serious account of how one busy American found in his middle years that his body was sending out distress signals, caused by a classical constellation of wrong ways of living. Too much work done too fast, too many fatty foods eaten in too great a hurry, and too much hard liquor brought him illness.

Not every successful American is fortunate enough to have a competent and sensible medical adviser when trouble catches up with him. Herbert Baus did. He was persuaded to lose weight, and to eat less fatty food and less salt. And, at first with no great enthusiasm, he began to drink a little wine in place of the cocktails he was used to. His experience when he did this can be duplicated by anyone who in good faith switches from the numbing blows of alcohol in concentrated doses to the gentle caress of wine.

If you have ever wondered what all the fuss was about as you listened to your wine-loving friends talk about their favorite subject, this book will tell you. If childhood conditioning in American Puritanism has led you to worry about the use of wine at the table or in cooking, it will reassure you. The triumph of Mr. Baus's book is that he makes his pleas for moderation and his description of the joys of sensible wine drinking with wit and grace.

If you choose, as Herbert Baus did, to join the happy fraternity of wine lovers, the most sensible of men, you will embark on a new way of living. This book can lead you pleasantly to the delights of wine—the most interesting, delicious, and harmless of alcoholic beverages. And most wine drinkers choose moderation in the enjoyment of food, in the work they do for a living, and in other aspects of life.

"Nothing in excess" was the motto of the ancient Athenians. That these proud and imaginative men did not always live by their own rule detracts nothing from its validity. This motto is still a sensible human being's best path. And I am convinced that as many celestial demerits will be chalked up against the person who witlessly denies himself the good things of life as will be charged to those who abuse themselves by gluttony—an excess of food, of drink, or of work. Herbert Baus is an entertain-

ing as well as reliable guide to that middle way. He knows, with
Montaigne, that wine is "the benevolent god who gives back
gaiety to men and restores youth to the old."

HAROLD C. TORBERT, M.D.

Contents

꧁꧂꧁꧂꧁꧂꧁꧂

Disclaimer

If you become an alcoholic or otherwise cause yourself injury by drinking wine, neither the author nor the publisher is responsible. We do not presume in any way to be your doctor, nor to supplement him, nor to gainsay him. We invite, even urge you to consult him if you have any questions about these matters. There are specific conditions where wine may be harmful. Your doctor is the best judge of whether such a situation exists in your case.

If you use reasonable good sense in taking advantage of one of the oldest and still most pleasing creations of mankind, your life can be immeasurably enriched and the odds are that you will improve your health. Judge wine's application to your own case and on your own responsibility, knowing only that it has helped far more than it has harmed.

How to Wine Your Way to Good Health

Introduction

❧❧❧❧❧❧❧❧❧

> Wine is the only pleasure known to me that is neither
> illegal, immoral, nor fattening; although the world
> is full of unfortunates who think it is all three.

Frankly, drinking for *health* never entered my mind until a few years ago when—in my middle fifties—a harsh interview with the family doctor convinced me that the time had come to seek something that was good for my health but which also might prop my morale.

Until then I suppose my attitude coincided with that of Allan Meltzer, the co-owner of Château Bouscaut, his Bordeaux escape from the miseries of Manhattan and the American megalopolitan grind.

"While my interest in wine is passionate and of some long standing," he wrote to me, "I confess that I have not given much, if any, thought to its relationship to health. To me, its production is man's work at its best and its consumption is one of the joys of life. I have always felt that that was enough to ask of anything and it never occurred to me to concern myself in terms of health, good or bad. If I had given it any thought it would have been that if wine is good for me, well fine, I am absorbing great quantities of it. And if wine is bad for me, I would not want to hear about it because I want nothing to interfere with this particular pleasure."

That probably speaks for most of us. But what happens when many of life's pleasures and the capacity to partake of them begin waning with the ruthless erosion of time, and suddenly one's favorite satisfactions are bundled up and summarily kicked out of one's life?

It started one night when, fortified with perhaps more than my wonted ration of martinis, I took my old poodle, Diesel, out for his evening stroll. I didn't get home, but Diesel did. My wife

1

panicked and came out beating the bushes for me. She found me in the bushes, knocked out cold. With the help of a young neighbor she got me home and to bed, rather well-banged up from having projected myself into a brick wall—probably from slipping on a manhole cover on our steep hill, although no one will ever know exactly what did happen that night.

The next day I had to face my doctor. After a long, re-assuring series of routine physical examinations which had invariably ended with the verdict, "You are as salubrious as a college athlete," the doctor said, "Your blood pressure and cholesterol are outrageously high, and some changes must be made." The businessman's syndrome had caught up with me at last. It could have been cancer or cirrhosis of the liver. Taking a constructive view of things, I chose to be somewhat relieved.

Some doctors are not adept at communicating. They just utter the vile news and leave you hanging there. Mine explained that blood pressure can have a dozen origins. It can stem from an organic disorder: kidneys, liver, heart, or whatever. It can be the penalty of dietetic indulgence; or it can result from what he called a "secondary nervous system," which "turns on" under pressure. In my case it was primarily a reaction to the constant and sometimes overwhelming pressures of my decades of political campaign management.

Popping pills could spell temporary relief, and he prescribed some. But the real solution for my dangerous blood pressure and cholesterol count was a more orderly existence, stressing a mandatory weight loss of thirty pounds. That spelled diet:

Eliminate salt. I used to drench my food in it—and mar-garitas with the lip of the glass smothered in salt was a staple of my good life.

Eliminate fats such as butter, the most flavorful cheeses, pork, processed meats, especially sausages, and the organ meats such as liver, brains, kidney, and sweetbreads.

Eliminate large breakfasts. A breakfast worth the name included bacon and eggs, or sausage and omelet, or pancakes smothered in butter and floating in maple syrup—with buttered toast or sweet rolls or both. Never more. That left fruit juice, yogurt, and maybe some cereal.

Eliminate desserts and sweets. Butter rolls, pastry and pie, cookies and cake, doughnuts and muffins, chocolate and cream. Fortunately, I was not much of a dessert man but I would fre-quently have a plateful of ice cream before the cocktail hour.

Throw away the frying pan. Frying increases the fat content of any food. French fries, fried chicken, fried eggs, and bacon were just a few of life's precious treats I was about to forego.

Add plenty of low-calorie foods. These included fruit, yogurt, skim milk, green vegetables, and salads, and chicken, fish, and lean meats—spartanly cooked. Cottage cheese is great, but it can't compete with ice cream.

Watch quantities; no more second helpings. Cut down the portion size. A serving of spaghetti is not two cups, it's one.

Beware of the "beautiful embellishments." A baked potato has 136 calories. A tablespoon of butter adds 100, almost doubling the damage. So skip the butter or sour cream. Try the potato with chives alone. A slice of bread has about 62 calories, depending on the type. A pat of butter adds 36, and a teaspoon of jelly piles on 16 more. A serving of asparagus contains 26 calories. The hollandaise sauce adds 191 more. A wedge of lettuce has 14 calories; the mayonnaise, 101 more. A cup of coffee has 5 calories. The cream adds 32 and the sugar 32, for a total of 69.

And so it goes. The "beautiful embellishments" wait in ambush. Whatever tastes better fattens more, so dismiss it.

My doctor saved the best news for the last. "You will never lose all that weight drinking hard liquor, so no more hard liquor." He delivered this haymaker in an impromptu little speech that I shall remember the rest of my life: "We are not talking about a six-day diet or a six-week diet. This will not solve your problem if you lapse into your old intake habits. This is for the duration. You are starting a new way of life, and it is to go all the way—if you want there to be a ways to go."

For all my years remembered I have reveled in the joys of the plate and the cup. I had been celebrated by friend and foe alike as a redoubtable indulger—concerned neither with discrimination nor capacity. Here was a cherished and cultivated pattern of living forever wiped out in one sweeping monologue by a determined doctor who laced his language with the somber syllables "or else."

Since my earliest boyhood I had been one-half blind and one-third deaf and had compensated for these shortcomings by taking solace in food and drink. To have the arena of taste also placed off limits smacked of the catastrophic.

It is the summit of stupidity to seek a professional's help if

ARISTOTLE SAYS: DON'T STOP NOW!

. . . In his *Problems* Aristotle declared that it is very dangerous for one who has habituated himself to heavy drinking to stop his tippling. To prove this statement Aristotle mentions Dionysius the Younger who ceased drinking after years of intemperance. He straightaway fell into a consumption which disappeared when he took up drinking again.

---

you are not going to heed his advice. When you upstage the doctor's orders you are not just kissing off a few votes; you may be entering the decisive precincts of life and death. But drop salt, fats, pork, sweets, the frying pan, martinis . . . what was left?

I had always prided myself on resilience, and now the solution hit me in a flash: switch to wine. But not just a glass or two. Drink all the wine I wanted. I would still be following the doctor's orders. Mercifully, if not intentionally, he had specified no more *hard* liquor.

I thought it best not to get into any dialogue with my doctor. You can ask too many questions, especially if you know your doctor is prejudiced against alcohol in any form for personal reasons. Besides, the regimen he had laid down was sufficiently draconian. So why not experiment and live a little? It might work. If it didn't, I would cross that bridge when I came to it. If it did work, the result would not only be a joy saver for me, it could be a boon to others. I decided to sacrifice myself.

For one accustomed over many years to three or four cock-tails before dinner and a flagon of wine with dinner to aid digestion (and conversation), and sometimes more of the same program for lunch, all the wine I wanted could mean up to two big bottles or more a day. However, it also would mean far less alcohol than before. My new drink was to be strictly table wine— 7 to 12 percent alcoholic content, not the sweet 20 percent wine —before, during, and after meals.

My weight sank as dramatically as the barometer with the approach of a storm. Every few weeks I reported to my doctor, who was both incredulous and elated as my progress registered on the scales. In four months I had shed thirty pounds. My blood pressure and my cholesterol went down with my weight and I was pronounced on all three counts to be within the high range of normal. All without missing a glass of wine in 120 days.

After this achievement, I had dinner one night with my doctor and his son and their families. The cat was bound to get out of the bag, and it did that night. After I left the doctor said, "Son, how can Herbert lose weight drinking all that wine?"

"Dad, the fact is he has already lost weight and keeps it lost drinking all that wine."

And no more has been heard about it since. After all, many years have passed and I have kept the weight off and kept the blood pressure and cholesterol down. There was much more to it than weight loss. Wine was proving itself not only an effective tranquilizer but a highly civilized one and the tastiest one on the market.

Do I miss the cocktail before meals? Not at all. A little *vin ordinaire,* perhaps over rocks, tastes just as good. Maybe better. In fact, I've been converting a lot of my friends.

All this suggests that I am pushing wine, and maybe I am. Why not? If my experience can offer to others a part of the good feeling it has brought to me, I'd like to share the message. I do not say you should not obey your doctor's orders. You'd be a fool not to. But only a fool swallows the orders of another mortal—even one with a medical degree—without evaluating them. I did evaluate, and applied my needs and the doctor's instructions to his words, "*hard* liquor."

Let me call to your attention that sometimes in this book I write (and quote others) about *alcohol,* and at other times about *wine.* Wine contains about three hundred ingredients, of which alcohol is only one, though the most important one. Therefore, much that is true about alcohol is also true about wine. Where the information or the quotation concerns alcohol I present it if the data is also germane to wine.

It cannot be said too often, that while wine is good, too much of it can be as bad for you as too little of it. Of course, wine cannot be an infallible solution to all the hazards of existence. But maybe wine can add a few years to that existence. And maybe wine can even add a bit of happiness to those years. I have seen dozens of books on how alcohol hurts for every one on how it helps. Since the latter are so rare, I decided to write one on how wine helps.

Wine has helped my health. It might help yours.

That is my story, with all the backup I could find in some serious research.

1

A Grape Way to Go—
Vignettes of History

Imagine the discovery of a substance that is sweeter smelling than roses and more seductive to the taste than nectar but is versatile enough to unshackle the human spirit from the grip of reality while capable of doing a number of other specific and practical things for you at the same time:

Do you need a germ killer, inside or out? X is an antibiotic.

Do you have heart problems? X as a vasodilator speeds the blood's flow and loosens up the coagulation of cholesterol.

Do you have a weight problem? X helps on several counts to combat obesity.

How is your appetite? X can accentuate or restore it and help you regulate its results.

Are you uptight? X is one of the gentlest, safest, surest, most savory sedatives known to man.

Are you bored, tired, distraught, unhappy? X can make the world seem and be a better place to live in.

Are you morose, sullen, antisocial? X will get you and your friends chatting and will keep you all that way for a pleasant evening.

Are you getting old? X can do much to alleviate the distresses of aging.

Imagine a substance that can do the gut things for you that hard liquor or hard drugs can do—and with a minimal tendency to addiction, allergy, satiety, or hangover.

Dr. William Dock, who originally envisaged the hypothetical impact of such a miracle drug newly sprung from a creative

7

modern laboratory, added that "humanity would be benefited for untold thousands of years."

Yet this miracle drug is already with us. It is called wine, and it has existed for five thousand to thirty thousand years (nobody knows how long). And, to paraphrase Dr. Dock, it has been performing these benefactions to mankind, often under doctors' orders, for all these millennia. It is as popular as ever in Europe, the Middle East, North Africa, and Latin America, where its contribution to good living has been accepted since the earliest times. But wine is just beginning to make its big move in the United States, where it enjoys a modest boom in some sophisticated metropolitan regions, mostly near the coasts, although it is still little known and largely unavailable in about 80 percent of the country.

Over the ages since it was discovered, alcohol has been used more often, and in greater volume than any other drug ever known. Wine is the oldest, the gentlest, the most civilized, and the most beneficial of all alcoholic beverages. Just how old is this stuff? When and how did it start? And who was its discoverer? No one seems to know, although there must be more than a few anonymous candidates for this honor. But the Chinese have an answer with a legend about how wine was invented for human health.

Many thousands of years ago the Emperor Yu devoted eight years of almost uninterrupted hard labor to fighting a succession of floods—instead of spending most of his time and energy figuring out how to get reelected, as rulers were to do centuries after his time.

Yu became a Chinese symbol for conscientiousness and was said during his ordeal never to have entered his own home and to have passed its threshold only three times.

The emperor worried so much about the continuing catastrophe that he could barely eat or sleep. The effects of this strain preyed upon him to the point that it was undermining his health.

Yi Tieh, a lady of the court, became increasingly upset as she observed her beloved emperor worrying himself to death.

One day, the legend goes, he pushed aside his rice bowl and chopsticks and complained, "I feel terrible. I can't eat. My appetite has vanished." Suddenly he smelled something as fragrant as the breath of spring. It was a preparation of Yi Tieh's, which she urged upon him.

The emperor then unwittingly indulged in history's first wine tasting. At least it was Chinese legend's first wine tasting. The inevitable happened. He liked it. He ordered a cupful. It released him from the clutches of his nerves. He ordered another cupful, several in fact. He felt better—better than he had felt in years. His appetite returned. He attacked his meal with zest. With it he drank more wine, cupful after cupful, as his cares were vanquished for the first time in many seasons.

After that, wine became a staple in the royal household. The recipe spread to the outside world. And mankind has benefited ever since.

But how did Yi Tieh conjure up one of the most important inventions in the lifespan of humanity? The Chinese have a backup legend to explain that, too.

In the Forbidden City lived the Jade Girl, more excitingly named the Jade Concubine, who earlier in life had been a servant to a goddess in a distant western paradise. The story goes that she brought the formula for wine from this paradise and committed it to Yi Tieh—although why she would arrange for a potential rival to receive the imperial credit for such a panacea is not clarified.

There is a little more to the story. The Jade Concubine is said to reappear even today. As late as 1946, she was reported to have been seen by a former attendant of the last Manchu empress, Tu Hsi. On beholding the Jade Concubine drifting through the palace hallway carrying a wine jar, the symbol of her identity, the attendant swooned and could not be revived for two days.

Cynics have been known to say this account is as good a description of a hangover as any. Certainly the whole legend, ascribing the discovery of wine to the vital needs of a ruler of a wise and ancient people, is as likely a story of wine's origin as we can hope to find anywhere.

The Persians have a myth which, if less venerable, is as

OLD CHINESE PROVERBS

Three cups of wine will settle everything and a drinking bout will dissipate a thousand cares.

If you satisfy your thirst you will overcome your troubles.

---

pertinent in traditionally linking wine with human health. It is about a consort of a Persian king who sought to kill herself with an unknown poison only to find in it an unexpected source of joy and sustenance.

It seems that king Jemsheed of Persia was fond of grapes and had not yet learned how much a mere grape can be improved by fermentation. He became accustomed to storing his grapes in jars so there would be enough for him to eat the year around. He was somewhat upset when, upon reaching for some of his favorite fruit, he found a seething, swirling liquid mass. Terrified that an evil spirit had somehow bewitched his beloved fruit, but unable to bear the thought of throwing it out, he labeled the bubbling jars "poison" and departed to solace his aching heart in his harem.

As can happen in a harem, one of the lovely inmates was sorry for herself because of comparative neglect. Her feelings had escalated into nervous headaches until she preferred suicide to such a pointless life. To this end she steadfastly engulfed some of her master's "poison." But instead of a funeral she had a siesta and awoke refreshed. She lost no time conducting a renewed assault upon the magical jar, and soon became fortified with enough courage to confront the king with news of her miraculous experience.

For discovering what grapes can really do for mankind, our heroine was readily elevated to top rank in the harem, and suffered no more from either tension or neglect. Wine is still known in Persia as "the delightful poison." Perhaps the old American invitation, "Name your poison . . ." emerged from this source.

We see that two of the world's most venerable cultures mythologize wine coming into being as a boon to health—and moreover, being discovered by woman, the giver of life.

In ancient India, wine was worshiped as a god named Soma. The Aryan conquerors of India excelled in the healing arts, pioneered in surgery, practiced bloodletting, and prescribed diets, baths, gargles, emetics, and inhalations.

Early Hindu surgeons used Soma to mitigate pain, and an ancient Sanskrit textbook advised, "The patient should be given to eat what he wishes and wine to drink before the operation, so that he may not faint and may not feel the knife."

The ancient Aryan religious lore are known as the Vedas.

Oldest of them all is the Rig-Veda, entirely devoted to the god Soma, crediting the god with great medicinal and joy-giving power:

> We have drunk the Soma, we have become
> immortal, we have arrived at the light,
> we have found the gods.

> Like a wise friend to a friend, O Expansive
> One, Amplify, O Soma, our lives for the
> purpose of living.

> May the waters guard my foot from slipping,
> and may the drops preserve us from sickness.

> O Soma, King, prolong our lifetimes, as the
> sun prolongs the days in spring.

While the exact source and composition of Soma is unknown and has been a bone of controversy among Oriental scholars for centuries, San Francisco's medical sage of wine, Dr. Salvatore Lucia, wrote: "At some point in Vedic history, the medicinal powers of Soma became attributed directly to wine, since the Rig-Veda speaks of wine as though it shared alike the powers of Soma."

In the Rig-Veda, "the god Soma heals whatever is sick," and "makes the blind see and lame walk." Soma is divine, purifies, confers health and immortality, and paves the way to heaven.

The Veda medical text, Ayur-Veda, described as the most ancient system of medicine, includes the Charaka Samhita, which deals with wine. Referring to wine as the "invigorator of mind and body, antidote to sleeplessness, sorrow and fatigue . . . producer of hunger, happiness, and digestion," the work declared that wine "acts as Amrita [Soma], it cures the natural flow of internal fluids of the body."

The Charaka Samhita eulogized wine as "worshiped with the Gods . . . the destroyer of sorrow, fear and anxiety . . . who is pleasure, happiness, and nourishment."

The Tantras lists five important elements of worship including wine, which is called the god-beverage with the power of Soma: "The Supreme Being is liquid form . . . the great medicine of humanity." Wine aids in the forgetting of deep sorrows and is "the cause of great joy . . . the mother of enjoyment and liberation." The god Soma was said to make the blind see, the lame walk, and the sick well.

The Bible and the Talmud keynoted the vital role of wine in the ancient Hebrew world. "Give strong drink unto him that is ready to perish, and wine unto those that be of heavy hearts," says the Book of Proverbs. (Scholars agree that "strong drink" in the Bible means undiluted wine.) "Let him drink, and forget his poverty and remember his misery no more." According to the Talmud, "Wine nourishes, refreshes, and cheers. Wine is the foremost of all medicines; wherever wine is lacking, medicines become necessary." Wine became the sacramental drink. In the tabernacle, the temple, and also in the modern synagogue, wine is blessed, and the children sip from the cup after the prayer of blessing which ushers in the Sabbath.

The Greeks and Romans originated the custom of drinking to the health of their benefactors and friends. Perhaps Dionysius of Eubulus started this tradition when he wrote in *Vinous Decalogue* that the first cup belongs to health.

The British philosopher Roger Bacon added insight to this happy ritual when, being invited to drink to the health of the king, he crisply rejoined, "I'll pray for the king's health and drink for my own."

Plato de Legibus said, "Among the Romans wine was considered as a medicine, and was given that the soul might acquire modesty and the body health and vigor. It was also believed that Bacchus had bestowed wine upon men as a remedy against the austerities of old age, that through this we might acquire a second youth, forget sorrow, and the manners of the mind be rendered softer, as iron is softened by the action of the fire."

No matter where you travel in Europe, you will find that the wine tradition goes back to the Romans. In sunny Spain, in France's Burgundy or Bordeaux, in Yugoslavia or Hungary, in Romania or on the Rhine and Mosel, and of course all over

An accident it cannot be
That men have toasted "health"
From century to century
And to it, drank their wealth!

Italy, it was all started by the Romans. The great wine industries of California, Australia, and South Africa hence owe their origins to the same peripatetic Romans.

There are some who say that whenever the Romans conquered a barbaric land in Europe, they deliberately taught the natives to make wine. Not only did this keep the peasants busy with the rigors of viniculture, but an extra dividend of the subsequent wine tastings was that the natives were no longer so restless.

The Roman conquerers in the already civilized areas of Greece, the Middle East, Egypt, and North Africa found the peoples long acquainted with the techniques and virtues of wine. That is, of course, where the Romans got the idea in the first place. The Romans, like the Japanese, didn't have to invent an idea to be masterful in its application and distribution. And the wine lovers of the West can thank them today.

2

❧❧❧❧❧❧❧

To Drink or Not to Drink

Ah, make the most of what we yet may spend,
Before we too into the Dust descend,
    Dust unto Dust, and under Dust, to lie,
Sans Wine, sans Song, sans Singer, and—sans End!

OMAR KHAYYAM

Born I was to be old,
    And for to die here.
After that, in the mould,
    Long for to lye here.

But before that day comes,
    Still I be Bousing;
For I know, in the tombs
    There's no carousing.

ROBERT HERRICK

The Anatomy of Alcohol

More nonsense has been written, spoken, committed, and legislated about alcohol than about any other substance to emerge from the laboratories during the long history of human folly.

There is as much misinformation, misunderstanding, and mythology about alcohol as about religion and politics. What we do not understand, we tend to shout about. Alcohol has a way of bringing out the best and the worst in us—in ways we cannot comprehend.

"The human condition being what it is," recorded Edward

Hyams, "only a very small number of very primitive tribes at the very lowest economic level have failed to develop some intoxicant to help them face the facts of life." Civilized men have always and will always find some way to manufacture liquor.

To be blunt, we are all born into a hell of a mess and nothing else we have found helps us to put up with it better than alcohol. We really don't know why, which could be a blessing; but what is so is so, and so be it.

Once alcohol has been established, seldom has a society rejected it. History has shown that an invention or custom will not survive and spread unless it does man some good. Alcohol does many things for man, of which the biggest overall good seems to be the boon of providing him with "an occasional release from the intolerable clutch of reality," as Berton Roueche crisply wrote in *The New Yorker*.

More esoteric was the language of William James: "The sway of alcohol over mankind is unquestionably due to its power to stimulate the mystical faculties. It brings its votary from the chill periphery of things to the radiant core. It makes him for the moment one with the truth. Not through mere perversity do men run after it."

Socrates told us, "So far as drinking is concerned, gentlemen, you have my approval. Wine moistens the soul and lulls our griefs to sleep while it also awakens kindly feelings."

Or, in the less masterful language of the twentieth-century academic, Robert Straus, behavioral sciences chairman at the University of Kentucky's Medical School, advanced political-sociological approval of drinking as a lubricant which breaks down the walls between groups: "Drinking facilitates communication between members of different statuses within the same social system, which in turn strengthens informal norms, relaxes the rigors of bureaucracy, and contributes to the smooth functioning of the social system."

What this world could use is a little more "what-the-hell-ism." We take life too seriously. I have never met a man with a sense of humor who was a bad man. I have seldom met a man with a sense of humor who lacked an appetite and a penchant for alcohol, for drinking is the handmaiden to a sense of humor. "A man cannot make him laugh," Shakespeare wrote of a character, adding, "but that's no marvel; he drinks no wine." History offers us something to think about when it tells us that of all the

leaders of nations the only one who stands out as strident teetotaler was Adolf Hitler.

What is all the shouting about? Why does this Dr.-Jekyll-
and-Mr.-Hyde substance, which has so many quiet devotees,
also have so many cacophonous critics? And why do not those
who disapprove of alcohol just go their quiet way and let the
rest of us live in peace with our particular tastes?

Dr. Giorgio Lolli wrote, "Usually . . . investigations have
been planned with the goal of finding whether, when, and how
alcohol does harm—not finding what alcohol does or whether,
when, and how alcohol may help." He pointedly added that
often such research is done with pure ethyl alcohol dissolved in
water, which is to wine as a bomb is to a shotgun.

"The admonitions against alcohol are unbelievable, and
date from antiquity," wrote Dr. Morris E. Chafetz. "If you drink,
some say, you'll become an alcoholic or a drunkard. At the very
least, your life will be shortened, or you will become illegit-
imately pregnant, or commit a crime, damage your brain, become an addict, smash your car, or otherwise go to pot. The
evils that spirits, beer, and wine portend are horrendous. Hide
the bottle from your kids, make special laws for its use, don't
let it go through the mails, and for heaven's sake don't advertise
it. Mind you, all this we deliberate, determine, and decide even
as we imbibe alcohol in great quantities."

Dr. Chafetz has held positions with the Harvard faculty,
the federal Department of Health, Education and Welfare, and
is a leader in the government's war against alcoholism as the
first director of the National Institute on Alcohol Abuse and
Alcoholism. He laid his impeccable medical credentials on the
line with some points of interest to any student or partaker of
alcohol in his beguilingly titled *Liquor: The Servant of Man*.

1. By focusing on the negative aspects, we tend to overlook the positive pleasures of alcohol as a social tool.
2. Alcoholism is a major health problem. Alcohol is not.
3. Pasteur said wine is the most hygienic and healthful
   of beverages and fermentation is correlative with life.
4. There is no sound evidence whatsoever that alcohol
   causes permanent direct damage to the body, or by
   itself causes any disease.
5. Many more people who drink alcohol do not commit
   crimes than do. Many people commit crimes who have
   not been near a bottle.

6. Whenever an activity enjoys widespread and continuous acceptance, it must have a practical meaning and use. Drinking has been so thoroughly accepted that there can be a little argument about its importance to people.

7. There has always been and will always be a need for some agent by which man can alter his inner being in relation to his environment.

8. The more brainy, vigorous, and intense the individual, the greater the need for both rest and stimulation.

9. If liquor can help overcome minor miseries, strengthen enthusiasm, and restore unity and freedom of flow, humans would be fools to ignore it as an aid to civilization.

10. Alcohol is one of the most valuable medicines in the world, especially in old age and in chronic illness.

11. Alcohol is a prime medium for permitting man to forget the shortness of life and the infinitesimal role he plays in the universe.

12. Alcohol has existed longer than all human memory.

The effect of alcohol on the human organism is subject to endless variables. The effects of alcohol taken on an empty stomach are far different from those produced by the same volume of alcohol taken with food. The effects on a light drinker can differ from those on a heavy drinker. The effects produced by the same amount differ for each individual In the same individual they differ from one day or one month to the next, depending on all the constantly changing attendant circum-

---

WHAT IS ALL THE SHOUTING ABOUT?

There is a lack of evidence that either the temporary or prolonged use of alcohol, even in large doses, is the specific or sole cause of any disease.

HARRISON MARTLAND

A man must drink rather a lot before alcohol is seriously harmful to him . . . the consumption of a little alcohol daily may even be a beneficial practice.

MILES WEATHERALL

stances. The amount of alcohol found in the body after drinking is primarily the result of interplay between three processes: absorption of the alcohol from the gastrointestinal tract; distribution of the alcohol by the bloodstream to various organs and body fluids; rate of disappearance of the alcohol through excretion (2 percent to 5 percent) mainly by kidneys or metabolic breakdown (oxidization: 95 percent to 98 percent).

Absorption depends on

- Whether you're drinking 151 proof Demerara rum or 3.2 proof beer or something in between.
- What chemicals other than alcohol are in your drink. For example, vodka and gin get to you rather in a hurry because they're much closer to pure alcohol than some other distilled liquors. When you're drinking beer or wine you're taking on both alcohol and a banquet and your absorption is much slower than hard liquor either straight or mixed.
- Whether you're eating while drinking. If you are, the food is doing a lot of the absorbing—relieving pressure on your liver and other organs. If you are drinking wine with your meal, everything—the wine and the food—will taste better, too. And alcohol concentration in the blood may be reduced by as much as 50 percent.
- How fast you drink. Slurp it down rapidly enough and it's something like hitting yourself on the head with an ax—sip it and it's more like caressing yourself.
- The emptying time of your stomach, and this can depend on all kinds of circumstances, including fear, anger, stress, nausea, stomach condition—in fact, your physical history for the preceding hours, days, weeks.
- Your body weight. Most of us think we weigh too much, and probably with good reason, but the more we weigh the more alcohol we can handle.

Once your system has absorbed alcohol, you're stuck with it until it has been oxidized or metabolized—which means burned and ejected from your body. This is mainly the job of your liver. If your liver is in good shape it will dissipate the alcohol at the rate of about one ounce per hour. Neither deep breathing, black coffee, saunas, calisthenics, nor any other capers or chemicals so far known to mankind will speed the process—

which is why sleep is the safest as well as most sensible follow-up to a bit of imbibing. It keeps you out of harm's way until your liver does its work.

Moderation

Every wine writer, every wine columnist, every doctor, every vintner—just about every pundit of any kind who advises you to drink wine or other alcohol adds that inevitable disclaimer —*with moderation.*

But what is moderation? What it is *not* is abstinence. Abstinence and alcoholism are the two extremes; moderation is the middle way, the good way in drinking as in politics. Moderation is an individual thing, much as the woman you love or the size of your shoes or the tone of your voice or your mannerisms. Moderation to one man is a glass; to another, a bottle. A bottle to one man is a pint; to another a magnum. Your size, your tolerance, your capacity, your hangover range, your age, your very mood at the time of drinking all help you measure it—and only you can measure it.

Goethe, even when taking the cure at Carlsbad, interpreted moderation to be two liters of wine a day. Brillat-Savarin considered that a healthy man could live long if he drank two bottles of wine a day—and when asked if he liked grapes, replied, "I prefer not to take my wine in pill form." The peasants of Languedoc required three bottles of wine a day to keep them going, but this was commonplace and examples of greater capacity are not rare.

Dr. Samuel Johnson revealed that he daily drank three bottles of port at University College, Oxford, and was none the worse for it. Dr. Alex Webster, Boswell's uncle by marriage, consumed five bottles of claret each day. The poet James Thomson was obliged by his guests to agree that the allowance of one meal should be one bottle a head but, regarding this as a niggardly amount, he placed a three-quart bottle before each man. General Bisson of France was cited if not decorated by Brillat-Savarin as drinking eight bottles a day for dinner, without skipping a beat. Also one Mytton was immortalized as drinking four to six bottles of port every day (that's 20 percent stuff compared with good table wine at 12 percent). He was said to shave with a bottle on his toilet, to work steadily at it throughout the day,

HOW MUCH IS TOO MUCH?

Men's bodies reach like those of growing plants. When a god gives plants too much water to drink, they cannot stand up straight and the winds flatten them, but when they drink exactly what they require they grow straight and tall and bear abundant fruit, and so it is with us.

SOCRATES

polishing off a glass or two at a time, and to put away another bottle at lunch. But the main press of his enormous ration was imbibed before, during, and after supper.

Brother Timothy of Christian Brothers winery in Napa Valley, California, was said to have escorted several friends to a restaurant and, for openers, to have asked the waitress to bring a bottle of wine. When she did he tut-tutted, "Miss, you did not understand me. I meant for you to bring us a bottle *each*."

You can overdo anything—the reverse of moderation. Sex is a health-giving, life-creating exercise, but overdone it can lead to debilitation, degradation, and disease. Food is life itself and the first frontier of comfort, but overdone it can lead to every kind of internal disorder, crowned by the ultimate disaster of obesity. Milk sustains our earliest years, but overdone it can lead to obesity more speedily and more dangerously than many foods of lesser repute. Hippocrates summarized it all: "When more nourishment is taken than the constitution can stand, disease is caused."

Illustrating the variations between individuals, a person weighing 110 pounds may take ten hours to metabolize one-half bottle of wine. A man weighing 200 pounds might metabolize four times as much alcohol per hour and get rid of two bottles in the same ten hours.

With a larger rate of intake by heavy drinkers, the disposal rate is often accelerated. Experiments have shown that heavy drinkers exhibit the lowest degree of impairment in relation to blood alcohol level, and abstainers exhibit the highest. Logically, moderate consumers were intermediate. "Practice makes perfect," to a degree, in drinking as in other sports.

Time is of the essence and timing is a key to victory in war, sports, business, and the practice of drinking. Good timing can be made into a good habit with good results, as noted by Dr. William Dock: "If the drug [alcohol] is not taken before noon, or after supper, it can be continued for years at reasonable and effective levels with none of the unpleasant or dangerous effects exhibited by nearly all agents with similar actions on the mind." Dr. Dock accentuated his emphasis of time as a strategic element of moderation by an added insight which makes good reading for wine lovers: "I have never seen harm done by the regular use of wine before or during meals."

The *Journal of Psychology* states: "Alcoholism rates are higher among populations that have negative attitudes toward alcohol consumption and whose members proportionately drink little as compared to those in populations whose members have favorable attitudes toward alcohol and drink ubiquitously."

MODERATION IS A RUSSIAN PROBLEM TOO

After *Newsweek* reported that young Yuri Brezhnev cut a wide drinking swath in Europe on an official trade mission, capped by an especially uproarious bout in Sweden, his father proscribed further foreign travel by the young man until he learned how to handle his liquor.

Brezhnev's Kremlin partner, Premier Alexei Kosygin, in 1949 almost put his neck under a guillotine of his own making when he blurted out in an alcoholic stupor, "Socialism could be achieved and Russia could be a great country if that pockmarked bastard [Stalin] could be removed." The gods who cherish drinkers were watching out for Kosygin. These treasonable thoughts never did reach the sensitive ears of Stalin.

In this kind of life, in pre-Moscow Russia [prior to 1450], there was no drunkenness. It did not exist as a vice gnawing at the people's organism. Drinking was gladness, pleasure, as is seen in the words attributed by an old Russian scribe Prince Vladimir: "Drinking is a joy to Russia, we cannot do without it."

I. G. PRYZHOV

Alcoholism

The big, frightening, controversial plague of the drinking world is alcoholism. How any malaise could have afflicted the human race so long and so overwhelmingly and still be so misunderstood remains a perennial mystery, while modern science is placing men on the moon and building arsenals that can wipe out half a world.

It will help if we fasten our minds on a few points.

"The drunkard drinks because he wants to. The alcoholic drinks because he has to," said Father Ralph S. Pfau, an Indianapolis priest who was himself an alcoholic for many years.

When the drinker is the boss, it is civilized drinking. When the alcohol is the boss, it is alcoholism. The drinker can drink daily, turning it on and off at will. The alcoholic can abstain totally for long periods of time, but let him take one drink and he has had it. He cannot stop. Once an alcoholic, always an alcoholic—or a teetotaler. Alcoholism is a disease of the mind, the body, and perhaps the soul, but not a crime or a sin or a vice. You don't put a man in jail for having a cold—although, if you did, it would keep him from spreading it around. Alcoholism is a mental health problem. The alcoholic is a casualty of our abrasive civilization.

The wisest as well as the most ignorant among us all too often overlook that it is not the alcohol which makes the alcoholic, but the misuse of alcohol. And if the alcoholic did not take the drinking route to self-destruction, he might well find something worse. If you think there is nothing worse, ask any of your friends whose homes have been burglarized or who have been mugged to help support some predator's dope habit. Or ask yourself why you dare not walk on the sidewalks or the parks of our great cities at night any more—and often not in the daytime.

"There are lots of ways of looking at alcoholism," noted Dr. Frank A. Seixas, medical director of the National Council on Alcoholism. "From the medical standpoint, however, we think of it as a disease—a disease of drug dependency."

The alcoholic may have a deranged mind or body. He may be a metabolic cripple. He may have a gland defect. He may have some sort of nutritional malfunction. He may have a physiological

HOW NOT TO BECOME AN ALCOHOLIC

Be born an Italian, a Jew, or a Chinese. The lowest incidence of alcoholism in the United States occurs among these groups; and their homelands stand among the lowest in the world. Their cultures have a view toward alcohol that is remarkably alike. They leave nothing about alcohol to chance.

They agree that alcohol has, like bread and meat, a place in human life. They have a rigid conception of what constitutes its misuse. They do not drink to get drunk, but to help enjoy life. They take wine as a food, and they use it with their meals. Wine is not a tool or an escape; it is a staple and a pleasure.

Drinking is never a sin, a vice, or a crime. They drink with a clear conscience, and have been doing it since child-hood with social sanctions and family sanctions and amidst their dear ones, not amidst strangers at bars.

---

shortcoming which becomes excruciating and sets up a craving. He may have a personality illness of a potential intensity. Any one or combination of these disorders can produce alcoholism. But alcoholism is just the route the alcoholic chooses to fly off the rails. His trouble is not the alcohol; that is his *attempted* solution.

About 80 percent of American adults drink. From 1 to 5 percent of these are alcoholics, depending on where you draw the line. It is a terrible problem. It can only be made a more terrible problem with the grotesque "solution" of politically enforced abstinence in any form. Syphilis is a terrible problem too, but the solution is not to prohibit sexual intercourse.

Dr. John R. Philip, of the New York City Health Department, expressed some thoughts worth remembering: "We must explode the myths, take it out of the realm of morals and religion. Kids had better learn how to handle drinking, just as they learn how to handle an automobile.

"Treatment should begin where it does for nearly all diseases—with the family doctor. Two hundred years of preaching alcoholism is a sin . . . has done more harm than good. Alcoholism should go into the mainstream of medical practice, to be treated like any other illness."

Prohibition—Rampant Extremism

One of the most inexorable perversities of human nature is that the surest way to make anything popular is to proscribe it. Any writer knows that the most direct route to a best seller is to have his play or book or film banned in Boston. Deprivation of something does not kill one's desire but rather inflames it. Conversely, people tend not to care inordinately for what they can obtain very easily. How many husbands rape their wives? According to an official report for England and Wales in 1903, cases of drunkenness were less numerous in towns and districts where saloons were plentiful than in towns and districts where they were few in numbers.

Utah, noted as one of the most repressive states in the Union on the subject of drinking, with the stuff rationed out sparingly in state stores, also has the image of leading most of her sister states in the incidence and severity of alcoholism.

Sweden's extremely powerful temperance lobby bombards young people at school, at home, on radio, and on TV with the idea that drinking is sinful. Sale of intoxicating liquors is confined to state monopoly stores, the *Systembolaget*. They are designed to discourage drinking since the shops are deliberately made gloomy and unattractive, hidden behind anonymous façades, usually without display windows. And they are few and far between.

So what? So drunkenness runs rampant in Sweden—even though Swedes drink only 9.2 pints of pure alcohol per capita annually, compared with 34.2 pints for Frenchmen. But the French drink evenly and regard drunkenness as a breach of etiquette while Swedes drink in Dionysian bouts and avowedly drink to get drunk. "Train journeys can be quite unpleasant, with schoolboys deliberately getting drunk and empty bottles rolling in the aisles. This sort of thing is a natural reaction to a repressive regime," commented the *London Observer*.

Although a lot of people and a lot of elected legislators still haven't learned it, twenty-five hundred years ago the Chinese sage Lao Tze wrote, "The more laws are enacted and taxes assessed, the greater the number of lawbreakers and tax evaders."

Anybody who tries to tell me what I may or may not drink is bigoted and dangerous. In telling me that I must conform my drinking style to his drinking style, he is doing the moral equivalent of telling me that I must worship his god in his way in his church. For thirteen years this fellow tried to dry up the country with a constitutional amendment which did more to give the United States a trauma about drinking than anything since the maritime adventures of Christopher Columbus.

Meanwhile, this unenforceable amendment made a laughingstock of all law and converted the American people into scofflaws who turned their ingenuity and energy into the game of sneaking behind locked doors to get a few drinks of the stuff that could be openly had at any public table in Europe or south of the Rio Grande.

On the other side of the coin, noted Dr. Celestin Pierre Cambiaire, drinkers have never tried to force anyone to drink. "It was never heard that any drinking nation passed laws to enforce drinking. In most civilized countries, men who use wine and liquors are the leaders of the land. It was never intimated that they wanted to deprive men of liberty and force them to buy and use intoxicating beverages. The French had abstaining Mohammedans in their colonies. They never passed a law to oblige [these teetotalers] to drink wine and spirits."

We have fifty states and fifty different sets of liquor rules and regulations, many of them wry and dry. If you are in St. Louis, Missouri, or Santa Fe, New Mexico, or many a city more on a Sunday, and you are visiting a friend then you can have a glass of wine. If you are in a public dining room, forget it. If you are in West Virginia you cannot ever have a bottle of wine on your restaurant table but if you are in a private club like all the knowledgeable natives are, help yourself to the wine cellar.

Once, arriving in St. Louis on a Sunday evening, I took my wife to Stan the Man Musial's famous restaurant hungering for a chateaubriand with all the trimmings.

"Let's start with an icy double martini," I drooled to the waitress.

"I'm sorry, we never serve liquor on Sunday," she said.

"Oh, fine. Bring me a bottle of good California red wine," I substituted.

"Sir, you do not seem to understand. We also cannot serve wine or beer on Sunday. Would you like a glass of milk?"

Angrily I erupted, "Well, I'll be damned. I spent five dollars on cab fare to get here for this when I could have gone to East St. Louis, Illinois, for less and had what we wanted to order. Well, we're going back to civilization and Missouri's Blue Laws can go to hell where they came from."

My next arrival in Missouri on a Sunday, to Kansas City, found not one amended Blue Law, but it found me ready. I phoned my favorite Stockyards restaurant and said, "I know you cannot sell me a martini or a bottle of wine, but may I bring my own wine and put it on my table?"

"No, that is not allowed," the voice politely said.

"Then I will mix my own martinis and serve my own imported wine while I enjoy a good steak right here in my hotel room."

Some states let you bring your own liquor to the restaurant table but the waitress can't bring a bottle to you if you forget your own. If you're crossing the border into certain states on a train, switch to iced tea. On a jet over such states you may be drinking, but if so, you're violating the law. Some states make you sit down while drinking; others let you stand. Some states restrict liquor sales to state-operated monopoly stores which look and smell like the interior of a precinct station—and can sell only to card-carrying natives. A lot of states prohibit the sale of alcoholic beverages on election days, causing the finest restaurants to serve drinks in cups to their favorite patrons. For years, until New York restored election-day drinking to legality, the exempt bar at the United Nations Building was the most popular watering place in Manhattan.

Drinking was universally accepted in our early days. The United States was a lusty nation with the bottle in the 1700s and early 1800s. Far from frowning upon alcohol, the early Puritans viewed it as a gift from God. Beer was served in the Harvard dining hall. The clergy drank.

When Lyman Beecher, a pioneer Prohibitionist, first proposed a program for combatting inebriety, his ministerial committee decided that nothing could be done to curb the growth of intemperance. Beecher was not easily put down, and he pushed through a program banning ardent spirits at ecclesiastical meetings, but allowing wine.

In 1826, Beecher launched the American Temperance Society. In ten years the organization claimed a million members and five thousand chapters. Although at first the program was "switch from hard liquor to wine," they later set up the society's goal as total abstinence—and lost half their membership.

Dr. Benjamin Rush, another temperance pioneer and author of the first medical tract on excessive consumption of alcohol, championed wine drinking while condemning hard liquor.

A long time before the United States proved that Prohibition stimulates more than it retards, the Koran banned the use of wine and gave the ancient Arabic peoples a chance to demonstrate the ingenuity of human nature. To be sure, the Koran was a bit ambivalent in its interdiction of alcohol. It also stated: ". . . of the fruits of the date-palm, and grapes, whence ye derive strong drink and good nourishment . . . is healing for mankind."

The Koran promised paradise to the true believers, and described paradise in language that any true drinker can well

---

SHAVING IT FINE

A good story is told illustrating the hypocrisy so often a bedmate to bigotry.

Upon being advised by his doctor that he should take a daily dose of brandy and hot water, the reverend president of a local temperance society replied, "What will people say when they learn that I have violated my own tenets of total abstinence?"

"That is easily solved," said the resourceful doctor. "Shave at night instead of in the morning. Keep your bottle of brandy in your dressing room. Have your shaving water brought in before retiring, mix your grog, and no one will be the wiser."

This plan was adopted with complete and medical success. Some time later the doctor was in the neighborhood and dropped by. Not finding his patient at home, he inquired of the housekeeper if the minister was better.

"The reverend is indeed better, sir," replied that servant. "But I fear in turn he may be getting a little queer in the head. You'd hardly believe it, but, you see, sir, he has taken to shaving at least twelve times per day."

understand: "They shall find themselves in a garden of delight. They shall recline in rich brocades upon soft cushions and rugs and be served by surpassingly beautiful maidens, with eyes like hidden pearls. Wine may be drunk there, but 'their heads shall not ache with it, neither shall they be confused.' "

The Koran's prohibitions did not prevent many of Islam's physicians from proclaiming the medicinal values of wine while inveighing against the evils of intoxication. Indeed, the Moslem tradition *encourages* the prescription, administration, and drinking of wine for health.

Avicenna, a distinguished Arabian physician and philosopher advised, "Young adults should take wine in moderation. But elderly persons may take as much as they can tolerate." At another point Avicenna aligned himself with those who think that if a thing is worth doing, sometimes it is worth overdoing: "Some persons claim that it is an advantage to become intoxicated once or twice a month, for, they say, it allays the animal passions, inclines to repose, provokes the urine and sweat, and gets rid of effete matters." But the sage issued clear warning that "frequent intoxication breaks down the constitution and the liver and brain, weakens the nerves, and tends to produce diseases of the nervous system, apoplexy, and sudden death."

Avicenna should know. It is recorded that he imbibed nightly.

Dr. Mahmoud F. Hoballah, director of the Islamic Center at Washington, D.C., expounded on the permissiveness of Mohammedanism in the face of medical exigency. "It is a well-known fact, accepted by all Muslim schools of thought, that when any food or drink has become necessary for a man because his health, his life or the duration of his life is dependent upon it, this kind of food or drink cannot be prohibited. The proofs to be cited for such a statement are many."

Alphonse Daudet writes of the Arab chief, the aga, who, tired of domesticity and "sick of love," visited the Algerian caravansary to watch the dancing and enjoy the wine of France. "Cursed is a single drop of wine," in the words of the Prophet Mohammed, says Daudet, who proceeded to show how the prohibition of the Koran could be circumvented. Into each glass of wine brought to him, the aga dipped his finger; as he withdrew it, a drop of wine adhered. Having vigorously shaken off the "cursed drop," the aga proceeded to quaff his wine without scruple, and with delight.

It was thus well understood in the Islam world that men will find a way to do and to justify doing what they are ordered not to do.

This was accepted in other cultures, too. In ancient China, Shu Ching, the Canon of History, declared, "Men will not do without kiu [a Chinese alcoholic beverage]. To prohibit it and secure total abstinence from it is beyond the power even of the sages."

Ghengis Khan, in addition to his endowments as a military master, showed himself sophisticated about men and alcohol: "A soldier must not get drunk oftener than once a week. It would, of course, be better if he did not get drunk at all, but one should not expect the impossible."

In Russia the drinking problem is labeled "the green serpent." The Kremlin attacks the green serpent in many ways, from legislation to propaganda, from temperance lectures to scientific experiments. But columnist Holmes Alexander wrote, "The identification of drinking with manliness and conviviality in so many Russian minds is stronger than all the propaganda and laws. The green serpent may be around longer than Communism."

Deploring "the wilderness of Prohibition" for "providing a windfall for gangsters" and leading "even prosperous and high-minded physicians to prescribe whiskey or port for friends who never had been in better health, and the venal fringe to write prescriptions for patients they never saw," Dr. William Dock put his finger on one of the most harmful, long-range "hangovers" from this era: "This created a sense of shame or guilt in the profession, which made many physicians banish all thought of alcohol as a valuable clinical weapon."

The assault on integrity that Prohibition fostered was exacerbated by the tendency of doctors to prescribe (and people to patronize without prescription) nostrums in which alcohol was the only effective component—with a pious pretense that they were nonalcoholic and therefore noncontaminated. Many will remember the sweeping popularity of the nostrum Hadacol, which produced an impressive fortune for its proprietor because of its surreptitious alcoholic content. This Prohibition-propelled tendency has long been attacked by the American Medical Association and the federal government for the mischief it continuously does, including its huge traffic in *untaxed* alcohol.

A popular song of not many decades ago memorialized this chapter of pseudomedical history and stressed that such stuff, for all its faults and tax-yield sterility, had a privilege that legitimate wine did not—it could legally advertise:

> So we sing, we sing, we sing to Lydia Pinkham
> And her love for the human race.
> She makes her Vegetable Compound
> And the papers publish her face.

Wine has been prominent in books of therapeutic preparations for several thousand years, but also has been notably absent from the eight revisions of the United States pharmacopoeia issues since Prohibition. As the whirlwind of Prohibitionism began to blow across the country, political pressure mounted (and continues to endure) against pharmacopoeia listings of wine and spirits.

In 1905 the *United States Dispensatory* recommended red wine as a tonic and an antidiarrheic agent in convalescence. But it reduced listings of wines from seventeen to eight in 1926, and eliminated wine completely in 1937.

The United States pharmacopoeia got alcohol back in briefly in 1955 as a "pharmaceutic necessity," but this reference disappeared again in the 1960 revision.

St. Chrysostom—St. John of the Golden Tongue—ascetic, martyr, and a Hercules among the preachers of the entire Christian era, said words in the fourth century that deserve to be heeded in the twentieth: "Shun excess and drunkenness and gluttony, for God gave meat and drink, not for excess, but for nourishment. Not that to drink is shameful. God forbid! For such precepts belong to heretics.

"For wine was given us by God, not that we might be drunken, but that we might be sober. It is the best medicine when it has the best moderation to direct it. Wine was given to restore the body's weakness, not to overturn the soul's strength."

Pointing out the folly of prohibiting wine when there are excesses, the saint continued, is akin to saying, "Would there be no steel, because of the murderers; no night, because of the thieves; no light, because of the informers; no women, because of the adulteries.

"In a word, you will destroy everything. But do not so; for this is of a satanical mind. Do not find fault with the wine, but with the drunkenness."

To protect the few who cannot take alcohol, it just will not work to forbid access by all. Prohibition stimulates more than it suppresses. That is why the 1970s noted a rising, sophisticated pressure to legitimatize marijuana as a psychologically effective measure to check its popularity.

3

༄ ༄ ༄ ༄ ༄ ༄ ༄

Wine and Other Liquids

I rejoice, as a moralist, at the prospect of a reduction of the duties on wine by our national legislature. It is an error to view a tax on that liquor as merely a tax on the rich. It is a prohibition of its use to the middling classes of our citizens, and a condemnation of them to the poison of spirits, which is desolating their homes. No nation is drunken, where wine is cheap; and none sober, where the dearness of wine substitutes ardent spirits as the common beverage.

THOMAS JEFFERSON

When men drink wine they are rich, they are busy, they push lawsuits, they are happy, they help their friends.

ARISTOPHANES

My education in sex and alcohol was in the best tradition of the American middle class. I was taught that sex led directly to vile disease, unwanted pregnancy, sure disgrace, and other mysterious disasters worse than death. Therefore, leave sex strictly alone, leave girls strictly alone to be sure of not getting involved with sex, and don't ask questions.

Alcohol was a poison that could lead to contamination, disease, automobile accidents, alcoholism, disgrace, and maybe even to sex.

The result was that up to a certain age I would as soon touch a female as play jacks with hot charcoals, and alcohol in any form was as approachable as a rattlesnake ready to strike.

The trouble with this system of education is that the child grows up to become curious. He goes to the streets for his education, where the truth begins to penetrate. Eventually the child finds out what he's been missing. Then "curious" becomes "furious" and he wants to make up for lost time. Thus prohibition—whether federal or parental—manages to keep the lid on for a time; but the truth will out, and prohibition ultimately can lead to overcompensation. At age nineteen I left home for adventure and discovery, fell off a horse at a fox hunt, broke a couple of front teeth, and sank another one through my lower lip. It hurt likes blazes and made my face a pretty sight to take to the fox-hunt ball that night; but I was determined to go anyway. A newspaper-reporter friend suggested that a bit of Virginia corn would provide effective medication for my wounds.

"What the hell, why not?" I exploded with new-found courage, as my gathering curiosity and my pain closed in upon me simultaneously.

The result was that the pain was greatly modified, I discovered alcohol, got a little drunk, met a girl, fell in love, danced all night, and had the time of my life. The "education" of my childhood and my home was forever detonated as the truth exploded. There was some good in sex and alcohol after all.

It was some time after this that by degrees (and by accident of course) I began to discover that there was such a thing as wine. The more I saw of that, the better I liked it, but always as an afterthought to generous hard-liquor consumption that preceded the meals and usually followed them too.

At a party long ago, I remember meeting the debonair Don Julio, a descendant of California's Spanish pioneers, impressively youthful and vital in his eighties or nineties at the time. I asked him to what he attributed his streamlined appearance and vibrant demeanor at such a point in years.

"That's easy," he said. "I drink wine with meals and never another alcohol except brandy, sometimes a little before meals and more often a little after meals. Brandy is really distilled wine, and I consider it a much more healthful way to go than drinking whiskeys, gin, or rum. That's my secret."

If the doctor says, "You're killing yourself!" don't fall apart. Something will get you, even if you do watch out. After all, we're *all* killing ourselves just living, so we might as well do it with as much joie de vivre as we can manage. Here is that much maligned, much misunderstood, much idolized liquid, wine—part myth, part science, part agriculture, part chemistry, part drink, part food, part drug, part experience, part conjecture, part anesthetic, and part good taste.

The magnificent thing about wine is that it helps, assuages, and delights others even as it delights you. There is no more pleasing thing you can do for yourself or for your brother than to pour a glass of wine that you both drink together.

For decades I had happily concurred with my worthy friends who subscribe to the wisdom of Alex Waugh: "I am prepared to believe that a dry martini slightly impairs the palate, but think what it does for the soul." But after a great many years of hard-liquor concoctions of every description, I switched to the thinking of St. Paul: "Drink no longer water; use a little wine for thy stomach's sake." Just change that a trifle: "Drink no longer booze; use a little wine for thy health's sake."

"Drink no longer booze" has now become my way of life. The result for me has been lower weight, fewer colds, no hangovers, relief for my blood pressure and cholesterol problems, and many individual and specific benefits including the happiest: I seem to enjoy it more and more as I ease into advancing years. Further, I have found that wine tastes better, is more fun to drink, leads to livelier and less garbled conversations, and is easier on the budget—if handled right.

The best of wine superiorities may be that exclusive wine drinking is much less likely to lead to alcoholism. Given the deprivations and frustrations of modern living and a culture that flashes the green light to alcohol, you often come up with alcoholism. But take your alcohol as 12 percent of your drink, a drink you instinctively sip instead of gulp, a drink you take mostly with your meals—and you are courting the seduction of alcohol without the hammer of intoxication and the risk of eventual alcoholism. In the words of Paul Claudel: "A cocktail is to a glass of wine as rape is to love."

I have a few friends who insist wine gives them worse hangovers than hard liquor; it gives them hot flashes; it makes their hearts beat faster in the middle of the night—and, in general, they prefer their distilled delights. They may be right. But it's a world of individuals and everybody should lay out his own course. My predilection is to drink wine, which I find, with Edward Hyams, "has been the least coarsening medium in which alcohol can be taken and the least likely to dangerous abuse" and also "is one of life's absolutely reliable pleasures."

For centuries, wine has been the preferred liquid of much of Europe and that part of the New World below the Rio Grande.

In a sort of cork-popping, bubbling, gurgling, civilized revolution, wine is enjoying a renaissance in the Anglo-Saxon part of the Western Hemisphere today. There has to be good reason for a phenomenon this enduring and pronounced. The reason? Where alcohol is good, wine tends to be better; where alcohol is bad, wine tends to be less bad and sometimes good.

I can't *prove* that wine is good for your health. There has been little substantiation based on what the scientists call "controlled-sample laboratory experimentation." Notwithstanding that wine is among the oldest drugs known, there still remains less known about it than about many other and much newer drugs. However, common sense and circumstantial evidence galore tell you that wine is good for your health. There is an impressive lore built up over centuries to support it. There have been outstanding doctors corroborating it. There have been case histories and laboratory experiments to substantiate it. There have been books and articles to contend it.

And though my preference may be emotional and unscientific it is supported by impressive expert testimonials. Dr. Celestin Cambiaire: "Wine is a weakened form of alcohol and has a tendency to protect those who use it against alcoholism." Dr. Pierre Viala: "A moderate use of wine is the best antidote against alcoholism." Dr. Jean Louis Faure: "Nothing is better to fight alcoholism than a moderate use of wine."

France's high alcoholism rate can be misleading. French alcoholism is low in the south, where wine use is high; and high in the north, where wine use is low. The Normans drink an explosive called Calvados, which is a form of 90 proof apple brandy having nothing to do with the grape or with wine but having a great deal to do with alcoholism statistics in France. When reminded that France has a rather high alcoholic rate, one wine-town mayor riposted, "I know of only one alcoholic in Châteauneuf-du-Pape, and he was born that way."

In England, James Boswell noted: "It cannot too emphatically be insisted that light wine is essentially a temperance beverage, and that its alcoholic content is . . . a characteristic of secondary importance. Wine is not the drink of the dipsomaniac but of the viveur." England's Dr. Robert Druitt, a member of the Royal College of Physicians, wrote more than a century ago: "I had always believed that health and morality would be largely promoted by the more liberal use of wine, and by taking from people all excuse for drinking distilled spirits. Civilized man must drink, will drink, and ought to drink; but it should be wine." His colleague and contemporary, Dr. Adam Clarke, added: "Ardent spirits exhilarate, but they exhaust the strength; and every dose leaves man the worse. Unadulterated wine . . . exhilarates and invigorates; it makes [man] cheerful, and provides for the continuance of that cheerfulness by strengthening the muscles and bracing the nerves."

For half a century Sweden allowed a man only from one to three liters of spirits per month but as much wine as he liked. Women, who had access to wine but not to hard liquor, registered only one-third of 1 percent of the total alcoholics. Today Sweden cuts usage of distilled spirits by pricing and taxing policies that encourage beer and wine consumption over the hard stuff. Government ads feature slogans like, "Next time, take wine instead."

From Australia, Dr. Max Lake wrote, "It was the very first issue of excessive drinking of hard liquor that influenced many . . . doctors . . . to examine the merits of wine. Their subsequent devotion to the cause of intelligent drinking was really a battle for moderation over excess—both the excesses of the rum swillers and of those zealots who demanded that liquor be banned altogether. A plentiful supply of light, wholesome table wines with meals is a diversion and virtual antidote to the drinking of hard liquor. I personally agree with the 'modern' view that there would be no alcoholism and drunkenness today if people kept to table wine."

In the United States, Benjamin Franklin assured us, "Wine is a constant proof that God loves us and loves to see us happy." Sprinkled throughout Franklin's abundant literary output were such gems as, "I every day drink a glass of infusion of bark in wine, by way of prevention, and hope my fever will no more return."

There is much evidence to prove that wine is less intoxicating than equivalent solutions of alcohol in other forms and combinations, although this evidence has only accumulated in recent times. It had long been misconstrued that the effects of wine, beer, and hard liquor upon the human system could be measured strictly in terms of the quantity of alcohol consumed. Therefore, much of the classical laboratory research had been conducted with pure alcohol. It is now established that the situation is far more complex and that findings based on plain alcohol solutions do not always apply to the respective alcoholic beverages.

Table wine ranges from 7 to 15 percent by volume, or 14 to 30 proof, versus hard liquor which is from 40 percent, or 80 proof, to much higher. Wine therefore consists of from 85 to 93 percent other components—which contribute innumerable factors to its benefits and to its enjoyment while cutting its impact as an alcohol carrier. Slightly more than two bottles of table wine would be required to match the alcoholic volume of a pint of 100 proof spirits. Remember, too, the alcohol in wine is absorbed more slowly than alcohol of the same concentration in water alone. And wine is usually consumed with food—which delays absorption and lowers the level of alcohol in the blood.

Consider that while my buddies are downing three martinis, thereby taking on four and a half ounces of alcohol each, I am drinking three glasses of wine, thereby taking on a trifle over one-fourth as much alcohol or a bit more than one ounce. Compute that arithmetic in terms of calories (528 versus 180) and intoxication, and it tells you why hard liquor clouts while wine caresses.

The spirits lover drinks for kicks, with the other pleasures secondary. The wine lover drinks for pleasure, with the kicks secondary.

Felix Marti-Ibanez, editor-in-chief of *MD,* wrote: "The cocktail lacks the perfection of wine. If wine . . . is a delectable experience, the cocktail is more like the explosion of a devastating megaton in the brain. Wine is an almost spontaneous masterpiece of nature; the cocktail is an artificial creation of man. The French use two different words for wine intoxication (*enivrement*) and liquor intoxication (*ivresse*). The word 'wine' comes from *vis* or force, strength, power. The connoisseur of wines rarely degenerates into an alcoholic."

Dr. Milton Silverman, international authority on alcoholism, wrote: "Because of its low alcohol content and its content of protective chemicals, and also because of cultural and sociological factors . . . wine may . . . be described as a pharmaceutical agent of major importance—and moreover, an agent which may serve as the most effective preventative of alcoholism known to medicine. Beyond a certin point, wine and plain alcohol differ. More wine continues to give more relief, while more plain alcohol or more of a comparable beverage begins to give more tension."

"The wine-drinking people of Europe are the most sober and temperate people in the world . . . and . . . the use of strong liquors, which are responsible for drunkenness, is very small. It is a good sign, therefore, to find Americans learning to use wine with their meals." This sounds like present-day wine ad copy, but it was written by Dr. Edward Fitch in New York before World War I.

Wine gets a bad reputation from the misleading American insistence on dubbing alcoholics "winos." To begin with, the wino would much rather drink whiskey, vodka, or gin than the bastardized wine he does drink—if he could afford it. To get the maximum jolt per dollar spent he buys the cheapest stuff he can—which often is fortified "wine." The wine the wino drinks is not the 12 percent table wine you serve with dinner or order at the restaurant. The wino gurgles a 20 percent sweet muscatel for the minimum outlay of money. To call such consumers "winos" is a travesty upon the English language.

Wine compares well with nonalcoholic beverages also. The store shelves are full of soft-drink formulas that have a far worse cumulated effect on the internal organs not to mention the deposit of ugly fat.

We must drink water and we cannot live without it. Let us

WATER, WATER EVERYWHERE

'Twas honest old Noah first planted the vine,
And mended his morals by drinking its wine;
And thenceforth justly the drinking of water decried;
For he knew that all mankind by drinking it died.

BENJAMIN FRANKLIN

And Noah he often said to his wife
When he sat down to dine,
"I don't care where the water goes
If it doesn't get into the wine."

ANONYMOUS

resign ourselves to that. But we smuggle aboard about eighty to ninety parts of water with every one hundred parts of wine we consume. If we must take on the prosaic staple, wine is a splendid disguise for getting it into our system.

This is well understood in much of Europe, where there is a wineglass (sometimes a thicket of wineglasses) at every table setting, in contrast with the United States, where the full glass of water is as de rigueur on most restaurant tables as silverware, paper napkins, and salt and pepper shakers.

Dr. Heinrich Kliewe quoted a German encyclopedia, vintage 1737: "Wine is after water the most natural and oldest beverage and has this advantage; water moistens and stops the thirst but it does not nourish or strengthen, while wine does all these things at the same time."

Mayor Diffonty of Châteauneuf-du-Pape, a town rather more famous for its bottled namesake than for any of its other distinctions, wrote a reverse Volstead Act inviting its citizens to stop drinking the water and stick to wine. Proclaiming his prohibition-in-reverse, Mayor Diffonty said, "A man who is lucky enough to be born in perhaps the finest wine community in the world would be crazy to drink water from a faucet. We do not have idiots in Châteauneuf-du-Pape because of the sanity of the wine."

The whole thing started when local health authorities reported that the Rhône and Ouveze rivers were not as pure and potable as they might be, or might once have been. (This condition is so widespread in our times of proliferating pollution that ecology consciousness has been suggested as a continuing—and potentially spiraling—thrust toward increased wine consumption.) The mayor carried on, "With the exception of children, for whom milk and fruit juices remain the appropriate drinks, citizens are vividly recommended to drink the wine of the territory, the only wine that can assure their proper longevity."

"No epidemics were ever traced to wine . . . or to moderate drinking or even to drunkenness," reported Dr. Celestin Cambiaire.

In fact, it has been often noticed that drunkards were almost immune to certain epidemics. On the other hand, very many epidemics have been traced to water and milk. While, in any country, one can drink a glass of pure wine without the least chance to come into contact with deadly germs of contagious diseases—

in many places, and in most country places, millions of disease germs are in contact with the water supply.

On the contrary wine kills all microbes which may injure man's health, and respects all those which are beneficial to man. Beer is by far more artificially produced than wine, and cannot be compared to it as a microbe killer.

Tea and coffee are not offered by nature to the white race living in temperate regions. They have to be imported. No race having tea or coffee as a national drink ever built any high civilization. [While this is interesting copy, a Chinese or Japanese might not agree.] Moreover tea and coffee taken in great quantities are harmful. They may cause various kinds of nervous diseases.

To most people milk has the image of being the most healthful beverage on earth, but Dr. Cambiaire has some second thoughts, and in these he has lots of company.

"Everybody knows that all disease germs thrive wonderfully well in milk," he wrote. "Grown-up animals do not drink milk. To drink milk men have to rob young animals of what nature intended entirely and only for them. No great civilization was ever built by milk drinkers."

Milk, like water, can be overrated and should be put in its proper perspective. Milk is the greatest food in the world—until the baby is weaned from its mother's breast. Thereafter, milk is not his mother's but an alien animal's—a foreign substance that during his life may be more apt to kill him than, for example, wine is.

Milk and its products—rich butters, sour cream, whipped creams, ice creams, and other goos, which the Germans with onomatopoeic aplomb call *schlag*—are major perpetrators of obesity, high cholesterol, and related cardiovascular killers. In its way milk can be as deadly as cigarettes—yet it never bears the public image of a poison. It comes packaged as a panacea good for everything that ails everybody. It kills with kindness.

Milk, of course, is not addictive per se but advertising, marketing, and lobbying have secured milk and its products as number one in just about everybody's icebox and menu.

The Italians have a number of good ideas which qualify their stance as one of the world's most civilized peoples. One of the best may be to switch a baby from his mother's breast to a wine bottle at approximately age three. The Italians, for all the

EAT, DRINK, AND BE WARY

As to the supposed superior health values of milk, it is a fact that milk is very indigestible for a considerable number of people, and is especially dangerous because . . . being touted as nature's 100 percent health food . . . few suspect the digestive difficulties it leads to.

Milk is tremendously important for infants and some growing children; because mother's milk is good for all infants it does not follow that cow's milk (vastly different) is good for all children and all adults.

The slogan "a quart of milk a day for every child" is good commercial propaganda. It is bad medical advice. Nearly 7 percent of children who go to physicians are sick because they are forced to take more milk than they need. Milk is an animal food *for the very young of the same animal,* and is not a satisfactory food for young animals after infancy. In most animals development of teeth marks ending of the period of using milk for food, and begins the era where meat, fish, eggs, vegetables, fruits, etc. are used unto old age.

"Comment on Overrated Foods,"
from *Consumers Research,* 1935

---

wine they drink, have very few alcoholics; and, for all the pasta they eat (or could it be all that milk they do not drink?), they are less inclined to obesity than many of their contemporaries.

While not suggesting that infants switch *directly* from milk to wine, as the Italians are said to do, *Consumers Research* endorsed wine as a food supplement.

The extensive use of wine at every meal, as practiced in many parts of Europe, is not a bad habit . . . wine drinking was one of those vital adjustments made by man to an imperfect food and water supply. A diet high in spaghetti, macaroni, and other pastas and devoid of the native wines of Italy or France would not be merely indigestible but would be dangerous to health and mental activity.

In older countries, the lesson of modifying grape and other fruit juices by the wine-making process has been well learned . . .

Were there a wine lobby to match the milk lobby, every child would be drinking wine before he got into high school and wine flagons would embellish every family dinner table and every restaurant in the land.

The milk lobby has recruited legislatures by the chamberful to join the sales and marketing legions of the cow business. Legislatures exalt milk while they hobble competing comestibles. For example, if your doctor says to cut out the butter for your heart's sake, just try to order a bit of margarine at your favorite restaurant. You could as quickly get cyanide; in many states it is illegal to serve margarine in restaurants. For years people had to buy white margarine with a little package of powdered dye that they kneaded in themselves if they couldn't bear to eat the ghastly, pallid stuff in its lardlike whiteness. Finally, sixty-five years of federal restrictions were lifted and most states also relented, so now you can buy oleo that already looks like butter.

Many dairymen still grumble bitterly, as did their champion, Wisconsin's state senator Gordon Roseleip, who growled, "I still think that coloring it the same as butter misrepresents it."

Wisconsin, "America's Dairyland," held out until 1967 before joining the other forty-nine states which had been permitting yellow margarine since President Truman signed the Margarine Act in 1950, and lifted a 10 percent tax on oleo. The nation laughed during the "Battle of Wisconsin," when the redoubtable Senator Roseleip, blindfolded, taste-tested margarine and butter in a senate caucus room and couldn't tell the difference.

By prohibitions against their competitors the milk people

THE RIGHT CHEMICALS

Pat Hansen, in her Ventura, California, real estate office, asked me, upon learning I was creating this book about wine and health, "But, Mr. Baus, isn't wine full of chemicals?"

"Assuredly," I replied. "So are vegetables, so are meats, so are all foods, so is every drink, and so is water itself.

"You see, wine is full of the *right* chemicals."

still try to force you to consume their product whether your doctor wants you to or not. So, when you eat in a restaurant, eat your bread dry—it's great that way. Or, if you like, dip your bread in vinegar and oil. This is less fattening and makes less cholesterol, and it has still escaped the milk lobby's attention.

A rather agreeable substitute, as a matter of fact, until the law says you must limit yourself to sour cream salad dressing.

Wine has flowed down human throats since before Homer called it "a divine beverage" and Plato said, "Nothing more excellent or valuable than wine was ever granted by God to mankind."

Wine, on balance, is a virtue, not a vice. But it is a virtue with some of the redeeming rewards of the most popular vices. It makes people *feel* good.

> God, in his goodness, sent the grape
> To cheer both great and small;
> Little fools will drink too much
> And great fools none at all.
>
> ANONYMOUS

4

ꙮ

Drugs: The Serpent's Tooth of Our Time

Wine is the greatest of all medicines; where wine is lacking, there drugs are necessary.

JEWISH SAGE

Temperance movements, later prohibition, then the advent of effective new drugs such as aspirin, hormones, vitamins, antibiotics, and barbiturates, drew the medical profession's attentions away from the medicinal uses of wine. But today, scientific research is reconfirming its health values.

ROBERT C. STEPTO

At the head of all sickness am I, blood; at the head of all medical remedies am I, wine. Only when no wine is available have recourse to drugs.

TALMUD

We live in a drug age. On the record, physicians are filling more than two hundred million legal prescriptions annually for psychoactive drugs (antidepressants, sedatives, stimulants, and tranquilizers). By the modest ratio of ten pills to a prescription, this means that two billion doses of these drugs are legally administered every year.

This flood of prescription drugs is dwarfed by the over-the-counter trade abundantly available at thousands of supermarkets and drugstore outlets—the psychotropic drugs to relieve pressure, induce sleep, keep one awake, make one alert, relieve pain, reduce sickness, stabilize one, fight fatigue, and so on.

With the older generations blazing the way in a hail of pills, the younger generation of any family today is as statistically apt to produce a drug addict as it was to produce an appendectomy a few decades ago. The army, which used to worry about AWOL curbs, is today worried about drug-addiction curbs. The newspapers are full of stories about the children of celebrities who are hooked on drugs—including some who became fatally addicted.

None other than the U.S. Department of Justice, Bureau of Narcotics and Dangerous Drugs, projected in 1972 that from thirty to fifty million Americans "will have smoked marijuana by 1976." Two Stanford University psychiatrists, in a survey of 1,314 doctors, found that 25 percent had smoked marijuana. In San Francisco, 27 percent of physicians under thirty-five classified themselves as current users and another 30 percent had used it in the past. New York City figures were almost as high.

Does playing around with the bush leagues of marijuana lead one to the big leagues of heroin? It's a major controversy, and the returns are not in. But pot does produce effects similar to LSD and other strong hallucinogens; it can induce bronchitis and sinusitis; there is evidence of insomnia and digestive problems; and British doctors have reported it may result in brain atrophy.

"It's pretty well established that the use of marijuana by young people is positively related to the experimental use of other drugs. The probability that the individual will experiment with strong hallucinogens and other drugs rises strongly with the use of marijuana. There is no necessary causal relationship. There *is* social relationship," wrote Leonard Gross in a tract based largely upon a study by Professor William McGlothin of UCLA for the National Commission on Marijuana and Drug Abuse. "Marijuana is the least harmful of the drugs currently being illegally used by young persons. [But] there are real dangers attached to its frequent use," Gross concluded.

What brings upon us the fury of this universal pill storm? This is a complex, multifaceted question, and even the experts cannot agree on the answers. Obviously, there *are* no easy, isolated answers, but several phenomena in the modern history of science and medicine are worth our examination here as we consider the possibility that wine has a contribution to make in fighting the monster of our time.

First, the growing power of science and technology to create drugs of greater power, effect, and specificity to help offset problems that seem to mount in magnitude as the globe gets older.

TODAY'S DRUG STORM: RELIEF WITHOUT PLEASURE

Alcohol has certain powers of certain therapeutic worth. It can lessen the leaden load of years. It can smother pain. It can summon sleep. And it can, above all, placate the troubled spirit and rest the racing mind.

But alcohol is not, and hasn't been for some years now, the only drug that can perform these several services. There are other analgesics (aspirin, Meperidine, codeine), other soporifics (chloral hydrate and the many barbiturates), and other ataractics (chlorpromazine, reserpine, meprobamate), which are not merely as good but, in almost every respect, almost immeasurably better.

Their only flaw, in fact, is excellence. Unlike alcohol, they are all (with the one exception of aspirin) so efficiently potent—and hence, at least potentially, so dangerous—that their use is properly confined to conditions of comparable stature. They are also, unlike alcohol, incapable of giving pleasure. They can offer only the chilly charity of relief.

BERTON ROUECHE

Second, the increasing reliance by doctors upon the pill-as-panacea. More than nine-tenths of psychotropic drugs in the United States are prescribed by physicians relatively untrained in drug effects instead of by trained psychiatrists. Many physicians are not trained to understand, let alone supervise, these new drugs. Deaths and other tragedies from use of certain types of drugs underscore this fact.

In *Mystification and Drug Abuse,* Lennard and Epstein wrote:

Patients seen in everyday practice present physicians with complaints that are obviously troublesome to the patient and a source of concern for him. But often a physician can neither discover a specific cause for the patient's complaint nor clearly define the complaint for himself or the patient. The physician nonetheless often prescribes medication.

Prescribing a drug legitimizes the doctor-patient relationship. . . . Through prescribing a drug, a physician also reduces a patent's anxiety by implying that he has defined the problem and can alleviate the complaint. . . . Prescribing a drug may also help a physician to maintain a sense of accomplishment and to allay his frustration.

Research has brought out that young people often ill as children and taken regularly to physicians, from whom they receive pills, form the group most likely to enter the drug scene during late adolescence.

What doctor would maintain a patient on a drug—often of no therapeutic value—especially if the drug were potentially harmful or addictive? No doctor, if he knew. But many doctors do not know. As a result, as many as one million Americans are hooked on barbiturates and tranquilizers and do not know it— let alone do they dream that a barbiturate habit can be more difficult and more dangerous to kick than a heroin habit.

"It may take only four or five pills a day for as little as three days for some people to get hooked badly enough to develop withdrawal symptoms if they stop," said Dr. Leon Marder.

Most of the victims get their drugs legally from their doctors, most of whom are as unaware as their patients that the patients have become addicted.

"It takes a very skillful person to exist on a heroin habit because of the difficulty and the expense of getting the drug. But barbiturate users have no problem at all getting their supply and the cost is relatively negligible. There are 1.5 million prescriptions for barbiturates and tranquilizers written each year. Most are unnecessary and misused," said Dr. Marder.

Commented the Los Angeles *Times* about Dr. Marder's thesis: "It is not for laymen to advise physicians on the practice of their art, but surely it would seem that more doctors should exercise greater prudence in dispensing these sedative drugs. Many patients won't like that. Far too many Americans have been conditioned to seek an easy escape from psychological problems. . . . It is a national problem of deep and disturbing implications, this pill popping—a problem whose full dimensions we still have not seen. But we have seen enough to accept the urgency of action."

Pharmacological education of doctors and their suppliers could alleviate this problem. Pharmacology does not play the role it should in medical education and has not since the reform in medical education sponsored by the Carnegie Endowment and the American Medical Association in 1910, chronicled Nicholas von Hoffman in the Washington *Post*. Since then, schools emphasizing pharmacology over anatomy, pathology, chemistry, and other sciences have been denied accreditation.

"In effect it was decided that it was enough for the modern doctor to be able to come up with a diagnosis and match the name of a disease with the name on a bottle of medicine," wrote von Hoffman. He suggested there is something more to this than slips by doctors.

"The most important therapeutic tool doctors have—pharmacology—could not have been taken out of their knowledge and control without a powerful drug industry. Over the last fifteen years the abuses and excesses of these people have been exposed often enough, but there is still a strong tendency to believe that what they do is an aberration, a temporary deviation from a more respectable norm. In truth they are built into the very structure of American medicine and have been for a century," wrote von Hoffman.

The third reason for the dramatic increase in pill use is the growing acceptance by the public of pill-as-panacea. What people want, industry will supply if it can—at a profit. Stock market statistics in drugs and chemicals in recent years will testify to the profits. Few developments will skyrocket a pharmaceutical, drug, or chemical stock farther, faster, or more prolongedly than the right new pill.

The public demand for drugs is not automatic. Think of the ads you see on television or in the newspapers and magazines for new preparations to make you sleep better, work better, look better, feel better, or play better. Take a look at any medical journal or other periodical read by doctors and make a swift tabulation as to what percentage of their fat advertising lineage is paid for by drug manufacturers. And, by the way, how many ads have you seen on television or in print—lately or in your lifetime—about how wine (or any other alcoholic beverage) would make you sleep better, look better, or feel better? You aren't going to see any, either, unless some seismic, unscheduled political movements take place. For the vintner to hint that his product will contribute an iota to your health would be illegal and could put him out of business. But the pill-pushing drug industry can advertise with impunity in the midst of the drug deluge which worries every thinking American today.

Almost every drug known to man can be advertised as a health commodity—and many are massively—except alcohol. Meanwhile, we all stew over the drug problem and wonder how it hit us.

Admittedly, today's drug research and development laboratories produce one miracle after another to repel disease, prolong life, and protect man in his battle against disintegration, deterioration, disease, and death. We are certainly more fortunate than our forebears.

Is our problem a legacy of the fact we have not had time to adjust to this chemical tidal wave? Mankind has not yet mastered the secret of moderation applied to the ancient miracle of alcohol; should we expect moderation overnight with the modern medical miracles that have all but overwhelmed us in just a few decades? Whatever has the power to cure has the power to kill. If overcure is our problem, we need time to cope with it and we need allies to buy the time. Education is one of those allies. Another can be wine, which so long held the center of the medical stage and perhaps still merits a place in the picture.

If today's drug culture is founded on the home medicine cabinet that is full of pills, who is to say that our ancestors may not have been in some ways better off with a wine-drinking culture based on a cellar that is full of bottles?

Maybe a combination of the two—with *moderation* in each—has a contribution to make.

Perhaps a wine renaissance can help fight drug addiction as it can help fight alcoholism. What many drugs can do to anesthetize and what many stronger alcoholic beverages can do to anesthetize, wine may well do—perhaps not as fast, possibly in some cases not quite as well or as specifically—but, in the loving company of family and friends, with vastly more pleasure and less penalty.

"The 'from nature's realm' characteristic of wine is also claimed by marijuana and other drugs," said Dr. Robert Kastenbaum of Wayne State University, Detroit. "But drug users lock themselves into their own generation gap; individuals of widely differing ages enjoy wine together. Drugs tend to increase the user's alienation from the community in general; wine links people to each other."

France's Patrick Le Chene, head of the Comité National des

Vins de France, said, "The American government thinks it's better to get drugged than drunk. . . . Wine may just be the best antidote to drugs that anyone has come up with."

"Ten years from now society will be fighting addiction to drugs nobody ever heard of today. The new chemicals will just further complicate the drug-abuse situation that is costing governments billions of dollars every year," predicted Dr. R. Gordon Bell, of Toronto's Donwood Institute, a group studying addiction.

The "welcome effect" of certain drugs consists of taking people out of themselves, leading to addiction.

"People want to change the way they feel, whether its tense, guilty, lonely, depressed, bored, or just plain frustrated. There are two ways of taking a chemical holiday. Some drugs reduce the unpleasantness of these feelings. Others give you the feeling that you are strong and can overcome them."

At this point, Dr. Bell opened the floodgates of the controversy about which is worse, alcoholism or drug addiction. He judged that alcoholism is more devastating than the effect of any other drug. Some chemicals are more addicting than alcohol (it takes years to get hooked on alcohol; it takes several jabs of a needle to get hooked on heroin), but no other has such terrible social consequences, he asserted. Some of the others have as bad effects on the addicts themselves, but none is so dangerous to other people.

Dr. Bell may not have weighed the full impact of the crime statistics, the burglary epidemic, the mugging plague, the police records. But he has plenty of company for his views. "The most severe drug-abuse problem we've got in the United States is alcohol," said Michael Sonnenreich, executive director of the National Commission on Marijuana and Drug Abuse. In *Town and Country,* Dick Kagan pointed to "statistical evidence" that alcohol is the third largest killer in the country, after cancer and heart disease; he quoted but did not name experts as saying, "If we were thoroughly to scrape the whole problem out from under the rug, [alcoholism] might turn out to be our number one health problem."

Well, maybe. The great debate rages. Alcoholism flourished for centuries without triggering urban jungles of burglary, armed robbery, larceny, mugging, assault, and spiraling criminal violence. Alcoholism has a long lead, there is no question, but it may be looking over its shoulder to find drug addiction gaining in the deadly race.

Governor Nelson Rockefeller put the situation in a balanced perspective: "Right now, addiction to alcohol is overshadowed by addiction to drugs in terms of public alarm and concern. This is understandable. It is a newer scourge. It is spreading swiftly among young people. And it demands all-out war. But alcoholism must not be allowed to become the forgotten addiction. For in the sum total of human misery that it causes, alcoholism continues to rank among the major social evils afflicting our society."

We have already introduced Dr. Morris Chafetz, a leader in the federal government's war against alcoholism. We quote him again as an eminently qualified authority to suggest that of all addictive drugs, alcohol is among the best and least harmful (just as of all alcohols, wine is best and least harmful):

> Although we have many chemical cannons to shoot at the patient, let us for the moment focus only on liquor's role.
> Liquor does not have the unpleasant or dangerous side effects of other drugs. Antibiotics have surely been a great blessing, but as with alcohol, too much of a blessing can be disastrous. Antibiotics are used too early and too often, and we may in time pay the price for this free and easy use.

Then Dr. Chafetz gave us all something to think about as we poke into our medicine cabinets for the pill bottles: "If the proper, controlled use of liquor came back into the practice of medicine, the sale of tranquilizers, and many other drugs, would plummet."

Alexander Webber got to the heart of the matter a century ago. "It is found that in a state of nature instinct points out to mankind, even in an uncivilized condition, a means of obtaining narcotics and stimulants in some manner or other, tending very powerfully to refute the pratings of teetotalers, *et hoc genus omne.*"

In other words, it's the nature of man to get drugged in some way or other and in some degree or other. So why not do it the best way—which means the most agreeable, most beneficial, and by extension least harmful way?

The civilized consumption of wine, used in lieu of hard liquor and/or hard drugs, can help combat *both* alcoholism and other drug addiction. What matters which is worse? They are both terrible.

One thing any individual can do to help both himself and the commonweal is to drink a little more wine *in compensation for* taking a few less pills and other drugs to accomplish the same ends.

It's a great deal more fun. And the serpent's tooth does not lurk in the wine.

5

Follow Your Doctor's Ardors

There are more old wine drinkers than old doctors.

GERMAN PROVERB

There's more old drunkards than old doctors.

POOR RICHARD'S ALMANAC

Doctors make the decisions for us, or at least the recommendations, having to do with life and death. But like their patients, they are mortal, too—although some of them don't always care to admit it.

Vintners tell me the medical profession leads all the others in appreciation and consumption of wine. They point out the number of "medical friends of wine" societies, and the predominance of doctors in the ranks and leadership of such organizations as wine and food societies and wine appreciation associations. The world teems with doctors who make a hobby of growing grapes and making wine.

Australian surgeon Max Lake is the winemaker at his own vineyard which he named "Lake's Folly." He is only kidding, you may be sure, for he commented, "I also judge in wine exhibitions annually and it is a judicial opinion that I make some of the best wine in the world." He further wrote, "I think you will be surprised at the fact that the Australian wine industry appears to have been almost totally founded by physicians and surgeons."

I was surprised—and delighted too. It is my considered judgment that all these wine-loving doctors in America and Australia and elsewhere would find some more healthful hobby if they thought the fermented grape was bad for them or for other people. By their own predilections such doctors appear

53

to shore up my conviction that wine is indeed good for my health. Where could I look for better support?

Medical Economics questioned a group of doctors, finding that 80 percent take a drink or so on weekdays, and even more on weekends. *Virginia Medical Monthly* said that most physicians now generally "regard moderate drinking certainly not as harmful, and often beneficial, to their well being."

Yet for all the doctors who make wine, and all the doctors who love to drink wine, and all the doctors who organize to drink wine with their peers, I found precious few who will publicly praise wine for health or will prescribe it to their patients even as they quietly swish it down at their own dinner tables. More than one doctor I know officially denigrates the values of wine, particularly as a health medium, despite a lusty appreciation for the pleasures of drinking it. One of California's leading physicians, conversing with me, opened with a twenty-minute, bone-chilling recital of the horrors of alcoholism as the number one blight of mankind. Then, making sure I turned off my tape-recording machine and agreed not to quote him by name, with equal intensity he switched to his favorite hobby and recited his adventures and satisfaction making his own wines, "including the finest Cabernet Sauvignon and Pinot Chardonnay in the world. But the vintners need not worry about me. I won't sell a drop of it. It's too good. I drink it all myself or give it to my friends."

The biggest bugaboo that turns objective health professionals into antialcoholics, at least for the record, is fear of alcoholism. Although doctors are better trained and more scientific minded than most people, doctors are still human. They react to prejudice like everyone else.

Because of their training and their experience, our doctors may be more sensitive to the hidden pitfalls of alcohol than most of the rest of us. We can appreciate a doctor hesitating to encourage wine drinking by others lest some unfortunate souls become alcoholics. Nevertheless, we would be shortsighted not to look at both sides of this situation. If our doctors do not preach what they practice, perhaps it behooves us to do as the doctors do, not as they say. We can follow our doctors' ardors!

Brillat-Savarin criticized doctors for "the barbarous severity which they use toward their patients" in connection with drinking wine. "The initial misfortune of falling into their hands is the prelude to a whole series of defensive struggles, and the re-

BETTER NOT TO LISTEN TO DOCTORS?

Father George M. Trunk at age one hundred was thought to be the oldest practicing Roman Catholic priest and also the oldest active newspaper columnist in the United States.

His pastor, Father Vidal Vodusek of San Francisco's Church of the Nativity Parish, told me Father Trunk drinks two glasses of wine at noon and two in the evening plus a bit of brandy after meals, topped off with three or four cigars a day.

Asked how long this has been going on, Father Vidal said, "They start quite early in Europe, you know."

When Father Trunk, at age seventy-six, came to San Francisco from Leadville, Colorado, a couple of miles above sea level, his doctor feared an altitude-adjustment problem and prescribed, "No more coffee, no more wine, no more brandy, no more cigars."

Reacting that "I might as well go to the undertaker," Father Trunk continued doing those things that brought him joy.

To me Father Vidal commented, "After all, it goes to show that sometimes it is better not to listen to doctors too much."

---

nunciation of all the minor joys of life. I rise to protest against the greater part of their bans and vetoes as being useless. I say *useless,* because the sick are almost never inclined to eat what would do them harm."

"If distressing sensations are by nature injurious, pleasant ones are equally wholesome," reasoned Savarin. Let "these bedside tyrants" be assured "that their prescriptions are almost always ineffectual," he continued; "the patient seeks to avoid complying with them, and his friends are ready with all manner of reasons to strengthen him in his resolve; and the death rate varies not at all in consequence."

Savarin gave two humorous stories to embellish his point.

Canon Rollet was a hard drinker. He fell sick, and the first words of the doctor laid a ban on all use of wine. Nevertheless, on his very next visit, he found his patient in bed, and beside him a table covered with a snow-white cloth, a crystal goblet, a noble bottle, and napkin ready to wipe his lips withal.

At the sight of these things he fell into a monstrous rage, and spoke of withdrawing from the case, when the poor canon spoke in doleful tones, "Ah, but Doctor, recollect that you forbade me the use of wine, you never cut me off from the joy of seeing the bottle."

Savarin also told the sad story of one M. de Montlucin, whose doctor "was far more cruel still; he not only laid his ban on wine, but even ordered his poor patient to drink water in large doses."

Soon after the doctor-despot's departure, M. de Montlucin's nurse brought him a large glass. After one mouthful the patient returned the vessel saying, "Take it, my dear; I have always heard it said that medicine must not be wasted."

Moralized Savarin: "I am more than happy to give my readers a piece of good news, namely that good cheer is far from being injurious to health and under equal conditions gourmands live longer than the rest of mankind."

Germany's Dr. F. Maret stipulated that modern medicine "has to take much from wine, from its myths, its magic and its high rank as a remedy. As medication in the strictest sense—it is nowhere registered anymore. But its position as a therapeutic aid has remained and only a pitiable, incorrigible teetotaler among the doctors will want to miss it in his therapeutic treatment."

E. von Leiden, European nutrition physiologist, warned that while some doctors may forbid wine because of a technical conviction that it is bad for a given situation, others will ban it because they are prejudiced against it on emotional, religious, or moral grounds: "Many doctors order or forbid alcohol more from their personal stand on the alcohol question instead of carefully considering the interest of the partient."

On the other side of the coin, a wine-loving doctor, Kenneth G. Cambon of British Columbia, admitting his experiences with wine and patients to be "blind to the science of statistics," commented that because he was an amateur winemaker, "it should therefore cause no surprise that I am now prescribing more and more wine."

I am much taken with the mystery of why so many doctors

DOCTOR KNOW THY PATIENT

It is more important to know what sort of patient has the disease than to know what sort of disease the patient has.

CALEB PARRY

who drink wine and love it are apt to shun mention of this in patient-doctor relationships, or who even lean over backward and, keeping their personal acceptance of the beverage a deep secret, discourage its consumption by less fortunate men.

We shall now touch upon how, from the dawn of recorded medical history until earlier this century, doctors used wine as medicine:

Hippocrates, the "father of medicine," pioneered application of wine to medical use. Employing few pharmaceutical preparations, he administered diets, laxatives, and "vinous medicine" to cure disease.

Many of the best doctors since Hippocrates had nothing but praise for wine, and much of it in extravagant terms. To be sure, they spoke without the backup of scientific methods (especially the so-called "controlled sample" technique), which has in so many ways befuddled our over-technical age. But their considered *opinions* on wine as on some other matters still would seem to deserve consideration today.

THE DOCTORS' CHOICE

Detroit's Dr. Joseph A. Johnston said of his penchant for relaxing with two martinis before dinner and two highballs after dinner, "It's a damned sight better than Seconal."

Peter and Barbara Wyden, in a survey of doctors' diets for *Holiday* magazine, commented, "Quite a few other doctors in our survey enjoyed their liquor late at night and for the same reasons."

Dr. Ancel Keys told the Wydens, "When I'm faced with dinner without wine, it's like some sort of punishment. We usually kill a bottle between the two of us."

Asclepiades, physician to Cicero and medical innovator (shower baths; graduated, open-air exercises; diet restrictions), was noted as a wine prescriber and won popularity with the name "Oinodotes"—giver of wine. Going to either extreme of the emotional spectrum, he would fill his insane patients with wine to induce sleep or administer it in cases of lethargy to excite and awaken the senses.

Combining medicine with pleasure, Hippocrates, Theophrastus, Mnesitheus, Erisistratus, Cleophantus, Dioscorides, Oribasius, and other leading physicians of the Greco-Roman world championed the use of wine for specific diseases and put together a medical system dominated by wine as perhaps the most important therapeutic agent—a status it retained with fluctuating degrees of emphasis until early in our own century.

Mnesitheus declared that the gods had revealed wine as the greatest blessing of mortals. He wrote of Dionysus, the god of wine: "In medicine it [wine] is most useful; it can be compounded with liquid drugs; it brings help to the wounded. Therefore Dionysus is everywhere invoked as physician."

Mnesitheus advised regular drinkers to occasionally go on a spree to purge themselves of hangovers, becoming the first recorded professional advocate of "the hair of the dog that bit you."

Dioscorides, physician to Nero, saluted wine as "good for all the bitings and stingings of all creeping beasts" and "good for the long continuance of windiness of the midriff, and against the bitings of the stomach, and 'nitchcock orf yesking' [hiccups]." Wine is good, he added, "against bending or stretching out of the stomach, and against the flowing of the guts and belly [diarrhea]." He recommended it also for "lustful women."

Celsus, whose encyclopedic *De Re Medicina* of eight books was lost until its rediscovery by Pope Nicholas V in the fifteenth century, prescribed systematically for every disease affecting any part of the body. Most of his medicines included some kind of wine.

Galen, after Hippocrates the most famous doctor of antiquity, founder of experimental physiology and author of almost a hundred books, put together a system of healing so comprehensive that it ruled European medicine almost until modern times. His elaborate list of vegetable drugs, most of them compounded with wine, won the historic name "galenicals."

In his first book, *De Sanitate Tuehda,* Galen wrote, "Wine

moistens and nourishes whatsoever is before made dry . . . and assuages and overcomes the sharpness of bitter gall, and empties out by sweat and drives forth by water"—meaning it flushes out the system and so is a good diuretic. "Wine drives away sadness and pensiveness," he continued. "If a man will use it wisely, it will digest and distribute or convey the nourishment, increase blood, and it will also make the mind both gentler and bolder."

Galen pioneered the conception of wine still honored today as a boon for geriatrics: "There are two profits which come to old men by the use of wine: one is, that it warms all the members of their bodies, and the other is that it scours out by the water all the wheyishness or thin wateriness of the blood."

Doctors of the ancient world had to function without the test tube, the laboratory, the machine, modern chemicals and drugs, electricity, and so on, but they laid the foundations for these marvels to come. Let us give them all credit for making the most of what they had.

Maimonides pointedly observed that wine "removes the superfluities from the pores . . . and excretes urine and perspiration. The benefits of wine are many if it is taken in the proper amount, as it keeps the body in a healthy condition and cures many illnesses. But knowledge of its consumption is hidden from the masses." Then, as so often now.

Perhaps the most famous medieval physician was Arnald of Villanova, who came along eleven centuries after Galen to produce the earliest printed book on wine. Arnald extolled wines even as he expounded wisdom pertinent to our own more drug-filled days: "The modest and wise physician will never hasten to drugs unless compelled by necessity." In his *Liber de Vinis,* Arnald became one of the first to praise and appraise wine's psychosomatic properties: "Its goodness is not only revealed in the body but also in the soul, for it makes the soul merry and lets it forget sadness." Wine is "becoming to the old because it opposes their dryness. To the young it is a food, because the nature of wine is the same as that of young people."

Arnald enumerated the systemic beneficiaries of wine: the brain, the digestive system, the blood, and "all the spiritual parts." Ailments alleviated by wine included cold flux, old age, short breath, heart trouble, muscular pains, "flatulence of the belly," failure to conceive, nausea, dysentery, and indigestion. Arnald appreciated wine, but not less the alcohol which is its

THE DOCTOR WHO NEVER LOST A CASE

Germany has a legend about a doctor who never lost a case. Coming in cases, he is named *Bernkastler Doktor*. As both doctors and wines go, he is one of the most expensive. As *doctors* go, he is easiest to take.

For generations it has been said of this "doktor" that if you drink him bountifully all sorts of woes will stay away from your door. If "an apple a day* keeps the doctor away" in some parts of the world, in the Mosel region of Germany they say, "a 'doktor' a day keeps your troubles away."

It all started when Archbishop Bomund II, Elector of Trier from 1351–1362, fell ill and appeared to be on his deathbed. A flask of wine was brought to ease his journey to the next world, but by a miracle it projected him back into this one in full health. This nectar of his salvation was named *Bernkastler Doktor*. It became written:

> Ye who are sick and sorrowful
> Arouse yourself and take a pull
> Of Wine—the finest Doktor.
> It's better than the best of pills,
> For Doktor wine can cure all ills—
> A great and kindly Doktor!
> For cheering draughts so justly famed,
> Its native hill is proudly named
> (Just like the wine)—The Doktor.

most spirited ingredient. "It prolongs life, and that is the reason it deserves to be called 'water of life.' Eau-de-vie [alcohol] stimulates all the faculties of the mind, especially memory. This

---

* Dr. Elmer L. Severinghaus, internationally recognized nutrition authority and medical consultant to the Vitamin Information Bureau, said that apples have no other great virtue than to supply a bit of sugar and some vitamin C.

A whole pound of fresh, unpeeled apples supplies 242 calories, and a mere 16 milligrams of vitamin C. A pound of peaches, even when peeled, adds only 150 calories but provides 29 milligrams of vitamin C and 5,250 international units of vitamin A.

water of life is a water of immortality; it prolongs life, dissipates the bad humors of the body, strengthens the heart, and keeps up youth."

Doctors did not have as much to work with in those days, to be sure; but in some ways they may have been easier to live with.

One of the first medieval medical schools was established at Salerno, Italy, immortalized by its health code in poetic form, "Regimen Sanitatis Salernitanum." It was medical gospel to medieval physicians. Wine was an integral part of the "Regimen," being the therapeutic agent most often invoked.

Pleasure as therapy was endorsed by double entendre in this passage, which also prescribes activities pertinent to the seasons:

> The Spring is moist, of temper good and warme,
> Then best it is to bathe, to seate, and purge,
> Then may one ope a veine in either arme,
> If boyling bloud or feare of agues urge:
> Then Venus recreation doth no harme,
> Yet may too much thereof turne to a scourge.
> In Summer's heat (when choller hath dominion)
> Coole meates and moist are best in some Opinion:
> The Fall is like the Spring, but endeth colder,
> With Wines and Spice the Winter may be bolder.

Dr. Alexius of Kamp-am-Rhine often said to his patients, "Drink wine, it cures you." When a very old lady to whom he had recommended wine died anyhow, his friends at the weekly medical meeting said, "You see, doctor, the woman died anyhow." Dr. Alexius replied, "She did not drink enough wine."

Ferdinand von Heuss, physician-vintner, lashed out against adulterated wines in colorful language, reported by Dr. Kliewe: "In a scientific paper he condemned them to Dante's Inferno, where bribed officials, forgers, and traitors forever have to drag the lead habits of their rotten beings through hell. Already in the early Middle Ages the devil's servants who tried to spoil the holy wine with impure materials were punished with the most severe church laws."

Excoriating new wine, Dr. William Turner, who wrote the first wine book to be printed in English, presented possibly the earliest plea for proper aging of wine and yet one of the most earthy ever turned out: "I must needs dispraise the manner of our delicate English men and women who drink the English wine only for pleasure whilest it is yet as thick as puddle or horse piss. New wine puffeth a man up, and filleth him with wind, and is hard of digestion, and breedeth heavy dreams, and makes him to make water."

Dr. Turner exalted white wines for their diuretic properties: "Aged men have more need for the most part for such wines as make a man piss much, because they have such plenty of water-ish excrements."

Quoting half a dozen of the most distinguished physicians of his day, a "gentleman of the faculty" in London wrote a letter containing "Observations Concerning the Medical Virtues of Wine" to Dr. Buchan, published in 1787: "There is no product of art or nature which possesses so many medical virtues as good wine. Wine benefits stomach and bowels, nervous energy, the blood, the vascular system. Wine is an antidote to indigestion, loss of appetite, infectious diseases, putrid colluvies, bad circu-lation ('a putrid state of the blood'), fever, languor, weariness, trembling of the hands, giddiness and frequent faintings, and af-fections of the blood. It is a nutrient and a restorative."

Assessing that "generous wine, properly administered, would be found the best medicine," the medical observer ex-pressed a thought that may deserve more consideration than it gets in our modern drug age:

> When all this can be effected by the most pleasant liquid in the world, we cannot but wonder at the absurdity of those who swallow disagreeable drugs at the risk of their lives. Nor is it less astonishing that physicians, who in all ages have acknowl-edged wine as a medicine, should not so much as give it a place in their prescriptions unless in a medicated form; I mean, com-bined with metals, gums, and other detestable drugs. Would they prescribe wine to their patients in proper quantities, and take care that they should have it pure, generous, and good, they would find it worth all the articles of the *Materia Medica* put together.

As the rising tide of antialcohol crusaders surged to front and center, a swirling controversy shook up wine's long reign as the "mother of medicines" and sowed the seeds of modern medi-cal reluctance to smile upon this ancient nepenthe of mankind.

Coincidentally, the scientific breakthrough in drugs and chemicals helped escort in the new era. Its coming was tele-graphed by Charles Tovey in 1862: "Modern practitioners do not appear to advocate the use of wine as a medicine to the same extent as the ancient physicians. Some dislike to give a professional sanction to what may be termed the gratification of a depraved taste, and fear that a habit formed during illness may be continued in convalescence."

Meanwhile, the medical profession came under increasing attacks, such as this accusation in *A History of Drink* by James Samuelson, an antialcohol attorney: "Another explanation has been given of the prevalence of drunkenness, namely, the practice on the part of medical men of too freely prescribing alcohol as a remedy for bodily ailments . . . indeed, we shall find presently that medical men of the higher order admit this to be the case. The downfall of many a man or woman has dated from the first dose prescribed by a heedless or mercenary physician."

The resulting doctor's dilemma was well delineated as Dr. Savory of St. Bartholomew's Hospital tried to state both sides of the intensifying dialogue:

I am sure that we could not altogether dispense with [alcohol's] use without frequent disadvantages to our patients, and even the occasional sacrifice of life. In cases where stimulants are required, sometimes others, as certain drugs, might be substituted . . . but . . . there must remain, I think, many instances in which alcoholic drinks largely promote recovery, and several in which the balance of life and death turns upon their prompt and judicious administration. When I reflect on the enormous evil of alcohol to the community—an evil in its physical and moral results beyond parallel—I wish with all my heart that I could, as a surgeon, say less for this most prolific parent of disease and crime.

Doctors and forces in favor of wine conducted a long and determined holding action.

In 1880, the British Medical Society sponsored a study that found an average longevity of fifty-three years for heavy drinkers, fifty-nine years for semiabstinents, and sixty-three years for moderate drinkers. "Wine is more conducive to good health than strict abstinence," interpreted Dr. Alfred Hiller of the Giannini Foundation.

A complaint being voiced by increasing numbers of doctors today, and by some of their patients too, was expressed early this century by C. W. Hawker: "The average medical man has oft a failing, and that a somewhat serious one. He seldom knows much about wine, for, for some unexplainable reason, a knowledge of the health-giving and curative properties of wines, and the special characteristics of the different varieties, is not included in the curriculum of the ordinary medical student. He is crammed with enough learning about drugs to fit him for the post of a qualified dispensing chemist, and he can cover a page with cabalistic chemical symbols without turning a hair."

Dr. Yorke-Davies, of the Royal College of Physicians in London, chronicled dawn of a new era in wine and doctor relations in his 1909 book, *Wine and Health: How to Enjoy Both.* "The ordinary medical practitioner takes very little interest in the medical effects of alcohol. He is more taught the use of drugs which . . . in ailments due to errors in diet and malnutrition are perfectly useless. Neither a prophet nor a watering place have any honor in their own country."

Half a century later Dr. Heinrich Kliewe elaborated on the new era:

> In old times most physicians recognized the beneficial effect of wine on the psyche and the healthy or ill body. If today wine plays a less important role as a remedy it can be traced to the excellent chemical preparations available for the treatment of different illnesses. But even today wine's importance for health cannot be denied.
>
> Since wine consumption considerably increases yearly, the physician today cannot basically reject it, but he should acquire specific knowledge about the effect of all ingredients of wine on the healthy or sick organism.
>
> Generally, most physicians today have a benevolent attitude toward wine at home and socially, but with their patients they often act like real wine opponents. Physicians thinking negatively about wine should at least consider, when they forbid wine drinking to a patient, if the gain in health which they achieve through the prohibition stands in the right proportion to the therewith affected decrease of joy in life.

Which suggests—"Physician, heal thyself."

Notwithstanding that wine—unique among medicines for tasting good and providing pleasure while it does its work—has suffered a long eclipse from the dark night of Prohibition, plus the emerging prevalence of more potent and direct chemicals, there are signs of a coming restoration in which we may again lick our chops as we mitigate our miseries. Wine still has a role on the medical stage.

In 1937, less than five years after the repeal of Prohibition, the International Committee for the Scientific Study of Grapes and Wine secured the opinions of 4,560 physicians in twenty countries. While 3,936 doctors held wine to be useful or even indispensable, only 425 professed a negative opinion. Thus 86 percent favored wine consumption and only 9 percent were against it—a margin that would make any candidate for office hysterical. And 956 of the doctors who advocated wine did not even themselves use it. The report did not say how many of the opposed 425 unofficially drank it themselves.

In the 1960s, a poll taken by Louis Harris and Associates for *Life* magazine, covering a cross section of five hundred urban, suburban, and rural American physicians, showed that 75 percent of doctors drink, and almost half (48 percent) drink wine with dinner.

Fresh evidence that today's medical establishment is constructively reassessing wine for health emerged when seven teams of nationally distinguished doctors joined in the National Study of the Medical Importance of Wine at the beginning of the 1970s. The project defined the great need for research to begin finding out more basic things about the world's oldest but still most baffling alcoholic beverage. In a timely ecological thrust, the report noted, "The lessons of history can clearly be applied once again. If present trends continue, water will soon once again be unfit for drinking. Wine can serve to purify our polluted waters or it can even serve as a suitable substitute." Research programs were proposed to examine the impact of wine on emotional tensions, cardiovascular disease, nutrition and metabolic disorders, and gastrointestinal disease.

The clincher was reserved for the last, summarizing recommendation, "Educating Health Professionals in the Medical Values of Wine": "While information on the medical importance of wine has accumulated for many centuries, the traumatic period of Prohibition in America has helped keep much of it out of American medical texts and journals. Despite the fact that wine is one of man's oldest medicinal agents and, as such, widely used in Europe, it is not yet included in the standard American curricula of physicians, nurses, and other medical personnel."

Wine has only been around for thousands of years, the report reminded us. It is time for the most advanced scientific nation in the world to approach the subject of wine and its inadequately understood potential benefits to mankind with candor and enlightenment rather than with the continued prejudice of ignorance, superstition, and fear.

A Hospital Is Not a Home

Coming and going, the hospital is the main port of passage between this world and the next. Even as trains invariably enter and leave a city through the ugliest, most disreputable part of town, the hospital is the most unlikely and unlovely sort of a portal to begin or end the only journey we'll ever make through life.

Have you ever known anybody who wanted to go to a hospital? One goes because he is sick or fears he is sick and hopes to be restored, but deep inside, every hospital patient takes with him into those forbidding walls a private dread that he may not emerge alive.

His ordeal has come and he must forsake the bright familiarity of home and the cheerful noises of spontaneous social contact as he enters an institution alien, gray, forbidding, inhuman, and inhumane.

This is when a fellow needs a friend. He has found it—in wine—in thousands of years of European hospital tradition. In ancient Egypt, even before the Golden Era of classic Greece, the physicians of Pharaoh Ikhnaton and his queen Nefertiti knew more about wine than many modern doctors, and they administered it in their temple-hospitals to help patient morale and convalescence.

Hippocrates, who began so much in the realm of medicine, incorporated wine into the regimen for almost all acute and chronic diseases—and especially during the period of convalescence. This practice persisted with the passing centuries to become universal today in Europe.

The tradition of serving wine in hospitals, convalescent centers, and nursing homes is at last getting a start in the United States with the emergence of apostles of enlightenment such as New York's Dr. William Dock, who wrote, "What is needed in our city hospitals . . . and other retreats for ailing or aged people is a regular alcohol ration, such as is normal everywhere in Europe."

Stressing the cruelty of denying a familiar comfort in this time of terror and tribulation, Dr. Dock continued, "Most physicians forget that the normal apprehension and restlessness of people sent to hospitals is exaggerated in many patients who are accustomed to a few drinks in the evening, or at lunch and supper, when they enter a hospital, where little or no potable alcohol is provided. Prescribing the continued intake of the usual beverage does relieve the mild but undesirable disturbance in the ordinary citizen when drinking is cut off by hospital custom."

Every doctor knows that recovery is a state of mind, and that the will to live is essential for recuperation. Dr. Morris E. Chafetz, agreeing with Dr. Dock, wrote, "A small amount of alcohol administered at proper meals may actually *hasten* recovery in the hospital." So, he continued, "Why can't the chronic-disease wards in our hospitals provide liquor in small doses to patients with evening meals, or perhaps schedule a cocktail party whereby the patients . . . can chuck the deadly routine and socialize a bit?

"It would only help counteract the tendency in all chronic sufferers to withdraw into themselves and to become married to their bodies and complaints—and thus miss out on the benefits and lightness that can come from sharing a delightful moment with other fellow beings."

Studies by Sarley and Stepto and also by Funk and Prescott demonstrated that serving wine in hospitals lowered patient complaints, made patients more cooperative with doctors and staff, and relieved patient anxieties and fears, although 3 percent of the patients at Wrightwood in Chicago refused wine "since they had never been wine drinkers and didn't intend to start now."

Addition of wine was most important with older patients and with those to whom wine drinking was already a part of their life-style. The wine made patients happier.

Beer is another fermented drink that has its champions as an institutional anodyne for the aging. Dr. Milton Greenblatt, Massachusetts commissioner of mental health, said that beer has a "remarkable effect in many elderly men and women in our hospitals. It cheers them up, it's nourishing, and it opens up their blood vessels so the blood travels through their systems a bit faster. That's especially important for elderly people who often have circulation problems."

Noting that patients at four Bay State hospitals are drinking some two thousands cans of beer monthly on doctors' orders, Dr.

Greenblatt said: "It's a social lubricant. It helps shy or withdrawn people start a conversation more easily."

Getting into the "spirit," several Massachusetts hospitals have established pubs for patients. Boston State Hospital opened a Pink Elephant. At Westboro State Hospital, it was the Lantern Room. Grafton State Hospital featured The Pub. This was an outgrowth of experiments by Dr. Ching-piao Chien, with four control groups suffering from depression or mental deterioration stemming from senility. One group drank beer, one fruit punch, one fruit punch with a mind-affecting drug added, and one continued to get its usual administration of thioridazine straight. "As Chien suspected, the most efficacious therapeutic agent turned out to be the beer, along with the social atmosphere of the pub and salutary effect of simply being allowed to drink," reported *Time* magazine. Would you believe that not one of the beer drinkers refused his daily glass, while punch drinkers turned theirs down one-fourth of the time?

Wine (or beer) can help the hospital as well as the patient, giving a lift on the public-relations and fund-raising fronts so vital to these traditionally cash-starved institutions.

Dr. Armando R. Favazza suggested, "Wine given to a hospitalized patient may do wonders for the hospital's image as a place where one comes for living and not for dying." It needn't cost much, either. "Wines, when bought in bulk, are negligible in price. Bulk wines are cheaper than fruit and vegetable juices and may be good replacements on the hospital evening cart."

During the postoperative period the patient is at lowest ebb and needs all the allies he can muster. Wine or champagne can supply both a shot in the arm and added food value. Wine can do a lot of things that pills can't do to expedite recovery, inside as well as outside hospitals. Convalescents snowed under by pills, powders, and tonics can also find in a good wine a rapid and rewarding way to health.

The top of the day in hospitals, as in the outside world, is mealtime—and here is when wine can do its best work. Joseph L. Zem, director of San Francisco's St. Luke's Hospital, inventoried the tortures great and small of the hospital inmate—drab costumes, needles and shots, thermometers, catheters, bedpans, blood transfusions, the whole dismal paraphernalia of hospitaldom—but contended that all this can be borne if the victim gets a gustatory respite. "The only thing he can relate to with any pleasure, any thought of home, is what he might be served for his meals."

Zem described St. Luke's menus, which read like those of a fine French restaurant, complete with four-ounce servings of wine at lunch and dinner. St. Luke's chef Battel got this fan letter from the wife of a pleased patient: "While [my husband] was there you fed him so well, and everything was so deliciously prepared, that although I'm a reasonably good cook, life is now difficult for me."

Los Angeles *Times* wine chronicler Nathan Chroman suggested a hospital wine cellar and a hospital wine list so the patients can have some real fun coordinating their wine and food. "A hospital sommelier . . . would be a welcome face, with a key dangling around the neck."

Dr. Robert Druitt reported that about a century ago the Alice Hospital in Darmstadt, Germany, during one-half year used 4,633 bottles of white and 6,332 of red table wine, plus 60 bottles of champagne. With 755 patients during that time, the 11,000 bottles of various wines averaged out to 15 bottles per patient.

A hospital is not a home, but at that rate even a hospital cannot be all bad.

It works both ways for the Hospices de Beaune, a charity hospital founded in 1443 in the wine province of Burgundy. Founder Nicholas Rolin donated a portion of his vineyard, now some of the best grape-growing land in France, to support the hospital. This has been parlayed in the last century into an annual wine auction that often nets the institution more than a half million dollars.

A number of Burgundy wine proprietors contribute a portion of their product to the hospital, with proceeds going directly as a charitable donation. This auction, held every November after the vintage, traditionally sets wine prices prevailing all over Europe.

Wouldn't you rather convalesce in a hospital that serves wine? Here is the stage of a struggle for health, often the last between life and death. Where better to fight—at some dour, drab, gray, penal-type institution or at St. Luke's—which is at the same time a fine hospital and one of the best restaurants in town?

6

❧❧❧❧❧❧❧

When Wine Is
Not Suggested

Regrettable as it may be, there are times and conditions when one should not or must not drink wine.

There could be a temptation for one so unfortunate to say, "The hell with it; I'd rather be dead than dry." Or, perhaps, if it is sufficiently temporary, he will just grit his teeth and bulldoze it through. After all, he is the patient, and it is his life.

If you suffer any physical abnormality or disease, discuss wine use with your doctor. Wine benefits some conditions and hurts others. We give the broad outlines and some case histories and medical opinions in this book, but the specific application to your case is between you and your doctor. So much depends upon the individual and his metabolism, his body conditions, his personal reactions, his medical history. One may take a bottle while another should take only a glass. There are no universal generalities. Your doctor must be the final arbiter and nobody, least of all this author, should undertake to second-guess him.

You may be lucky and have a doctor who appreciates wine and/or (more important and probably more rare) *who understands it*. Or you may be unlucky and have a doctor who is prejudiced against wine (or alcohol, and there is a difference although not all doctors recognize it) for religious or personal reasons. Therefore he fears to let you have any wine even in situations where it is generally acceptable. He sincerely believes it might hurt you or it might set you back or it might create complications or, in most such cases, it might move you in the direction of addiction. Doctors who are against alcohol tend to discount the comfort and the overriding benefits that a little wine can bring. The happy circumstance—in those many situations where the use of wine is an open question and generally accepted—is to have a doctor who has an open and flexible mind backed by a genuine knowledge and understanding of both the advantages and limitations of wine.

There are times when alcohol is bad. There are times when water is bad, milk is bad, air is bad. Whether alcohol, and specifically wine, is good or bad must be decided by your doctor. If, on the one hand, he judges that alcohol can cause addiction and that it can have an adverse impact in certain diseased or abnormal conditions, hopefully, he also weighs that alcohol does not cause disease and that it can help prevent or help combat some diseases.

The doctor's fallible role evoked these words from Dr. J. M. Eylaud, which deserve consideration in a time of decision: "Medicine is an art and . . . there are, not diseases exclusively, but diseased patients with very personal reactions each worthy of being considered with objectivity, interest and care. The doctor must not forget that his art includes intuition, prudence, circumspection."

We present below some red lights established by medical experience and knowledge. We hope none of these apply in your case. In all of the following situations (and perhaps a few more), wine can be harmful:

Alcoholism. No liquor of any kind or degree.

Allergy. You can have an allergy to alcohol, and of course you do not throw a can of kerosene on a burning fire.

Drugs. Drugs and alcohol sometimes are an explosive mixture. If your doctor has you on a drug program, make sure whether you can tolerate wine.

Eczema.

Epilepsy. Wine can cause attacks. But Rodin, Frohman, and Gottlieb gave alcohol to twenty-five adult epileptics without an increase in attacks. While even a little wine is usually forbidden epileptics, the question should be measured to every epileptic individually, and the decision made by the doctor.

Genitourinary disease, including prostratitis or other prostate trouble.

Inflammation of mouth, throat, esophagus.

Kidney infection.

Liver inflammation, cirrhosis, hepatitis.

Lymphogranulomatosis. This and some other tumor diseases can be intolerant to alcohol, reacting with severe pains, bleeding in the tumor area, sudden unconsciousness, local sensation disorders, itching of the skin, and loss of feeling.

Mental problems. With organic or abnormal mental difficulties any wine is forbidden. The same holds true for the pathologically inclined. Any alcohol consumption is to be rejected with alcohol intolerance and hypersensitivity after damage of the brain or with mental deficiency, hysteria, or other abnormal psychic tendencies.

Multiple sclerosis. White wine and concentrated alcohols are forbidden, but moderate amounts of a simple red wine may be permitted, according to Dr. Heinrich Kliewe.

Nerve disorder, neuralgia, neurosis. Although psychotic and neurotic patients complaining of insomnia, anxiety, tension, inner restlessness, obsessions, irritability, and uncertainty can find a mitigation of their troubles with moderate alcohol doses, wine should be rejected with peripheral neuralgia or with infections of the nerves.

Pancreatitis.

Porphyria.

Psoriasis.

Stomach cancer or inflammation, gastritis, ulcers.

Sometimes the doctor says it best. We will let two good doctors close this chapter. Drs. Ferguson and Michael Marie of New York's St. Vincent's Hospital wrote in *GP* (General Practitioner) magazine:

> There is only one contraindication to alcohol, and that is alcoholism. This is generally accepted, and many wise physicians have used any illness in this unfortunate group to prohibit the use of liquor. Since the alcoholic population is exceedingly large and voluble, it is no wonder that people are heard to say that their doctor has prohibited drinking because it will aggravate their arthritis, acne, gallbladder condition, etc., when the actual reason for the prohibition is a real or potential alcoholism.
>
> Many disease states have an occasional but recognized tendency to react unfavorably to alcohol. This reaction might be properly called an idiosyncrasy. Since it occurs infrequently it seems unwarranted to prohibit alcohol to all patients with these particular conditions.

In cases of honest doubt or earnest difference of opinion, two consultants can be better than one. As Dr. J. M. Eylaud so neatly thumbnailed it, when Hippocrates says "yes" and Galen says "no," the best conclusion may be "maybe."

7

❧❧❧❧❧❧❧❧

The Balm of Youth

I proceeded from my mother's breast (and I lingered there for
three years), straight to the wine bottle. . . .

ANGELO PELLEGRINI

It is not *whether* one drinks that is important—for one will either
drink or find other outlets to fill the same imperious needs—but
when and *why* and above all *how* one drinks.

So it boils down, as do so many things, to a matter of education. Education, really, is the process of learning the answers:
when and why, who and where, and above all how. *Whether* is
usually a foregone conclusion.

What better time to start education than when young? And
what better way to conduct education than to learn by doing?
What surer approach to mischief, in drinking or in any other important part of life, for that matter, than to say no when the
young already drink or will surely discover from the streets or the
dormitories or somewhere out there that it's fun, as I did. Prohibitions don't fool anybody and only shrouds the forbidden activity with an aura of arcana, making it a protest against adult
treatment of young people as fools and inferiors.

The Italians, the Jews, the Chinese, and to some degree the
French learned this wisdom a very long time ago, and apply it in
the home. The kids start drinking wine in a mild way often before they have teeth to chew. They are part of the family's activity, and no great fuss is made about it. When they grow up
they have been educated and conditioned, and wine is as natural
a part of their lives as breathing and eating—there is no problem.

Whereas in Italy and the other more civilized lands the
whole family partakes of wine as a living symbol of the abundant

74

ITALIAN WISDOM

Wine is one of the means of holding generations together.

I visit my young lady friends when they are in confinement in the maternity ward. I somehow sneak in with a bottle of wine. I moisten the baby's lips with my best wine, then the mother and I drink the rest of the bottle.

We are fortunate in having a good family. There are three children and none is alienated. I am positive that one of the great bonds that holds us together is what they learn in our home about bread and wine. They have learned to appreciate and respect wine and use it with prudence.

And there was evidence [when my son was] ten years of age that his attitude toward wine was beginning to shape up. One day I heard him offer his friend, two years younger than he, a taste of wine. "Wine!" exclaimed the little fellow, shocked and amazed. "Do you drink wine?" "Sure I drink wine," said the boy. "It's not poison, you know."

I must remember that I myself learned about wine just as I learned to walk; it was a part of growing up. And I must remember, too, that my memories of it are among the happiest of my youth.

And [my children] are now beginning to come to me with this sort of request: "Father, may I take a bottle of wine to Mr. Brown? He just loves it." The request is not only granted, it is applauded. It indicates that the children are coming of age. They themselves are now associating wine with fellowship, realizing that it is a beautiful thing to be shared with one's friends. It would never in the world occur to them to ask for a bottle of whiskey as a gift for Mr. Brown. Never!

ANGELO PELLEGRINI

---

earth and of togetherness, some Americans view it as a threat to survival of the family as an institution. The generation gap and youth revolt are orders of the day, and the establishment is commonly regarded not as the bastion of society but as the enemy.

Where have things gone wrong? For one thing, we may have forgotten the social importance of *eating* together—the love, conversation, fun, settlement of dispute, élan vital. This is the gut machinery of the family unit in the happy lands, and drinking wine with meals is the social lubricant that makes the machine purr. Lacking this, young people turn elsewhere for community experience. Some turn to drugs. These instruments of alienation and self-immuration are used to lock the young into their own generation and lock others out. Wine, however, can be a bridge between generations.

It is said that the United States began to awaken to the world of wine in World War I, when a million young men were

---

SIGNS OF THE TIMES

Assyrian Times: 2800 B.C.

Assyrian tablet: "Our earth is degenerate in these latter days. There are signs that the world is speedily coming to an end. Bribery and corruption are common. Children no longer obey their parents."

Greek Times: 2350 B.C.

Socrates: Children pursue luxury and show disrespect for their elders, loving "chatter in place of exercise. Children are now tyrants, not the servants of their households." Children "no longer rise when their elders enter the room. They contradict their parents, chatter before company, gobble up dainties at the table, cross their legs, and tyrannize over their teachers."

Today

An antialcohol lecturer exhibited to a group of children a live worm, a bottle half full of water, and a bottle of gin. When he placed the worm in the water, it continued to wriggle. Then he filled the bottle with gin, and the worm turned to stone.

"Now, children, what does that show?"

A precocious youngster raised his hand. "It shows that if I drink a lot of gin I won't have any worms."

---

exposed to the culture of Western Europe with more progress made in World War II and subsequent occupation by American armies. Whatever the reasons, table wine enjoys growing appeal with America's young, with food and at parties. "American kids once had to go to Europe to acquire a taste for wine, but now they take it for granted and buy it in gallon jugs," wrote Ron Schwerin in *Esquire*.

When young people drink they particularly favor wine, the *San Francisco Chronicle* reported about its own city, then noted a nationwide trend: "Wine is popular with young people because they are more aware than their parents were of the dangers of drinking hard liquor at an early age. It's part of the new consciousness of better health."

Notwithstanding the hopeful indications that our young people are displaying signs of becoming smarter than we are— they are already smarter than we *were*—we continue to make it as hard as possible for them. Perhaps, as Dr. Chafetz wrote, "So many adults have had such miserable, unhappy, confused adolescent periods that they are unconsciously determined that their children must pass through the same kind of hell. They limit their teenagers' pleasure by all manner of fearful warnings and statistics; they make sure that they get the habit of running in the same old rut, existing without really living; and most important, they make their children forever guilty and fearful of alcohol and sex, or sex and alcohol."

Prohibition was not flushed from the American scene by its constitutional repeal in 1933. As late as 1971, our biggest state (in both population and wine production) saw its state legislature, by a three to two margin, reject constitutional revision permitting eighteen-year-olds to drink. California's legislature took this action three weeks after extending adulthood in other prime areas to those eighteen and older. Thus a Californian at eighteen is a legal adult when it comes to sexual intercourse, dying for his country in war, or voting for the senator who in turn solemnly voted that he is still a child when it comes to drinking a glass of beer in public. One conservative senator argued that drunken driving "would skyrocket" if a twenty-year-old were legally empowered to buy a drink. Was this adult public servant telling us that these "kids" are in fact not drinking because of a law that a senate kept on the books? Or was that senate as ridiculous as it seemed? Perhaps not; it was just a group of men like so many of their peers, terrified of what they did not understand: alcohol and alcoholism.

Incidentally, the state of New York has no more problem with its eighteen-year-old minimum than neighboring Connecticut and New Jersey have with their twenty-one-year-old rules, and New York steadfastly resists their pressure to raise its drinking age. England has a sixteen-year-old limit and gets along just fine.

I join doctors, psychologists, and others more expert than I in such matters to suggest that we dump the twenty-one-year age limit for drinking. It is a farce and an idiocy. It doesn't inhibit drinking compared with the moral mischief and deliberate cheating it instigates, because it takes little more ingenuity for a twenty-year-old to get an illegal bottle than it does for him to breathe. What it does do is drive young people (as the Eighteenth Amendment drove their grandparents) to drink clandestinely, to flaunt the law, and to do it in places and with company neither in their best interests nor society's.

A questionnaire to Stanford University students reflected a liberalized attitude toward drinking as a practice that a lot of people need—with the stipulation that it must be well controlled and not harmful to others. Two-thirds of the freshmen expressed the belief that teen-agers drink mainly to defy authority, an opinion held by three-fourths of the seniors.

A significant comment from the study by Stanford's Institute for the Study of Human Problems: "A lot of people tend to drink too much here due to the enforcement of very strict rules which make drinking something more exciting and special. The regulations really make minors break the law and if they do it together they have something important in common."

Just what is the ideal age to start youthful drinking? We are told that the Italians build a very happy family culture upon starting infants at age three. I have friends who expose their toddlers to a sip or two at the family social hour, and it is one of the happiest family groups I know.

Reuters' 1972 study of French drinking habits concluded that "While thirteen years is a rough consensus, the argument ranges between extremes from farmers who think five is a good age to start to senior executives who keep wine from their children until they are at least fifteen."

San Francisco's Dr. Mark Lewis Gerstle, director of the Adult Psychiatric Clinic of Children's Hospital, lamented, "The delightful soporific and tranquilizing effects of a half bottle of excellent burgundy or sauterne are advantages of which [the adolescent] is ignorant, and when told or even observed, leave him skeptical or incurious. I have heard such comments as 'you have to swill the stuff,' 'it takes too long to get a lift out of wine,' 'it has no kick,' 'why not take a straight shot,' 'it's neater and quicker.'" As a result, the kids go into hard liquor or, seeing "themselves in rebellion against the materialistic strivings of their parents [they] turn the whole marijuana scene into . . . a protest tool, which they use to mock a middle-class culture which they really disdain. This leads them into a drug culture, a shadow world, a psychological dependence whose implications to themselves and society are very disturbing."

All this suggests that wine can enrich the lives of the young—while they are young and increasingly as they mature—if successfully introduced into their lives in a way and at a time to preclude any youthful predilection to the harsher outlets of hard liquor and/or hard drugs.

Wine can bring the generations together, as we can learn from older and wiser cultures. Wine has a significant role in our potential mastery of alienation tendencies in the individual and the possible weakening of the family unit, suggests psychologist Robert Kastenbaum.

"Part of the appeal in drugs to the young," Kastenbaum writes, "is the opportunity to be 'in' on something. But the wine lover is 'in' on an exceedingly rich lode of potential knowledge and experience. One can spend a lifetime of exploring wines and understanding something of the world he lives in through wine."

What can be better for one's mental and physical health than wine? And this appeal lasts a lifetime, gaining proportions, dimensions, depth, new revelations, and more rewarding applications with the years.

8

The Milk of Old Age

. . . Making use of the wine which Dionysus has given men to lighten the sourness of old age; that in age we may renew our youth, and forget our sorrows.

PLATO

Was it not Talleyrand who observed that the young can never appreciate good brandy? Is there not somewhere in one of Meredith's novels, a character that remarks that one has to be as old as a good wine to realize its magnificence? Science, from Hippocrates onward, allows the aged their cup of wine, and although alcohol is an ingredient in it, and an indispensable one, it is not the only ingredient that gives it the high quality that Horace extolled, and that every lover of good wine lauds.

C. LOUIS LEIPOLDT

What goes up must come down. Night follows the day. By quickness or by luck we may escape many a reckoning and get away with many a peccadillo or sin more mortal. But not a one of us will (or ever has) escaped old age—except by bowing out before it arrives.

One does have a choice of aging disastrously or aging gracefully. A person can grow more beautiful and more fascinating with age. A liberal allowance of wine is helpful to the aging process.

Even as wine can prepare us for sleep daily, so can it over a lifetime help prepare us for the big sleep. Every delight we have known wanes with the fleeting years—save only wine, which we may enjoy increasingly. And as our longest, effective pleasure it has the quality, in replacing all the rest, to let us miss them less and less. It even manages to mitigate the deepening veil of melancholy, at least for a little time each day.

The spice of life while young is the enormous vista and

the incredible alternatives of the future. After that has been breached by age, wine helps the traveler accommodate to the realities of life already lived, and provides more exquisite if more limited vistas of the remaining future.

It may be that an old man finds more spiritual than physical satisfaction in wine—for here is at last one thing that improves with age!

The Talmud (Megillah 16b) asks, "What is meant by 'the good things of Egypt' which Joseph sent back to his father?" and answers, "Old wine, in which the minds of old men find comfort." The Talmund also states, "the older a scholar grows the more his mind becomes settled" and that the mind, reflecting upon the similar enrichment in improved wine, "finds comfort in it."

Wrote Athenaeus of Nestor: "And of all heroes, the greatest drinker is Nestor, who lived three times as long as other men; for he evidently used to stick to his wine more closely than other people."

Regimen Sanitatis Salerni, the major medical encyclopedia of the Middle Ages, after excoriating the drinking of water as "hurtful to the stomach" and the cause of many evils, recommended wine to all, but chiefly to old folks:

> One may give an old man as much wine to drinke, as he can bear without hurt, that is as much as his natural and due appetite desireth. For like an old Boots and Buskins [that be dry and wrinkled] are more supple and plaine with oyling; so likewise old folks by drinking of chosen wine.
>
> Ancient folks are cold and wine heateth; their spirit is heavy, and they bee full of melancholy, and wine maketh them merry, and represseth melancholinesse. And commonly, old Folkes sleep ill, and wine maketh them to sleep well.

Dr. Edward J. Stieglitz of Washington commented in a more scientific vein: "Alcohol is a vasodilating substance. It is of considerable assistance in the management and control of arteriosclerotic change in elderly persons. In my opinion the judicious use of whiskey or other spiritous liquors is therefore indicated in the management of many aged patients. Alcohol in moderation supplies quick fuel, relaxes tensions, and tends to increase the appetite. A glass of wine or a highball before dinner and another at bedtime is often most constructive in increasing vigor and endurance in the elderly."

"Wine promotes the metabolism, diminishes the impact of

exhaustion, stimulates breathing and circulation, spurs appetite and the digestive glands, and improves hormone gland performance—being in all these matters especially beneficial to the aged," said Dr. F. Maret.

Dr. Morris Fishbein pointed out that about 10 percent of Americans are over sixty-five years of age—a percentage that will continue to increase with the advancement of medical science. He suggests that wine is better for them than the psychiatrist's couch. "They develop all sorts of mental and disturbed states. This syndrome, called endogenous depression, in which you're ready to quit or to do away with yourself, is an example. I am not certain but that a reasonable use of wine could give about as much help as one gets from a psychic energizer or from a good psychiatrist." Dr. Fishbein referred to wine as the psychiatrist-physician of old age and his contemporary, the famous Canadian physician Sir William Osler, rhapsodized: "Milk is children's wine and wine is the old man's milk."

Wine can be better than medicine. Dr. Morris Chafetz commented on "the most common prolonged illness known: incurable, inevitable old age. Hardening arteries, faulty digestion, insomnia, generalized aches and pains, feelings of uselessness, all are the symptoms of the elderly." He told this anecdote: "My grandfather, who is eighty-nine, has suffered all of these pangs at one time or another, but on those occasions when he has had dinner at our house he always leaves in good humor, having charmed us with his reminiscences and thoroughly enjoyed himself. His circulatory complaints disappear, his appetite, digestion, and mood are excellent. Sleep after such an evening refreshes him."

It seems that grandpa has had a few drinks—all that is necessary to produce what his nurse reports as a "miraculous

---

H. L. MENCKEN: GOOD NEWS

My doctor tells me that in his judgment—and he's one of the best doctors in America—alcohol to a man over sixty is not only harmless but a positive benefit. He said it has an effect on the heart muscle that seems to be very salubrious. This is good news to me.

WINE IS GOOD FOR OLD GIRLS, TOO . . .

Mrs. Grazia Vacca, Sardinia's oldest woman at 107, was toasted by her three children, more than one hundred grandchildren, great-grandchildren without numbers, and an army of friends as the "nanny of all Sardinians."

At the party, with a glass of wine in hand, she toasted herself: "I don't want to die. I want to live many more years."

Her recipe for longevity: "Fresh air and water, good meat and wine."

---

change." Dr. Chafetz diagnosed: "Getting out to see his family helps, of course, but so does the liquor. You see, at home he cannot have it—because his nurse is afraid he will become dependent on it!"

Dr. Kliewe, who established his objectivity by being frequently critical of wine, called it "the old boys' darling." Describing the onslaught of age with its reduced heat production, lowered appetite, undernourishment, malnutrition, diminished cell and glandular functioning, slowed metabolism, delayed absorption, impaired excretion, and other penalties, he said: "Without a doubt, wine, which contains several hundred matters, can supplement most of the missing or insufficient existing substances and contribute in a stimulating and regulating way to the metabolism. Next to many other minerals it also contains the substances especially important for the aging person—potassium, calcium, magnesium, phosphorus, and iron, also the trace elements iodine, copper, fluorine, cobalt, molybdenum, and others."

Certain vitamins, especially the B group, can be supplemented by wine, which offers such valuable ingredients as acids, nitrogen compounds, sugars, oils, and alcohol.

With age the stomach may begin to break down and the digestive juices may run low. This is where wine can do some of its best work, giving a sort of daily "engine overhaul," as it were. Germany's Dr. F. Maret suggested: "With growing age, when the secretion of the digestive juices usually decreases, wine is especially useful. It favors the intake of high-protein and fat foods, and according to more recent research wine can lower a heightened cholesterol level in the blood. So wine justifies its good reputation as 'the milk of old age.' "

The wisdom of continuing or even increasing alcoholic portions to those who had drunk all their life was expounded by Dr. Abraham Jacobi: "When an old man is ill, no matter the cause of his illness, he should take the amount of alcohol he has been in the habit of taking each day. It may even be necessary to increase the dose. It may be disastrous to change an old man's mode of living. There are many old persons who are suffering for want of alcohol in some form. To relieve them it may be necessary to resort to narcotics; there is a close relation between the two." However, Dr. Jacobi made his preference starkly clear: "Alcohol is less harmful, as it does not check secretions and excretions."

Perhaps the number one curse of aging, which befalls many, is to get laid away in an institution of some sort. "Abandon all hope, ye who enter here," well might be writ over the entry door to one of these terrestrial pugatories where old people pass away the rest of their time without excitement, without usefulness, without meaning, and without joy. Several studies have shown that if there is a ray of sunshine in these gloomy tombs of the breathing, it comes out of the wine bottle.

In addition to the subjective benefits of bringing joy, helping digestion, encouraging sleep, and stimulating appetite, in such institutions wine can bring "togetherness" between one inmate and his fellows, and between generations when the younger

---

WATER, THE TROUBLEMAKER

Wine, beer, or booze—name your poison, if you're getting along in years. But watch out for that water!

Andrew Hastings of Louisville observed his one hundredth birthday in the spring of 1972 by downing two fried eggs, rolls with peanut butter spread on them, a steamy serving of sauerkraut, and a can of beer. He finished it off with a shot of booze.

Hastings had a simple explanation for his choice of food and drink: "Water will rust your insides."

WINE AND LONGEVITY

He who drinks one glass a day
Will live to die some other way.

LATIN PROVERB

Wine works the heart up, wakes the wit;
There is no cure 'gainst age but it:
It helps the headache, cough, and tisic,
And is for all diseases physic.

JOHN FLETCHER

---

people visit. It makes the patient again feel like "somebody." And it helps the staff, by making them more acceptable to the patients and making the patients seem more like people, like personalities, in fact.

An immortality elixir wine may not be, but the belief that it is a longevity agent seems supported by a flood of empirical evidence accumulated over centuries. While wine will almost never kill the patient and rarely cures him, it so often makes him happier and hence determined to get well that it can be credited with helping to preserve its own patrons. Not to mention wine's services in helping discourage many miseries that bedevil life, an area we will explore in these pages.

The landmark story of Luigi Cornaro was such an epic in the annals of longevity that it made *Encyclopaedia Britannica*. A Venetian nobleman, vintage 1467–1566, he was so dissipated by age forty that his physicians gave him up for dead unless he would summarily mend his ways. He got the message and reduced his diet to a daily ration of twelve ounces of solid food plus fourteen ounces of wine. Later he cut back to an egg daily plus a liberal measure of wine. He lived to be ninety-nine.

At eighty-three Cornaro wrote *The Sure and Certain Method of Attaining a Long and Healthful Life,* which ran through many editions of its English translation. Other books were written by him at ages eighty-six, ninety-one, and ninety-six. Addison commented that his works were written "with such a spirit of cheerfulness, religion, and good sense, as are the natural concomitants of temperance and sobriety."

TO WHOM AM I SPEAKING

An elderly couple were noted among their friends both for their vitality and their penchant for drinking a robust portion of wine.

The wife, visiting her doctor for a checkup, was startled to hear him report, "Lady, you're pregnant."

"But that's impossible. I'm sixty-eight."

"I don't care if you're one hundred; you're pregnant."

"But, doctor," she protested. "My husband is ninety-five."

"Well, then, young lady, pick up the telephone and congratulate him."

She dialed home and when he answered, she burst out, "Darling, guess what; I'm pregnant!"

There was a prolonged silence at the other end of the phone, until he replied with dignity, "To whom am I speaking?"

"Moderate drinkers seem to live longer than teetotalers," wrote Dr. Herbert L. Gould in *Medical Times*. "Some evidence seems to support the belief."

Dr. Raymond Pearl of Johns Hopkins University matched a group of ninety moderate drinkers against their blood brothers, who abstained. "Significantly, the experiment had to be abandoned when the last of the nondrinking brothers died," commented Dr. Gould. "But Dr. Pearl had enough results to report that moderate, steady drinkers had a somewhat lower rate of mortality and a greater expectation of life."

Professor M. Hochrein, a famous heart specialist of Ludwigshafen, tested thirteen hundred citizens of that German city who exceeded eighty years of age and found that all who had reached this respectable age in good condition had been wine drinkers since their youth. The wine-drinking population averaged ten years older than all others.

Dr. Hochrein accounted for the phenomenon: Light wine up to one bottle per day levels blood pressure, wine does not overload the system with liquid, the alcohol content of wine is not sufficient to render the heart toxic, wine is an easily assimilated conveyor of energy, wine contains "all the important mineral elements and valuable vitamins as well as calories"; wine acts euphorically, it is antispasmodic, it is antineuralgic, its acts as a sedative and can dampen pain.

The Abkhasians, who live in a remote part of the USSR, are famous for their longevity. For them to pass ninety and one hundred is commonplace. While 2.6 percent of them live to be over 90 according to latest figures, the comparable rate in the Soviet Union is .1 percent and in the United States, it is .4 percent.

According to the Ethnographic Institute in Sukhumi, arteriosclerosis, where it occurs at all, is found among these people only in extreme old age. Abkhasians themselves credit their longevity to their traditions in sex, work, and diet. Sex usually starts after age thirty and lasts until long after seventy, some fathers siring children after one hundred. One centenarian said, "A man is a man until he is one hundred, you know what I mean. After that he is getting old." As for work, they never retire and work until a very old age—mostly on the farm.

Overeating is considered dangerous, and fat people are regarded as sick. Abkhasians eat without haste, taking only small bites. They do not smoke or drink coffee or tea. But they do consume a locally produced dry red wine. Everyone drinks it, usually in small quantities, at lunch and supper, and they call it "life-giving." It is credited, among other things, with destroying bacteria and preventing the development of arteriosclerosis.

A bishop of Seville, hale and hearty while still in the saddle at well over one hundred, would be asked the inevitable question: "Bishop, how can you enjoy such great health at your great age?"

"There is only one reason," he would reply profoundly. "Every day since I can remember I have consumed a bottle of wine, except, when I have not felt well. Then I have consumed two bottles."

If you are growing old, you may have more to look back on than to anticipate, but wine can do much to fulfill your continuing need for "great expectations."

It has been said that younger wines excel in antibacteriological action against infectious diseases, while older wines perform better against the chronic physical degeneration of old age. The aging person needs both—after all, there should be some compensations for growing old.

Wine does practical things for you, too. Your digestive

system is running down, but wine will sharpen your appetite and make bearable your increasingly stringent diets. Wine will help you eliminate food waste and surplus. Your energy will not be automatic as it once was, but wine bolsters your springs while, by its slower release of alcohol into your bloodstream, it diminishes or avoids the stress that might accompany stronger drinks.

You will be subject to increasing threats or breakdowns in your circulatory system, including its main pump, the heart— another of the deteriorations of time that fortunately responds constructively to the intake of wine.

Your doctor will probably advise you to cut down on both sugar and salt. Again, the chemistry of wine renders it eminently suitable for diets calling for reduced sugar and salt input. And, because it tastes and feels so good, wine helps you put up with dietary stringencies.

Wine's large iron content can impressively alleviate your lowered blood hemoglobin count. Wine's supply of vitamin B_1, the antineuritic agent, is a support against neuritis, often the blight of the elderly.

Reduced supply of hydrochloric acid, another inevitable penalty of the aging process, reduces functioning of the gall-bladder and small intestine—conditions often relieved by wine.

"Any person over forty is his own best physician," it has been sagely said. If you have been drinking wine for years and still like it—perhaps more than ever—you know it is good for you. Prescribe it for yourself. Even the critics of alcohol recognize that an old person accustomed to the solace of wine should be permitted, even encouraged, to continue or increase the application.

As you grow older so many things—sometimes it seems like everything—that you used to do for fun are either eliminated or on the way out. The big exception is wine, which you can enjoy more and more in compensation for less and less of other wanted joys. Wine can help you appreciate what's left and reduce the pain of missing what's gone.

Your pocketbook may be limited, but the less expensive table wines—available in bulk at your wine shops or supermarkets for your own rebottling—can be easy on your budget while every bit as helpful nutritionally, biologically, therapeutically, and spiritually.

WHILE YOU'RE YOUNG

For many years I have known a dentist who is a hearty and robust practitioner and praiser of the art of living. He wouldn't touch wine but I long ago forgave him that foolishness since he was a bit of a hypochondriac who ruled out a number of the good things, because one time or other he thought they made him sick.

But he reveled in boy–girl stories and aphorisms, and one of his favorites was this advice to the new generation:

"Get a lot while you're young."

He didn't mean real estate. I'm afraid he didn't mean wine, either! But so many medical masters, including a number who are ordinarily cool on the virtues of wine, have advised that old people should be allowed to drink to their established capacities that I think my friend's line has a serious extended application here.

And then, finally, as has so often been demonstrated on all continents and in both hemispheres, wine has that crowning capacity to help you live longer to enjoy it more. Hippocrates reminded us centuries ago that the aim of medicine is to have our patients die young—as late as possible. Wine contributes to this in more than one way, perhaps most importantly by making the old feel young as late in the game as possible.

THE CARROT OR THE STICK

There is a world of difference between ordering an old man to take his medicine and inviting him to have a drink.

SALVATORE LUCIA

9

❧❧❧❧❧❧❧

The Happiest Marriage:
Wine and Food

This wine should be eaten;
it is much too good to drink.

JONATHAN SWIFT

Drink a glass of wine after your soup,
and you steal a ruble from the doctor.

RUSSIAN PROVERB

They that drinke wyne with meals, it doth profit them and
maketh good digestion; those people that use to drinke wyne
seldom times, be distempered.

WILLIAM BULLEIN

It is well known among physicians that the best of the nourishing foods is one that the Moslem religion forbids, i.e., wine. It
contains much good and light nourishment. It is rapidly digested
and helps to digest other foods.

MAIMONIDES

Wine and food celebrate not only the happiest marriage, but also
the oldest. And they still enjoy an ecstatic honeymoon, as anyone who has harbored them together can attest.

Pasteur called wine "the most hygienic and healthiest of
drinks." Wine is more than the ideal mate for food, it is itself a
liquid food with multitudinous and mighty merits.

Food, of course, is the first necessity of life. Man spends
a big percentage of his conscious lifetime eating food, and a

larger percentage of his time chasing it. If the meal is not man's most sacred ritual, it is at least the one he is most loath to miss, and it may be the only one with which he is never bored.

Man eats not only to live, he eats to enjoy, he eats to relax, he eats to socialize. This is where the wine performs its stellar role. Wine contributes the subtle dimensions that make a meal more than an exercise of grinding two sets of bones over mouthfuls of groceries. The marriage of wine and food is a happy one because it makes the meal it graces a sacrament.

"We do not regulate our meals according to the food value of their constituents; we want a pleasant meal and a pleasant drink," reported *The Hospital* magazine in June 1907: "The physiological value of pleasurable eating and pleasurable drinking is none the less real because we can't measure it calorimetrically.

"At meals we have not only to do with the science of dietetics, but with the art of gastronomics. Wines may or may not add to the food value of a meal. Even if wine were not a food, in proper and suitable doses it is an accessory to food and a handmaiden to dignity."

Dr. Robert Stepto told a group of his peers that "When wine is used as a food in combination with other foods, the nutritional, physiological and psychological benefits are maintained at maximum levels and any potential hazards are at a minimum. Wine can be included beneficially in the normal diets of most people and can be included in certain therapeutic regimens upon the advice of the physician."

"Wine is a chemical symphony," summarized Professor M. A. Amerine—of more than three hundred different identifiable components. Wine's role with food is a hearty one, which

— helps arouse your taste and appetite;
— helps the cook prepare a good meal;
— helps you digest;
— facilitates your elimination as diuretic and laxative;
— fuels, energizes, helps maintain your body machine;
— fortifies you in many ways and at many renewed times.

What wine does before you eat is as good for your health as what it does while you eat. As an appetizer it can deliver the kick of the cocktail without its penalties, stimulating the flow of gastric juice and arousing your anticipation of the nutrients to come.

In the kitchen, wine adds flavor as a seasoning. It helps mature (predigest) and tenderize the meat while it accentuates and intensifies the flavor. While wine contributes variety and depth to the taste, it also helps to dissolve albuminous mucci of certain fish and to absorb the grease in various meats and poultry.

"If a table without wine is sad, a kitchen without wine is incomplete," declared Edouard Longue of the French Institute of Life. "The effects of wine go beyond its useful actions in the diet of healthy humans. It is equally spectacular in its utility in the diet of those who are ill or convalescent."

Illustrating wine's subtle role in cooking, Longue described the ancient custom of placing several spoonfuls of wine in the bottom of a hot soup plate before pouring the soup. This is called *chabro* or *chabrol* in France. "Dietetically speaking this practice is excellent especially if the soup is thick or fatty. The tepid acids activate the saliva and help the enzymes to work and start the secretion of the pancreatic juices. But this action also has a symbolic side. It shows an unconscious desire to marry wine and food and a simple pride in being able to do so right at the start of a meal." Where could you possibly rather be when eating and drinking time comes than at the right table in France? It all comes together in an old saying: *Poisson sans boisson, c'est poison*—or, Fish without wine is poison.

The principal chemical elements of wine are worth a quick alphabetical review to give an idea of its varied riches.

Acids. More than a dozen, separated into two groups, one growing with the grapes and the other formed during or after fermentation. Most important is tartaric, rarely found in fruits other than the grape, which imparts to the alcohol in wine more richness than is found in any other fermented beverage. Tartaric, tannic, and acetic acids stimulate the flow of gastric juice, giving wine (especially white) its superb quality as an appetizer. Carbonic acids accentuate taste, suppress nausea, and promote diuresis (urination). Some wine acids are antibacterial. Polyphenols help control the rate at which alcohol is absorbed from the intestines and are believed to reduce cholesterol levels. White wines usually contain more acids than red, and serving whites chilled helps reduce the intensity of acidic flavor.

Alcohols. More than a dozen, of which ethyl has the highest volume and glycerol next. Alcohol to a degree replaces fats and carbohydrates in the diet. It contributes energy and stimulation. At 7 to 15 percent in table wines, and up to 20 percent in sweet wines, it is the most important ingredient physiologically and quantitatively.

Aldehydes. Formed when alcohol is oxidized. These have a therapeutic effect and contribute to flavor. Each alcohol has its related aldehyde.

Calories. About ninety calories to a serving of four ounces. Wine may add weight when consumed alone, but tends to act as a one-for-one replacement of some other food calories when consumed with meals. Experiments show persons voluntarily, often unwittingly, reduce the amount of food intake when wine is part of their meal. Thus wine serves as a healthful nutritional element. For maximum beneficial effect, it is best for wine to be included regularly with meals, rather than at random.

Carbohydrates. From .1 to 1.5 percent of sugar is present in grapes before fermentation in table wines; twice that much or more is found in sweet wines. Dextrose helps prevent fatty infiltration of the liver, preliminary to cirrhosis. Levulose aids in the maintenance and repair of the liver and is an intermediary substance in metabolism.

Carbon dioxide. During primary fermentation, this gas matches ethyl alcohol in volume. Much is lost by volatilization. It is most abundant in alcohol-rich wines. Preserved in some of finest whites, carbon dioxide adds delicacy and flavor. It is always added to sparkling wines, including champagne, and works as a nausea deterrent.

Enzymes. The activity of enzymes can be weakened by an unbalanced diet, lack of sleep, alcohol misuse, a lowered adrenal hormone production, and the process of aging. Because of its many ingredients, wine can improve enzyme activity.

Esters. Several dozen in older wines. These contribute no known health value, but they contribute the major flavor and bouquet of wine.

Glycerine. This sweetens and replaces the flavor of sugar, hence it brightens carbohydrate-restricted diets.

Hydrogen ion concentration (pH). The pH of wine resembles that of human gastric juice more closely than that of any other beverage, a property that allows wine to be easily assimilated.

Minerals. Wine contains traces of all thirteen major minerals necessary for survival. Wine's minerals supply building material for cells, help regulate metabolism, maintain body juices, and aid convalescence.

Wine is especially rich in iron (builds cells, carries oxygen, fights anemia); potassium (heart rhythm, metabolic equilibrium, muscle tone, hemoglobin regeneration); and phosphorus (bone-building, fights feebleness and anemia). Sodium content is low in wine, making wine good for salt-free diets.

Wines also have calcium (strengthens tissues, regulates blood, seals cells); magnesium (bones, teeth); manganese (blood-building, nerve metabolism, gland secretions); zinc (insulin, blood sugar); chlorine (stomach and pancreas juices); boron (cell-breathing); silicon (tendons, connective tissue); fluoride (tooth decay); copper (enzymes, antibiotic); vanadium (re-strains cholesterol formation and accelerates its decomposition);

WINE FOR MINERAL HEALTH

Number and amount of the existing bioelements [in wine] is considerable and corresponds to the number and amount of two multivitamin preparations of the pharmaceutical industry meant for convalescents and old people.

Without a doubt, wine, which contains several hundred matters, can supplement most of the missing or insufficient substances, thus contributing to the metabolism in a stimulating and regulating way.

Also a great part of the demand for vitamins, especially in the B group, can be satisfied by the ingredients in wine. [Many qualities lost from food by improper preparation, and also necessities left out of diets, can be found in wine.]

By comparing the daily use of an adult in these inorganic elements and the quantities present in the different sorts of wine, one can conclude that it is possible to cover the daily need of man in the elements and also in the minerals by the consumption of certain wines.

DR. HEINRICH KLIEWE

---

iodine (thyroid hormone regulation); cobalt (helps iron utilization, builds vitamin B_{12}); molybdenum (enzymes).

Nitrogen. This does not occur in effective quantities, but without its presence fermentation would not take place and there could be no wine.

Vitamins. These chemicals usually must be present in animal or human bodies, in very tiny amounts, if certain essential biochemical processes are to be carried out. The vitamins found in useful amounts in wine are vitamin B (riboflavin, pyridoxine, niacin, and pantothenic acid) and vitamin P (which strengthens the capillaries). Vitamin C is abundant in grapes but oxidizes easily and thus largely disappears in the fermentation process. Thiamine, another B vitamin, takes the same exit. The prominence of B vitamins in wine is one of the features distinguishing it from distilled liquors and from beer.

Numerous tests with animals support the conception of wine as the most nutritious of alcoholic beverages. Michel Flanzy and Jean Causeret at France's National Institute of Agronomic Research administered alcoholicly equal doses of alcohol, brandy, and red wine to three control groups, while a fourth received no alcohol. Only the animals that received wine were similar in growth and organ composition to the rats that were given no alcohol.

Dr. Curtis P. Richter, in similar experiments reported in the *Quarterly Journal of Alcoholic Studies,* also found that rats grow well while consuming wine. While again the alcohol consumers grew at a much slower rate, after 269 days the wine drinkers grew at a very rapid rate and none showed any nutritional deficiency—even though they ate only about half as much food as the control group.

A Grape Way to Go

"Grape nuts" is a code term for a group of food faddists, one of whose bibles is *The Grape Cure* by Johanna Brandt. Eighteen editions of this book had been issued by 1953, and probably a number more since then.

It is hard to think of a human failing not responsive to a diet of grapes only, according to this tome. Grapes were cited as the only hope for those suffering from inoperable cancer. Human ailments ranging from sex problems to syphilis were enumerated as candidates for the grape cure, including arthritis, diabetes, gallstones, cataracts, ulcers, TB, pyorrhea, and blood diseases. Grape juice rinses were suggested for nasal catarrh and grape juice enemas for rectal cancer.

Some of the maxims presented bear thought.

> When thirsty, drink a glass of water.
> When hungry, eat a bunch of grapes.

> Acidosis is at the root of most of our bodily ailments. It is caused by the use of cooked foods, meat, starch, white bread and white sugar.

Only the sick get weak on grapes, it apostrophized. You're not on a grape cure when you are eating other foods with your grapes. A few spoonfuls of medicine cannot undo the effects of years of wrong living. The book became almost human with, "Never force grapes down your own or anybody else's throat. To be beneficial they must be enjoyed."

This book-length salute to grapes did not once mention wine. But it attributed the miracle properties of grapes to a roll call of chemical properties: low in salt, contain arsenic, carbon, calcium, iodine, sulphur, magnesium, boron.

All well and good. Most of those properties are transferred to wine. Some of the properties in grapes are lost in the fermentation process, others are diminished, others are magnified, others are changed—and some well-known attributes of wine are not even present in grapes. No one can deny that wine tastes better and makes one feel much better. Perhaps the most valid appraisal would be that thousands of years of human history and cumulative human wisdom based on experience have produced incomparably more (and better known) "wine nuts" than "grape nuts."

Dr. Celestin Cambiaire said: "No one can deny that there is some food value in grapes; wine contains all the nutritive elements of whatever parts of grapes people eat, besides all the extracts of skins and seeds, which are not fit for table use. In this manner wine contains more nutritive elements than the part of the fruit . . . used as a food. Nothing has been destroyed by the change of the grape into wine [this is debatable], and something has been added [this is incontestable.]"

For all of its nutritional value by itself, wine's starring role on the nutrition front is its double-play combinations with food.

ALCOHOL PAVES THE WAY FOR EATING

Not only is greater enjoyment obtained from the meal. The enjoyment is due itself to the fact that alcohol has given him repose of spirit from the endless little worries of the day's work. He has sat down to dinner fighting the battles of the day over again, preparing for the work of the future, and seeking methods of warding off possible dangers to himself or to his plans. But for the moment these thoughts and cares are no longer of any value to him; the time has come for repose and repair; and to obtain complete digestion and assimilation he needs to free his mind of them. Under the influence of alcohol past troubles cease to repeat themselves and to reverberate in his mind. The worries of the day fall off and he acquires rest and content, in which he takes a more sanguine view of the present and of the future, and leaves difficulties and dangers till the morrow, when he will be prepared to deal with them refreshed and restored by the night's sleep.

E. H. STARLING

This includes its propensity to settle the nerves and the digestive apparatus for the meal to come, its creative contributions to the culinary process, and its help in digestion and elimination.

The aperitif hour stimulates the juices which so beneficially pave the way for the main event: the meal. We must eat to live. If we can make a good time of the process, we enrich life while we sustain it. There is no other exercise so inevitable, so diurnal, so capable of civilized enjoyment. To enjoy our meals is to lay a foundation for good health.

Wine chronicler André Simon said: "Gastronomy speaks the language of common sense when it asks all, whether they be rich or poor, to make the unescapable daily business of eating and drinking an amusing and profitable hobby rather than let it become a dull duty."

It's creative. It's easy. It's fun. Drink wine with your noontime and evening meals, thereby sustaining body and spirit together.

10

The Milk of Venus

Wine, it is the milk of Venus.

BEN JOHNSON

Then sing as Martin Luther sang:
"Who loves not women, wine, and song,
He is a fool his whole life long."

WILLIAM MAKEPEACE THACKERAY

"Where there is no wine, there is no love," quoth the Greek tragedian Euripides. It is a beautiful line, but not always so; but then, what *is* always so? Other poets have also pointed out that where there is too much wine there can be no love—or its expression, at least.

Still, wine can help get the game under way by quashing some of the inhibitions that impede contact. Ovid, the Roman poet quite expert in such matters, expressed it succinctly: "Wine gives courage and makes men apt for passion." He warned with equal sagacity that wine "prepares the heart for love, unless you take too much." But Ovid was more in favor of wine than against it as a love potion:

It warms the blood, adds luster to the eyes,
And wine and love have ever been allies.

The Old Testament does not hesitate to qualify wine as an aphrodisiac, mentioning among other things that the daughters of Lot used the beverage to seduce their father. The Talmud sends up a clear signal:

One glass of wine makes the woman pretty;
Two glasses and she becomes hateful;

98

At the third glass she lusts invitingly;
At the fifth glass she becomes so excited
That she will solicit an ass upon the streets.

What has always fascinated me about this famous passage is whatever happened to that fourth glass? Perhaps among the many specific controlled experiments concerning this versatile beverage, that one should be included. Or, any man curious enough may choose to make the test himself.

Another ancient religious book, the Shastras of the Hindus, tells us that in the early days wives were allowed only to smell wine, but mistresses were permitted—even encouraged—to drink it.

A Byzantine application to cure frigidity in women said, "Offer food which produces warmth [such as] yellow, scented old wine, which is barely sweet. Suitable also is wine diluted with sea water." Better, we think, would be a good Pinot Chardonnay, although they say that a bottle of champagne is faster.

Dr. Angelo Pellegrini always brings one of the best bottles from his wine cellar as a gift to a bride and groom at their wedding. "When you are settled in your own home and you have your first dinner together," he would tell the young couple, "I want you to drink this wine and I want you to drink all of it and then I want you to write me a letter and tell me what it led to."

Dr. Pellegrini closes with the observation, "I have a considerable collection that I will someday make public."

In early Rome, many authorities agree, and Plutarch spells out, women were not to touch wine at all. Resulting sexual irregularities was the reason, and a law of Romulus provided the death penalty for women who either drank or committed adultery. It was different for the boys. Romulus absolved one Egnatius Mecenius for beating his wife to death with a stick because she had drunk from the wine vat. Fabius Pictor tells of a Roman lady who, caught opening the purse in which the keys of the wine cellar were kept, was starved to death by family decree.

Fauna, wife of Faunus, a mythical king of early Italy, departed on one occasion from the impeccable propriety of her ways and got disgracefully drunk emptying a whole jar of wine.

Faunus beat her to death with myrtle switches—and missed her terribly after it was too late.

As late as Cicero and Augustus these restrictions endured. Horace's Neobule complains that she may not drown her love-longing in wine, and Ovid's Hero laments that she could better endure waiting for Leander if not denied access to wine.

But times change, and they did in the course of Rome's two thousand years. The death penalty fell into disuse. Paulinus tells us of a daughter of Augustus who behaved scandalously with wine and was sent into exile with the added penalty of having to give up wine. Perhaps this was deemed a fate *worse* than death.

Christian writers left evidence that women of the Roman Empire drank enough to worry the church authorities. Tertullian speaks of wine drinking being common among Roman women. So, even in Roman days, women increasingly invaded the male precincts until they became more and more equal with men in more and more things.

Arabian Nights tells about one King Omar bin Al Nie'uman, who plied a damsel with wine and then offered her hashish so he could fulfill his "base purposes." Personally, I think hashish a bit extreme. "A loaf of bread, a jug of wine, and thou" is a matchless combination.

A friend told me of the remarkable incident that ensued when he permitted his favorite nephew and brand-new bride to spend their wedding night in his apartment.

"I should have gotten out, to be sure, but pressure of business compelled me to stay in town and that turned out to be a good thing. The apartment was plenty big, anyway, and I established the lovebirds in a wing to themselves. At 3:00 A.M., unable to sleep, I rose to have a few glasses of wine in an effort to compose my nerves. Suddenly there appeared my nephew, disheveled, discomposed, and his eyes red with tears. Grown man that he was, he was still weeping."

My friend offered his nephew a glass of wine with the injunction to relax and collect himself. The nephew complained, at first almost hysterically, that nothing was working, nothing was happening, it was a tragic mess and everything was terrible.

After a few glasses of wine together both gentlemen felt much better and the nephew went off to bed—with a fresh bottle of wine and two glasses, of course.

The newlyweds emerged from their chamber a considerable

time after the cock crowed looking somewhat tired and as happy as could be. And the nephew assured his uncle thankfully that the night had left nothing to be desired.

But every coin has two sides, and one planning to use wine in his amorous arsenal will find that immoderation has harsh penalties in the realm of Venus. Alcohol is a sex depressant, not stimulant. Alcohol first dismisses inhibitions, but continued application dismisses potency also. Aristotle said a long time ago, "Too much drinking makes one very improper for the acts of Venus."

"What three things does drink especially provoke?" asks Macduff in Shakespeare's *Macbeth*.

"Nose-painting, sleep and urine," responds the porter. "Lechery, sir, it provokes, and unprovokes; it provokes the desire, but it takes away the performance. Therefore much drink may be said to be an equivocator with lechery; it makes him, and it mars him; it sets him on, and it takes him off; it persuades him, and disheartens him; makes him stand to, and not stand to; in conclusion, equivocates him in a sleep, and, giving him the lie, leaves him."

Students of the matter have contended that while overindulgence in *alcohol* can indeed lead to impotency, wine is much less apt to be guilty of preventing a swain from rising to the occasion. A wine-loving friend told me, "I can consume far more wine than booze and still perform well. In fact, I credit wine with having the unique characteristic absent in other alcoholic beverages of enabling me to quaff large quantities, feel sexier than hell, and still carry out my intentions to the fullest."

A bit of drinking, in any event, can have a very constructive impact on performing as well as approaching the art of Venus. Besides loosening inhibitions, it slows the male orgasm, to the enduring gratitude of both parties.

Drinking and sexual intercourse can either complement each other or compete with each other in making a common contribution to health: releasing tension and generating a euphoria of contentment and satisfaction. They share an anesthetic effect, they are ego builders, they lead to the most delicious kind of sleep. Sometimes, happily symphonized, they work to heighten the pleasure of the other. But at other times and situations, they are and must be mutually exclusive. Southern Europeans are said to find an outlet in the tradition of sexual play; Northern Euro-

ALCOHOL OR SEX?

The story is told of a confirmed teetotaler who was offered a glass of cognac at the end of a good dinner. He proudly and loudly expounded, "I would rather commit adultery than drink a glass of cognac."

The wise and hospitable host quickly broke up the resulting hush by riposting: "Who wouldn't!"

---

peans tend to find the same release with more emphasis on alcoholic intoxication.

Alexander the Great's penchant for heavy drinking was related by Athenaeus to his reduced inclination for women. Alcoholics are notably not womanizers; the reverse is equally true.

Shakespeare's contemporary from a more gentle climate, one Boniface Oinophilus de Monte Fiascone, with sure twentieth-century youth psychology, rebelled against his own family by writing a book extolling drunkenness. He made the point that "drunkards are not generally given to lewdness" and emphasized that "in those countries where they do not drink to excess they are very much addicted to debauchery."

This must pose a pretty dilemma for the straightlaced brothers and sisters who deplore both alcohol and amorousness as paths to sin and shame.

In an old fiction, Sedley bids his Phyllis farewell to seek refuge from her snubs in the bottle. If wine is the handmaiden of love, it can also be a consolation for coldness of an amorous object it does not arouse:

> 'Tis wine alone that cheers the soul,
> But love and ladies make us sad.

In *Songs of the Vine,* quoted above, Hutchinson also hands out a bit of advice:

> The whining lover that doth place
> His fancy on a painted face,
> And wastes his substance in the chase,
> Would ne'er in melancholy pine,
> Had he affections so divine,
> As once to fall in love with wine.

Love or wine? Wine or love? Or both? For me, and for the vast majority, I'm sure—both. And certainly both for the Duc de Richelieu, grandnephew of France's Cardinal Richelieu, who at eighty-four took to his bosom his fourth wife, a winsome young widow. At ninety-two he died in the full bloom of sexual vigor, but not before crediting his vitality to the habitual imbibement of Chateau Lifite.

Lord Byron posed the question, which has delightfully fueled another great and healthful pleasure—conversation: "Is wine favorable to love or is it not? I tremble to decide—more especially as those toping poets of mine differ among themselves on this point of critical importance. . . ." Certainly wine and sex have much in common. Each contributes much more to a person than it takes away. It could be said of both what Cardinal Richelieu himself said of wine: "If God forbade drinking would He have made wine so good?"

Wine and love—the oldest, greatest, most controversial mysteries of mankind.

11

※ンン❀ン❀ン❀

Wine as Therapy

Just as we have hydrotherapy, or the treatment of certain diseases by water, so we have winotherapy, or the treatment of certain diseases by wine.

DR. MAURIAC

There seems to be reasonable argument that if opotherapy (the grape cure) has merit, why not enjoy the process while getting as much if not more cure out of it? This school of thought would suggest—try ampelotherapy (the wine cure) instead.

Dr. Louis Reynaud of Châteauneuf-du-Pape and his fellow doctors of that distinguished wine-producing region almost unanimously agreed with Mayor P. Diffonty when he said, "The amateur should consume not less than one bottle a day, or perhaps one and a half." And somewhat more, of course, for a wine drinker who has won his spurs.

Dr. Reynaud explained why: "Our women get sick more often than our men because females drink less wine than males."

In the tradition of wine for health there are many remedies, startling, quaint, and even incredible—there are some better in the reading than the doing, just as there are some you may never have thought of but may find worth trying. For example, the Swiss had an old cure for pain of all sorts: drink some wine that has been warmed up with a red-hot iron. The wine will cure the pains and the red-hot iron will ward off evil witchcraft. (However, white wine at a chilled temperature and red wine at room temperature will taste better.)

We shall attempt to marshal, in reasonable detail, some specific applications of wine as both preventive and healing agent to specific organs and systems of the body, and to specific ail-

WINE: KILLER OR CURER?

Of course, even wine—to say nothing of liquor or cocktails —can kill people. Yet the great Spanish endocrinologist, Gregorio Maranon, found no evidence in his personal statistics on 100,000 patients that wine had played any appreciable role in causing their diseases, perhaps because, as Cervantes said, "Wine taken in moderation never does any harm."

Maranon came to regard wine with its "almost divine dignity" as a "semidivine remedy for human sadness." A semidivine remedy because sadness and tedium are the genesis of many of man's ills. For Maranon, living was a matter of defending oneself against a life that steadily harasses us to death, and wine was the best nurse against such sadness.

Obviously wine can kill the drinker, just as the bull can kill the bullfighter. The important thing is to decide whether it is better to flee the bull by jumping the barriers or to stave him off with adequate cape passes.

FELIX MARTI-IBANEZ

ments and diseases. Where wine may be harmful, we try to touch that also. Naturally, when in doubt about wine as a cure for pathological conditions, call your doctor.

Perhaps wine's overriding virtue, medical and general, is its psychosomatic capacity for making a person happier and more receptive to his lot. Wine can assist the doctor by making the patient more willing to do, and take, the other things he may need. Since the patient is more likely to follow a regimen that includes a little pleasure for him, here is an area in which wine helps both doctor and patient to a more effective relationship. Also, by improving the patient's outlook, wine has been known to foster the will to live, in the recuperating case. We think that if wine did no more than this—and it does much, much more—its existence would be medically justified if not cherished.

We tend to be what we think we are. We tend to be what we (sometimes subliminally) want to be. Therefore, a hypochondriac obsessed with a feeling he's ailing can be half sick from thinking he is. Health depends not upon the physical condition alone but also upon a mental attitude. Some will to die because of loss of a loved one, or general debility, or boredom, or frustration—and so they do die. Some will to live despite grievous blows—and so they defy and defer the inevitable.

Health is more than half a state of mind. The happiness wine brings must be its major contribution to therapy. "Wine rejoices the heart of man," wrote Goethe, "and joy is the mother of all virtue." And health is the price of virtues.

With happiness, we have everything. The keystone to happiness is health. The keystone to health is happiness. Where you find them, you find mental health—more than half the battle.

"Get happy" was a synonym for drinking I remember as far back as college days. For many a doctor, "get happy" is the first rule and greatest hope for his patients. Wine is the gentlest, kindest, sagest of the mind-altering drugs that we take to straighten out our brains, which are reeling from life's problems, battles, crises, and cruelties. If we are healthy, wine can help sustain us. If we languish, wine can help revive us. If we are stricken down, wine can help restore us.

Dr. Heinrich Kliewe capsulized, "A doctor should not be petty in dispensing red wine for patients suffering from incurable disease—for psychological reasons too. Wine in its overall effect beneficially influences the physiological functions of almost all the organs of the healthy person and has a health-retaining and -promoting effect."

Dr. Alexander Henderson, the London physician who wrote a history of wine in 1824, opposed any use of it except as medicine. But he made up for this in extolling its therapeutic properties: ". . . It acts as a cordial and stimulant; quickening the action of the heart and arteries, diffusing an agreeable warmth over the body, promoting the different secretions, communicating a sense of increased muscular force, exalting the nervous energy, and banishing all unpleasant feelings from the mind."

A broadside medical endorsement of wine for therapy came from Dr. Robert Druitt in 1865: "The persons who should drink pure wine are the healthy population in general, and especially the young and vigorous . . . the thousands of persons who complain of irritable throats and bronchitis; those . . . likely to boils, scrofula, skin diseases, chlorosis, or other cachexies; the gouty and rheumatic and phthisical above all others; and those who are in want of good, pure blood."

Wine and Anemia

Wine has long been advised for anemic patients because of its significant iron content. England's Dr. Yorke-Davies of the Royal College of Surgeons recommended "those wines containing iron" in his *Wine and Health—How to Enjoy Both* (1909). The presence of iron in measurable quantities in all types of wine was first demonstrated in the 1880s by Carles at Bordeaux. In 1938, George Marsh and K. Nobusada of the University of California found that about 80 percent of the iron in wine is in the reduced, or ferrous, form, making it physiologically available and thus helpful to anemics suffering from iron-deficient diets.

"Since old times red wine has also been well liked because of its beneficial influence on abnormal changes of the blood and the blood-building organs," wrote Dr. Heinrich Kliewe. "Especially red wine from vines grown on volcanic ground is supposed to be beneficial for anemic conditions. It is traced to the relatively high phosphorus and iron content of these wines."

Dr. Kliewe suggested that red wine can supply 50 percent of the body's daily demand for iron. He cited tests by McDonald and Pechet of the Harvard Medical School with rats receiving radioactively marked iron through a stomach tube. "The authors found that iron resorption is not impaired by other ingredients in wine. They therefore consider wine a valuable therapeutic agent for the treatment of iron anemia."

Some physiologists have stated that iron-rich wine alone can supply all of the iron necessary for metabolic needs, according to Dr. Salvatore Lucia's *Wine as Food and Medicine,* which also mentioned wine's richness in phosphorus as good for "the feeble and anemic."

Pointing out the iron deficiency even in a "fully adequate diet," Dr. Chauncey D. Leake reported clinical studies to determine more exactly the helpful potential of wine. "Whereas an ordinary adequate diet may contain from ten to twenty milligrams of iron per day, under healthy conditions only about one-tenth of this is absorbed. In iron-deficiency anemias there is suggestive evidence that wines may aid in the rate of iron absorption."

Wine and Arthritis

"For arthritis . . . I have found that—because of its analgesic effect—an alcoholic beverage may be prescribed as an adjunct to aspirin or other medications," commented Dr. Dougnac.

"Consider arthritis," wrote Dr. Herbert L. Gould. "Because of its pain-reducing effect, an alcoholic beverage is often prescribed by physicians as an adjunct to aspirin or other medications."

Wine and Back Pain

If one inherits the curse of back pain as his weak point, as many tall people are inclined to do, he has two consolations. One is that a sore back is never fatal, and the other is that a sore back is never contagious.

One of the perversities of this form of malaise is that wine can do it no direct good and could be harmful if, by relaxing inhibitions, it should incite the sufferer to overextend himself and perhaps intensify the irritation. Wine can do indirect good in two ways, however. First, it relaxes and dulls the pain. Second, as an inducer of sleep and a more relaxed attitude, wine is the ally of the doctor who will usually tell a patient with a painful

---

BETTER THAN ASPIRIN?

A small drink will do much to brighten the end of the day for the arthritic patient and usually gives definite relief from pain . . . It's a sort of very pleasant form of aspirin, you might say.

RUSSELL L. CECIL

In a survey conducted by W. M. Solomon, among rheumatologists, it was found that 80 percent of their patients routinely use aspirin to ease pain of rheumatoid arthritis. The survey further revealed that but few of the physicians polled restrict use of beverage alcohol, which appears to have value as an adjunct to aspirin or other therapy.

GP magazine

---

back to spend as much time as possible in bed—because, like a cold, a bad back benefits more from bed rest than most anything else.

Wine and the Bones

A medieval book of medicine said: "Ache by the bone, and all manner of bruises. Take a good quantity of wormwood and cut into three or four parts, and boil it in the best wine that you may have . . . And put therein a piece of new woolen cloth . . . wrap the sore therein, and do thus oft and always hot, and he shall be whole by God's grace."

If this is not a likely application today, one who is bone-weary or bone-sore can find the same general relief in wine, which attends any who is in pain or overtense.

Wine and Cancer

Cancer may seem unlikely to be alleviated by wine, but it has been heartily recommended by one of America's wisest physicians, Dr. William Dock: "For some patients total abstinence from alcohol is essential, but this is rarely the case in heart disease, cancer, or stroke."

Cancer being one of the most painful and feared of all diseases, its victims can take comfort in Dr. Dock's words:

After resection of cancer, or when the patient is being treated for neoplastic disease with radiation, isotopes, or cytotoxic agents, a steady intake of alcohol can provide calories, up to 800/day from 150 ml of alcohol. Similar quantities of alcohol and sugar can be given in appropriate drinks with and between meals. This will calm the nerves, diminish pain, and make it easier for patients to doze or sleep during the tiresome days in hospital. It also is invaluable during the long months when the cancer patient, at home, is adjusting to the resection, the risk of recurrence, or the certainty that his disease is chronic and uncomfortable.

Dr. Thomas E. Douglas, Jr., agrees in *GP* magazine: "Much fear of cancer stems from thoughts of uncontrolled suffering. Give a patient pain-relief and assurance that he will remain relatively comfortable and you give him peace of mind." For such a patient, drinking "Sometimes improves appetite, lessens anxiety, and provides a more restful sleep."

In 1932 the French League Against Cancer published a statistical report that in France's heavy wine-producing districts death by cancer killed from 26 to 96 per 100,000 inhabitants, while in regions without grape growers the figure was from 106 to 141 per 100,000.

Dr. F. Dougnac commented:

A liter of the red wine of St. Emilion, for example, brings to the organism 0.142 gr. of magnesium, the element of defense against cancer, and 0.017 gr. of silicon, the element of repair of cancerous lesions.

Is it then so bold to think that the lower proportion of cancer in viticultural regions is perhaps due to this constant daily supply of vitalized magnesium and silicon? Without doubt, this supply is not considerable. But we well know that small doses frequently renewed often have a physiological and therapeutic action as efficient as large but infrequent doses.

It is a fact that the ravages of cancer are less widespread among the races that drink wine than in the dry nations.

R. Cruchet supports this with statistics: from 1921–1926 the cancer mortality in wine-consuming France had been 76 per 100,000 while in the dry United States the rate was 96. At that time, due to Prohibition, the United Sates was probably hitting an all-time low in wine drinking.

"It has not been clarified if the lower death rate from cancer in the wine districts of France (about half of that in the other areas) should be traced to the anthocyanins contained in red wine, or if cancer-repugnant characteristics can be credited to the slightly radioactive potassium or magnesium in wine," wrote Dr. H. Kliewe.

"It is possible that they can restrain the formation of a tumor and improve the general condition of the body in combination with other existing ingredients in certain vines like lactic acid, iron, phosphorus, vitamins, and others, which are often little effective in their pure form or in artificial compounds."

Wine and Glycogen-Storage Disease

A disorder of carbohydrate metabolism, this disease may be fought by adding wine to the diet. In 1965 Dr. Charles Lowe and Luis Mosovich experimented with four young patients at the Children's Hospital in Buffalo, New York.

A significant improvement was found with the administration of alcohol—decrease in blood lactate, some improvement in blood sugar, increase in rate of galactose removal, and enhanced response to glucagon.

Wine and Muscles

Severe muscle spasms growing out of some diseases and injuries may be assuaged with alcohol, according to Leake and Silverman. "Alcohol may be helpful . . . in controlling the spasm and alleviating the severe pain which accompanies it. Here the analgesic properties of alcohol may be of particular benefit.

"Often, substantial quantities of alcohol may be temporarily required," the authors stated, because for some patients this may "represent a desirable substitute for the opiates and sedatives which otherwise would be indicated."

Wine and Premenstrual Tension

"One of the oldest household remedies is the use of alcohol . . . as a mild aid in the prevention of premenstrual tension and the control of menstrual pain," wrote Leake and Silverman. "If these beverages are actually effective in such conditions, presumably they would serve by helping to relieve premenstrual edema, and their action as tranquilizers would tend to alleviate emotional tension."

Wine and Skin

Introduced into the body orally, wine can play an efficient role in the treatment of skin diseases. Total abstention from wine has never brought the slightest modification to lesions under observation when there was no other change in diet or therapy.

However, alcohol in forms other than wine brings about facial erythrosis (skin inflammation) among patients suffering gastrohepatic problems. Bad nutrition, overeating, and a sedentary existence—not wine-drinking, have been cited as the principal cause of skin trouble.

Dr. J. M. Eylaud often found it necessary to add wine to the diet of skin patients for psychosomatic reasons: "A skin ailment, visible or not, is always very depressing. This nervous depression encourages persistence of the ailment." Therefore, by relieving the depression, wine can be of great benefit to a skin patient.

Wine and Gout

In generations gone by the very image of overindulgence was a pot-bellied English burgher limping painfully from gout with a bottle of port clutched in his aching hand. Now another myth has died—for it has been found that the cause of gout is not wine at all, but inflammation of the joints from faulty uric acid metabolism. Far from causing gout, wine-drinking can relieve the sufferer.

In this context, could there by any semantical significance in the French meaning of "gout"—i.e., taste, style, preference? Pertinently in the French Region de la Security Sociale XII in 1959 a survey found that almost twice as many women suffer from gout and its cousin, rheumatism, as men—although men drink more wine than women.

Dr. E. Mauriac stated that "people suffering from gout are very numerous in countries where wine is drunk very little, whereas they are fewer in countries whose beverage is almost exclusively wine." Professor H. Rendu found that "true alcoholics suffer almost never from gout."

The real perpetrator of gout is overindulgence in foods rich in purines (especially meats) and that old nemesis, emotional tension. So here wine as relaxer and an ally in the battle against obesity can again come to the rescue.

Ephriam Engleman, director of the University of California Arthritis Clinical Study Center, in 1957 mounted a nationwide research program to test the deep-rooted belief that wine caused gout. The study team compiled detailed drinking records of 200 gout victims plus 269 other sufferers with non-gouty complaints. The intake of wine was lowest in the gout group, with 61 percent of them having used little or no wine during their lives. And those whose wine consumption was highest had never suffered from gout.

J. H. Talbot's book, *Gout,* stipulated that there is meager evidence to support contention that alcohol aggravates gout. On the contrary, most gout victims are able to be attack-free while enjoying a temperate alcoholic intake. In a number of cases alcohol contributes a marked analgesic effect.

12

⚜️⚜️⚜️⚜️

Wine as Antibiotic

Philosophers often tell us that the smallest problems are the ones most likely to get a man down. Doctors carry the same message, because one of our smallest enemies is one of the biggest killers: the microbe. How to kill germs without killing or damaging their human host has been a major medical dilemma through the ages.

But one medicine has done it well for many thousands of years. Wine assassinates the miniscule enemy while exalting the body fortress. Why wine, which does so much for man, should be such an effective germ-killer is one of the good mysteries of life. In this one respect, maybe we are just lucky.

Wine Disinfects Food

Wine can be health insurance as well as aesthetic delight applied as a food disinfectant to repel that scourge known as "Montezuma's revenge," "Delhi belly," "turista," or just travelers' diarrhea. In my whiskey and gin drinking days I couldn't cross the border without contracting this siege of alien bacteria, but since my all-wine regimen I've withstood journeys of several months duration through Europe and again through the Orient without a gastrointestinal tremor.

This I credit to two things. One is wine's capability of disinfecting foodstuffs, always in full force and effect because I drink wine with every meal. Secondly, instead of drinking cocktails containing ice made of possibly-infected water, I have always quaffed preprandial glasses of wine, in itself pure and purifying.

Columbus was five hundred years ahead of me. He issued to each of his forty sailors a daily ration of 2½ liters of red wine, contributing to both their intestinal equilibrium and fortitude in the face of the terrible dangers of their historic voyage.

EAT OYSTERS AND LIVE

When it has unfortunately happened that persons have been
poisoned by eating oysters at private banquets, it has constantly been revealed at the inquest that the guests who took
wine with their oysters have felt no ill effects, while others
who took no wine have died.

FRANK HEDGES BUTLER

The ancients bathed strawberries in wine not only because
it made them taste better, but because they grow on ground level,
strawberries are quite likely to be infected. People in whom strawberries bring on urticaria (skin rash) have been able to eat them
with impunity if they are soaked in wine for ten to fifteen minutes.

Drinking wine with oysters and other shellfish is an aesthetic
thing to do, but at the same time wine's properties against Eg-
bert's bacillus (typhoid) makes it a preventive defense.

Salads in some countries are proscribed for vulnerable tourists who do not want to get laid away for a few days with a volcanic stomach. If the lettuce leaves and other raw vegetables are
not assiduously cleaned, they can harbor infectious disaster. The
fussy gourmet tends to scorn a glass of wine with the salad
course. While there is no substitute for a proper leaf scouring in
the kitchen before serving in the dining room, in the absence of
adequate scrubbing a bit of wine with your greens can be delicious insurance against several days of severe stomach cramps or
worse. A related defense that also tastes good is the presence of
wine vinegar in your salad dressing.

Tests have shown that after consumption of trichinous pork,
wine is supposed to kill 80 percent of the encapsulated trichi-
nella. Dr. H. Kliewe reported on investigations by McNaught
and Piera: "The capsules would be dissolved by the gastric juices
and the parasites killed by the wine. It should be similar with
meat containing larva, where the consumption leads to tape-
worm. The effect is traceable to the direct alcohol–acid effect of
wine and also to its secretion-promoting influence on the stomach–intestinal glands."

The French have an ancient ritual of soaking rabbits and
other game in wine before cooking them, especially when the

weather is not very cold. Rabbits often carry disease germs and wine kills those germs. This also helps to explain why French cooking tastes so good.

Wine Purifies Water

The best-tasting water you can drink is that which constitutes four-fifths or more of the volume of the wine you drink. M. Aribaud wrote in *Revue des Boissons* that wine possesses antiseptic properties "sufficient to make it preferable to any other liquid" and that red wines "kill the germ of typhoid fever in two hours, and sauternes ruthlessly destroy within five minutes the colibacillus, which is much too often found in oysters."

The Old Testament reported mixing wine with water to purify the water and to dilute the wine so it could be consumed in greater quantities.

Violle and Rosé found in a study in Marseilles that a combination of red wine with heavily chlorinated water made the water fit to drink as to both decontamination and flavor. Previously, the beleaguered inhabitants had preferred to risk epidemic rather than subject themselves to the ghastly flavor of water mixed with then-available germicidal solutions.

Dr. William Edward Fitch wrote in *Pediatrics* of 1,893 experiments in Vienna's Institute of Hygiene showing that pure wine will kill the bacteria of cholera in five minutes, and that water containing these bacteria can be drunk safely if it spent five minutes in contact with one-third of its volume of wine.

"If casks or bottles had been washed with water that was contaminated, after being filled with wine for a few hours the germs would be killed," wrote Dr. Fitch. "It is important to note diluting the wine does not destroy its antiseptic value. Mixing water that was contaminated with wine a few hours before drinking would purify it by destroying the disease germs that might be present. The value of wine during epidemics of cholera or typhus has been shown by the fact that those who used wine escaped, while the water drinkers were stricken with the disease."

Dr. Celestin Cambiaire recommended that for satisfactory results in decontaminating water, the quantity of water should not exceed the quantity of wine. "If water is added, the germ-killing power of wine diminishes in proportion. This diminution in microbe-killing power may be compensated by a corresponding increase in the duration of contact."

This explains the old custom of making thin wine, or *piquette,* by adding water to wine left in the bottoms of barrels and letting this thin wine stand for some time before using it.

Dr. William J. Mayo of the Mayo Clinic, speaking about the widespread fears of alcoholism, had this to say: "It is assumed that drinking . . . is due to an evil inborn longing, to be stamped out only by the exercise of individual control. Is this actually a fact?"

He answered his question emphatically. "In France and Italy the drinking of billions of gallons of wine has saved the people from extinction; they could not have lived had they drunk their polluted water. The Teutonic races turned to beer to secure a sterile drink; England had ale and wine, and temperance countries such as Turkey had tea and coffee. . . . The drink habit is one of many forms of individual protection resorted to by nature to save men from filth diseases which cause death or what is worse than death; intellectual deterioration."

In the *Annales de L'Institute Pasteur,* bacteriologists Bodin (1898) and Sabazes and Mercadier (1907) established that ordinary claret will kill the typhus and cholera bacteria in two hours, and in four hours when the wine is diluted. A white wine will kill these bacteria in twenty minutes, and champagne in ten minutes. Dry wines have a greater microbe-destroying power than sweet wines, leading Dr. Cambiaire to comment: "Science comes again to sanction the age-long preference people had in wine-drinking countries for dry wines. It must be added that sweet wine is harder to digest."

Traditionally, American tourists drink only bottled water when traveling in Mexico, Europe, and elsewhere because tap water isn't supposed to be pure like the water at home. Lest we get overly smug, we should be reminded that we are living in chemically corrupt times of ecology, water shortage, and the advancing threat of pollution. In the 1970s, the U.S. Forest Service found that pure waters flowing down the east slopes of the Sierra Nevadas in the huge Inyo National Forest were contaminated by fecal bacteria beyond levels tolerated by both federal and state standards. Thus, even in high mountain regions the ecological outrage of cesspools overflowing, insufficient chemical toilets, wastes accumulated without proper outlet, including those deposited on the ground, have all combined to contaminate the pristine streams.

It was speculated that a harsh solution of rationing access to the area and limiting the number of people allowed to visit it might be required. Perhaps a more popular *and* chemically reliable alternative would be to require visitors to follow the advice of St. Paul and "drink no longer water." Instead, invite them to import their own wine from California's verdant valleys across the Sierra and drink *that,* which is free of impurities and even capable, if mixed with the said impurities, of detoxifying them.

A New Yorker, worried about the city's last water shortage, wrote to his favorite newspaper quoting a news account from Spain: "In Spain's mainly rainless plain of Le Manch these days you may not be offered water. But a roadside inn proprietor apologizes for the spring drought and offers motorists as much wine as they can drink—free. One drought year wine was traded for water, two for one."

The New Yorker suggested, "Were wine in this country as cheap and accessible as in Spain . . . we could perhaps help solve overnight the serious water shortage in New York. All the mayor would have to do is to follow the example of the Spaniards and declare New Yorkers should be served wine instead of water at the city's expense during the water shortage."

Wine versus Poison

Pliny recommended wine as an antidote for the bites of scorpions, snakes, spiders, bees, hornets, wasps, and even of rabid dogs. He also suggested its use to nullify the effects of poisonous herbs, and speaks of Antony's starving soldiers eating such herbs on their retreat from Parthia and dying in great distress for lack of wine, the accepted remedy.

Dr. Heinrich Kliewe notes wine's mitigating effect on animals experimentally given deadly doses of snake poison. Occasionally the recovery is complete. He mentions the good effect of wine against poisoning with strychnine, digitalis, or belladonna. "When various amounts of pure alcohol or whiskey were given the effect was considerably inferior," he found.

"Moderate wine consumption does not work against the course of an antibiotic treatment. It is practically valuable," Dr.

Kliewe wrote, in recommending combinations of wine and other antibiotics. "The often-observed intolerance signs like nausea and vomiting are largely avoided by the combined application of wine and antibiotics."

Wine and Surgery

Wine, the most esthetic of beverages, can also double as an anesthetic. There are much better anesthetics available today—quicker, more total, more merciful—but at one time alcohol was all the surgeon had to alleviate the pain.

Leake and Silverman wrote in *Alcoholic Beverages in Clinical Medicine:*

> The record of [alcohol's] application in anesthesia goes back to the beginning of surgery, and it was still widely used in the nineteenth century to make possible amputations and even "cutting for the stone."
>
> As one surgeon put it in the days before ether and chloroform: "You made your man drunk, and the porters and students held him down, and you had to set your teeth and finish the job fast."
>
> Although the application of alcohol as a general anesthetic is usually unjustified, the use of alcoholic beverages as analgesics for the control of pain has been widespread for many centuries. Mullin and Luckhardt have claimed that such beverages under appropriate conditions can control pain for two to three hours without seriously affecting sensitivity to touch.

Hugh of Lucca, a famous medieval surgeon, championed the healing of wounds with wine only. His son, Theodoric, rejected oils and salves as too slippery to encourage union of tissues, poultices as too moist to foster healing, and powders as objectionable because they locked in decomposing matter. Instead, he insisted on wine as the best possible dressing for wounds. Arnald of Villanova, Henri de Mondeville, John of Arderne, Hieronymus Brunschwig, Paracelsus, Ambrose Pare, and Richard Wiseman were other surgeons of the Middle Ages to champion wine as an antiseptic for surgery.

About two thousand years before Christ a Sanskrit medical passage advised that "the patient should be given to eat what he wishes and wine to drink before the operation, so that he may not faint and may not feel the knife."

Nero's surgeon, Dioscorides, prescribed wine "for such as

cannot sleep, or are grievously pained, and upon whom being cut, or cauterized, they wish to make a not-feeling pain—but being too much drank, it drives out ye life."

Today, when sophisticated chemicals have replaced wine as an anesthetic and antiseptic during surgery, it is still advantageous to drink during convalescence for those unable to accept food without nausea. It helps by providing quick energy, inducing relaxation and sleep, stimulating appetite, and aiding digestion.

Once the operation is over the patient may have syncope (fainting from temporary cerebral anemia). Wines rich in sugar, ether, and alcohol, and especially champagne, are beneficial for shock, especially when the patient suffers from nausea and vomiting. In the postoperative phase, wine is beneficial when used as a food for convalescence, an anticolibacillosis (helps intestinal inflammation), a supplier of vitamins, and as a cathartic (diuretic, laxative, purgative). If azotemia sets in (excess nitrogenous waste or uremic poisoning), wine will help tremendously in the function of urine elimination.

In addition, the patient has just emerged from a traumatic event, and is punch-drunk and at a low ebb. Many a patient has been lost during this stage when he is too weak to fight back and often just does not give a damn. Wine can contribute a twinkle to the eye, a little spice to life, a will to live. Surgery is a violent, often lethal assault against the anatomical fortress while its defenses are down. If wine can fan the flame of life and instill a little determination to win, it can be the most crucial factor. Besides, who more than the patient who has been pushed almost over the brink deserves a little fun?

Of course, there are many instances alcohol is prohibited. How well I remember after my prostatectomy that alcohol in any form was out. As so often happens, I wanted no part of it anyway; we have an instinct against suicide. But where it can help— what a shame not to call in the reinforcements.

Wine and Infectious Diseases

Our Italian winery workers were full of red wine and garlic. They never caught anything. The germs couldn't get close enough to them.

KARL WENTE

Take a new glass, fill with red wine before the sun rises; take it outside, put it on the roof under a shingle; then, also before the sun rises, take the glass inside, and let the patient drink the wine; break the glass.

SWISS FOLK REMEDY

The effect of wine as an antibiotic has been compared with the action of penicillin. Alexander Fleming, who discovered penicillin, was also a student and advocate of the antibiotic power of wine. Tests have shown the antibacterial action of wine to exceed that of penicillin against certain bacteria within a fifteen-minute period, because the penicillin was unable to act within this brief time. It has been found that younger (and cheaper) wines are more effective against diseases of bacterial origin, while well-aged wines perform better against chronic disorders of physical degeneration from the aging process.

Neither the alcohol nor the acids alone in wine can explain its bacteria-killing effect, wrote Dr. Heinrich Kliewe:

It is probable that the bacteria-killing and -retarding power of wine should mainly be traced to the reciprocal promotion of alcohol and acid. These two main factors should be supported in their effects by anthocyanins, bouquet matters, aldehyde, sulfuric acid, and tannic acid.

The fact that white or red wines can kill or retard harmful intestinal bacteria explains the statement that in earlier times typhoid, paratyphoid, dysentery, and cholera epidemics were successfully fought with wine.

Then it is understandable that bacteria taken in with water or other liquids and foods are damaged by wine during the stay in the stomach."

Wine's use in typhoid has been said to modify abdominal symptoms, diminish diarrhea, restore tongue humidity, appease thirst, replace normal skin moisture, encourage peaceful and refreshing sleep, and regularize the digestive functions. Interestingly, warm red wine has been injected into the bloodstream to treat both typhoid and dysentery.

Wine has also been effective as a preventive of malaria. F. T. Bioletti spent half a year in a malaria-ridden district testing with three groups of laborers. The first two groups numbering Irish, German, Negro, and Chinese men drank beer and whiskey and suffered severe, frequently fatal attacks of malaria. The third group, including sixty Frenchmen who drank wine, only developed one case of malaria for the duration.

Wine also had its day as an agent against eruptive fevers (smallpox, scarlet fever, measles). Fonssagrives wrote more than a century ago, "The adynamic accidents which frequently complicate eruptive fevers have successfully been treated with high dosages of wine while other methods have failed. We can see the pulse strengthen and the eruption, which tended to retrocede, take again its normal evolution. Fodere says that, in a scarlet fever epidemic that raged against poor children, he saved many of them by giving them only wine. Wine acts as a stimulant and as an analeptic [restoring] agent."

Dr. J. M. Eylaud summarized wine's role, even today: "Wine acts favorably in these disorders thanks to its alcohol and to its other components which work somewhat like penicillin in some diseases. Whatever the case may be, wine, because of its popularity with people, must be part of modern pharmacopoeia to be used, humbly perhaps, and/or with other medicines in the treatment of all infectious ailments complicated by fever."

13

⚜⚜⚜⚜⚜⚜⚜⚜

Wine and Diabetes

"Alcohol turns to sugar; a diabetic cannot have it."

Many a physician has told this to his diabetic patient. People accept it as gospel. And thus is born and nourished one of the hard myths about alcohol that is accepted by big chunks of the population, subject or not to diabetes. Actually, wine has been allowed, even prescribed, for diabetics for centuries—and still is today, especially in Europe. Impressive research has validated this use.

While diabetes affects only a limited segment of our population, it is potentially important to all of us, since it is a derangement of the metabolism of carbohydrates, and also of proteins and fats. In effect, diabetes is a disorder of all basic metabolic processes. Therefore, studies of diabetes and of ways to prevent and correct it have a meaning that reaches beyond the single disease. It often leads to cholesterol and arteriosclerosis complications; it often stems from prolonged obesity, and it has many cause-and-effect relationships with other illnesses.

Any solution of sugar can turn to alcohol, but the reverse is not true. There is some controversy as to whether alcohol increases or lowers blood-sugar levels—and within the flexible borders of this controversy some specialists advise drink while others inveigh against it, with the decision sometimes getting further entangled in moral, religious, or emotional prejudices. Most authorities on diabetes today will permit, and many will encourage, alcohol use by diabetics when under proper control. This would include control of general carbohydrate intake. In a condition where patients are deprived of much that makes life easier or more fun, if a little wine can lighten the burdens there are many experts who believe that this can and does do more good than harm.

ALCOHOL FOR DIABETICS

In no disease is the employment of alcohol more useful or more justifiable. It furnishes an agreeable form of food in a diet which is often disagreeable, and the quantity of nutriment which it contains is by no means negligible. Authorities agree that the patient can take large quantities of fat more easily in conjunction with alcohol.

MORRIS CHAFETZ

No disease exists where clinically administered alcohol for diet needs is more often indicated than in diabetes.

FERDINAND C. HELWIG

Long before insulin came along to help diabetics, and even after, alcoholic beverages have been prescribed for diabetic patients. Many European clinicians in particular make wine an important component of the diabetic diet for both the psychological and physiological well-being of patients. In America, this practice subsided after Prohibition but it is gaining popularity again.

One of the first of the modern controlled experiments on using alcoholic beverages in the diabetic diet was conducted in 1906 by Benedict and Torok of the First Medical Clinic of Budapest. Calculated diets of three diabetic and two normal subjects were tested. Diabetic subjects reflected markedly less glycosuria and a marked decrease in ketone excretion when fat was replaced by cognac. Wine and beer registered similar results plus impressive evidence that their presence accelerated the oxidation of carbohydrates. The conclusion of these scientists was that diabetic diets, except in cases of nephritis, should include Rhine wine, dry champagne, or light beer in quantities from one-half to one full liter daily.

Later studies by Burge, Soula, Baisset, and Serianni established that small amounts of alcohol decrease blood-sugar levels in diabetics; that the ingestion of grapes seems to act favorably on carbohydrate metabolism in diabetics; that wine consumption with a meal produces a lower sugar level in veins than in the capillary blood vessels, whereas alcohol has no such effect; and that perhaps the grape possesses an ingredient like insulin, which has an effect on carbohydrate metabolism.

In 1952 Weinstein and Roe of George Washington University School of Medicine found that fructose, abundant in the sugar present in wine, is utilized more rapidly than glucose in the bloodstream of animals and humans. Therefore, fructose may prove valuable for the diabetic patient.

Before the development of insulin therapy, beverage alcohol was widely used; and even since insulin, the work of many scientists has borne out the value of alcohol in reducing the blood sugar level. Dr. Morris Fishbein went so far as to declare, "With alcohol in the diet, it is possible to use a smaller amount of insulin than would otherwise be the case."

Although generally in favor of wine for diabetics, Dr. Kliewe stressed that certain diabetic complications can preclude wine, and that the type and amount should be carefully controlled. "At the most the doctor could allow one or two glasses of a low-alcohol wine. The decision would be easier for him and the patients if the wines recommended for diabetics were labeled with calorie and alcohol content, kind and amount of sugars."

That is exactly what is being done in Germany today. Under the German labeling law passed by the Bundestag in July 1971, there are three categories of regular German wine: (1) German table wine, the equivalent of France's *vin ordinaire;* (2) quality wines of different regions, covering wines better than those in the first category; and (3) quality wines with different attributes, paralleling the French *appellation contrôlée* label and including such as Kabinett, spätlese, auslese, beerenauslese, and trockenbeerenauslese. These are the *red* labels. But perhaps for the first time in the wine history of any nation, there is a special category for the sufferers of diabetes. Around the necks of the bottles especially for diabetes sufferers appears a unique *golden* label.

Inscribed on the diabetic wine label is its chemical content: .1 percent glucose, .2 percent fructose, 272 calories of alcohol, total, 278 calories. "The wine corresponds in its quality and composition with the rules of the DLG [German government] for awarding the diabetic wine seal," reads the label. "Consult your doctor for the consideration of this wine in your diet!"

Dr. F. Dougnac added up the opinion of a dozen well-known French medical authorities in citing these reasons for wine's value to a diabetic's diet: prevents body dehydration, acts as a reserve food replacing carbohydrates, has vitamin B which supplements insufficient glycolitic diastases (caused by insulin shortage), stimulates combustion of sugars, attacks the formation of ketonic bodies and therefore helps prevent diabetic coma, facilitates digestion of fats replacing carbohydrates, and favors metabolism of nitrogenous foods.

Sugared and sweet wines are prohibited for diabetics, while cider, champagne, and beer are little advised (too much dextrin). With many complications, a diabetic's doctor may reduce or eliminate the wine ration, and in no case should the diabetic exceed his ration.

Thus wine can not only help fight diabetes after it arrives, but can help stave off its advent as outlined in Chapter 20, which describes the contributions of wine in fighting obesity—a sure sign of potential diabetes.

As long as the patient and his doctor remember that sweet wines should not be used, alcohol in excess can cause trouble, and that any unusual reaction of dizziness, flushing, nausea, and tachycardia may be noted by some patients taking both sulfonylurea drugs and alcohol, it is true that some diabetics *can* have wine and profit medically from it.

14

❧❧❧❧❧❧❧❧

Wine and the
Digestive Apparatus

Wine's chief use being notably to impart vigor to the digestive organs, thus to aid them in their power to nourish the body and consequently the mind; this may be required by very many in their normal state of health, without which debility would progress.

ALEXANDER WEBBER

Wine and the Stomach

The digestive apparatus is the motor that makes the man go. Many unfortunates live without one or more limbs. Many deaf or blind lead very useful lives. We all know the world is full of people without any brains. But without a gut (and a heart) a man is ready to join the eternal shades.

An automobile engine can reduce efficiency or break down completely if one of its parts is malfunctional (carburetor, spark plugs, magneto, generator). The digestive apparatus is the same if a part breaks down (kidneys, liver, stomach, intestines).

The digestive system is liable to be assaulted from lesions, ulcers, nerves, infections, bad food, excessive alcohol, irregular schedules, and dozens of other conditions. A general rule of thumb: if the digestive system is in good order, wine is a joy and boon to it. But if something is out of order, the odds are that wine is out of bounds or should be carefully limited until order is restored. Wine itself is a food as well as thirst quencher. However, its greatest contribution to the visceral system is what it does to supplement and ennoble eating.

A man has lost his will to eat? Wine can help restore his appetite. A man is tense at mealtime? Wine can help him enjoy the eating and the company. A man is having trouble getting rid of his food and drink efficiently and on schedule? How many of us know that a breakdown here can wreak havoc with the titillations of the table! How many of us have been shunted off by no medical advice or bad medical advice or too much advertising for chemical laxatives?

Dr. J. C. Geiger commented, "Wine taken with a meal means that the alcoholic content is much diluted, possibly to 3.2 percent. Wine with a meal produces a feeling of well being, which in turn has a salutary effect upon the digestion. After a hard day's work, life seems much pleasanter and we may face the realities of life with a more serene countenance."

Classic authorities agreed. Nesitheus called wine a diuretic and digestive. Palladas mentioned wine as a remedy for stomach trouble. Strabo said that wine was good for diarrhea. A. P. McKinlay commented that a chief medicinal use of wine in ancient times was as "a regulator of the excretory organs." He said, "The Emperor Augustus and nearly all his successors liked Setinum wine, for there was thought to be no danger of flatulence or indigestion from its use."

Elaborated the *Australian Brewing and Wine Journal:* "Wine can augment appetite and excite gastric secretions to a degree no other beverage can do. Wine can assist metabolism and

---

WINE VERSUS CATHARTICS

A famous French author once said his most overwhelming impression in America was our overabundance of cathartic ads.

"In Europe, especially in wine-drinking countries, you don't see such things. People should be ashamed of such things. You are a nation of dyspeptics."

Asked if this was caused by the high pressure, the tension, the strain, the diet or—

"None of these," he interrupted. "Your diet is not to blame—except for one very important thing—you don't drink wine."

---

nervous equilibrium and the daily elimination of waste matters."

The biggest point of all seems to be the unwinding. That is not easy to accomplish after a modern high-speed day. If the meal can be made a haven, however brief, from the burdens of responsibility and the turmoils for survival, perhaps no single greater comforter can be found in the pursuits of good health. never.

Many experts agree that wine does this more satisfactorily, more safely, more enduringly, and more pleasantly than any other agent imagined or devised by the assiduity of man. The culture of western and southern Europe, where wine is a way of life and has been for centuries, suggests this is something no man should overlook. If you haven't tried it—better late than never.

Wine and the Kidneys

What is man, when you come to think upon him, but a minutely set, ingenious machine for turning—with infinite artfulness—the red wine of Shiraz into urine?

ISAK DINESEN

Way back in 1827, Richard Bright included overindulgence in alcohol as a contributing factor to nephritis, the kidney-infection disease which is also called Bright's disease. An impressive number of medical authorities since that time protested that, on the contrary, the concentration of alcohol in the urine bears little or no relation to the volume of urine excreted. Fahr and Fishberg amassed experimental evidence that alcohol has no deleterious effect on the kidneys, with Fishberg reporting that he was unable to find any greater incidence of nephritis in patients who died of delirium tremens than in those who succumbed from accidental causes.

Thus, one of the medical myths broadly accepted even today—that alcohol is always forbidden in kidney trouble because alcohol causes kidney trouble—can be discarded.

The reverse is happily true. Alcohol's strong affinity for fats makes it little attracted to kidney tissue. Bright's disease calls for a monotonous low-protein, high-carbohydrate diet. Wine can help in several ways, researchers say: by making this boring diet more acceptable, by helping supply nutrition to a sufferer

who may not consume dangerous protein, by encouraging diuretic flushing of the kidneys, and as a preventive of acidosis
and an adjuvant to the alkaline reserve.

Wine and the Liver

One of the most indestructible myths in the drinking folk-
lore of mankind is that alcohol causes cirrhosis of the liver and
other kinds of liver damage. Dr. Morris Chafetz contradicted,
"There is no available information to incriminate alcohol directly
in cirrhosis of the liver." Indeed, cirrhosis has often been found
among Moslems, Mormons, Seventh-day Adventists, and other
teetotaler groups as well as among big drinkers.

"Certainly not all disease of the liver, especially fat liver
and the different forms of cirrhosis," wrote Dr. H. Kliewe, "can
be traced to the, even sometimes escalated, wine use. . . . Many
people who drank very little or no alcohol at all have a fat
liver of cirrhosis, and many alcoholics have none." It's something
else if someone already has cirrhosis, Dr. Kliewe warned—
then "the physician has to decide if and how much wine . . . is
allowed."

The liver's job is to extract poison from elements that enter
the body, then get rid of them. The liver is a tireless and thorough
performer, and can labor for years to harmlessly siphon off
those components of wine or other alcohol which would otherwise overwhelm the body.

It is inadequate nutrition, especially lack of the vitamin B
complex, that damages the liver. If one drinks to the exclusion
of eating, he is damning his liver. But if one drinks wine sensibly
with meals, wine may actually help the liver.

University of California medical professor John V. Carbonne reported on a scientific inquiry into the wine–cirrhosis
relationship. "We designed a study to determine if there is a
detrimental effect of liberal quantities of wine on the convalescence of patients . . . with cirrhosis . . . or if the sedative, appetite-stimulating, and perhaps other properties of wine would
be of therapeutic value."

Five male alcoholics with liver disease were tested.

"The administration of wine appeared to have no adverse
effect on liver function. Instead, liver function improved significantly in the five cases studied. The most striking improvement

occurred in those subjects with the greatest functional impairment."

Concluded Carbonne, "The management of the agitated alcoholic with liver disease requires sedation. Liver disease limits the type and amount of sedation which may be given safely. Since wine has a sedative effect and an appetite-stimulating effect, it may prove useful in the management of the cirrhotic patient who is apprehensive and agitated during the initial stages of treatment."

Leake and Silverman enumerated the villains of cirrhosis: malnutrition, especially protein and vitamin deficiency; virus infections; parasitic infections; overexposure to lead, carbon tetrachloride, and other toxic hydrocarbons. Wine and alcohol have nothing to do with any of these, except to contribute indirectly to malnutrition *if* the drinker does not eat enough. Cirrhosis also occurs "with excessive consumption of sugar or cola beverages."

Another rugged myth that flourishes perennially is that liquor of any kind is strictly prohibited for months, or years, or forever in victims of viral hepatitis. Despite this, wrote Drs. Matthew Ferguson and Sister Michael Marie, there has been no controlled study to indicate that alcohol itself has any toxic effects on the normal or posthepatitic liver. They cite the Armed Forces European Hepatitis Center study as the only one available (as of 1949). It concluded that patients drinking relatively large amounts of alcohol in the period of convalescence (six to twelve months after acute hepatitis) "showed no more evidence of posthepatitic liver damage than those who consumed smaller amounts of alcohol or none at all. The available literature offers no controlled data to contradict this. It is interesting to note that the recent international symposium on viral hepatitis does

---

BEWARE OF SOFT DRINKS

The person who drinks twenty bottles of sweet, carbonated beverages a day is as likely to develop Laennec's cirrhosis as the person who drinks a pint of whiskey every day.

N. JOLIFFE

---

not even allude to the question of alcohol following hepatitis. The well-known animal studies which indicated alcohol itself is hepatoxic have been adequately refuted by less well-known but more complete laboratory studies."

Wine and the Intestines

Since alcohol is a fat solvent, some have suspected that alcoholic beverages might stimulate increased absorption of cholesterol, fatty acids, and other lipids from the digestive tract into the bloodstream. No evidence of this has been found in normal individuals or even in those with atherosclerosis or coronary disease.

A frequent aftermath of bowel surgery for gastric or duodenal ulcer or cancer is the malabsorption syndrome, often another curse of the aging process, reflected by indigestion, intestinal pain, diarrhea, appetite loss, weight loss, and fatty excrement. T. H. Althausen and his associates at the University of California demonstrated that the consumption of white wine with meals can restore fat absorption to normal—probably because of certain enzymes in the wine. Other studies have shown that alcohol increases the propulsive propensity of the colon, aiding natural evacuation.

Wine and the Pancreas

Alcohol will appreciably increase the flow of pancreatic juice (bile), whether administered orally or rectally. Aid in digestion of fats is one bonus. The increased pancreatic juice is usually paralleled by an increase in the output of pancreatic enzymes, highly active factors in digestion.

With pancreatitis, wine or other alcohol is clearly forbidden.

Wine and Ulcers

While wine may be ill advised because it will burn open ulcers in the mouth, throat, esophagus, or stomach, no rigid rule can be set with gastric or duodenal ulcers. In some cases, alcohol is prohibited. Some physicians permit small quantities of wine when the ulcer is healing to provide relaxation and a mild tranquilizer. This is up to the individual patient and doctor. Some doctors permit the patient to decide for himself whether the benefits or the local irritation is the commanding factor.

While president of the American College of Gastroenterology, Dr. Mitchell A. Spellberg wrote a book for ulcer sufferers called *Living with Your Ulcer*. Only wine was recommended among the alcoholic beverages. The volume even included a chapter entitled "The Ulcerous Gourmet," featuring a number of wine recipes.

Wine's best application to ulcers may be as preventive medicine by defusing the high-tension syndromes that cause ulcers. Though there exists no laboratory proof that a diurnal drink or two helps prevent ulcers, it is known these inner wounds are found oftener in abstainers than in heavy drinkers.

In 1972 the British Medical Association published a book written by Dr. Clifford Hawkins entitled *You and Your Guts*. Pungent points prevail throughout the book, for example, burping is good for you. "Eat what the hell you like" is wise counsel and should be proffered more often, the book advises.

I have often found that life would be simpler, sweeter, and safer if we would follow the commonsense rule: Eat what you gut tells you, drink what your gut tells you, do what your gut tells you.

Plenty of medical opinion in my probings suggested that perhaps "drink what the hell you like" might also be wise counsel that should be proffered more often. And if you like your wine, you will find more often than not that your wine likes you.

15

Wine and Hangover:
The Moment of Truth

Gueule de bois: "mouth of wood," in France.
Tømmermenn: "I have carpenters" (in my head), in Norway.
Stonato: "out of tune," in Italy.
Katzenjammer: "wailing of cats," in Germany.
Hangover: too-much-itis, in the English-speaking world.
Non compos fermentis: wine-drinkers' hangover.

I have said, and quoted impressive medical testimony in support, that alcohol causes no diseases but complicates some and helps fight others. But it has its own disease, and that it does cause. You drink what you can handle and you feel good, and the next day you feel clear. You drink too much, that is to say you "hang one on," and you get a hangover. I have never known a hangover to kill a sufferer, but I have known many a sufferer to wish he were dead.

It is partially a mental thing. When you get a hangover, you did it to yourself. There is a sense of guilt. And you are at the same time disgusted with yourself and puzzled that something which made you feel so good the night before, and made it seem so easy and natural to take some more so you would feel still better, could raise so much hell the morning after.

If your wife says something to you, she is shouting. If a child drops something, it is an explosion. If the phone rings, it is a fire engine. If somebody thinks something is funny and laughs, it is an insult.

What caused your hangover? Your own personality. The quality you drank. Who you drank with. What you were doing while drinking. Smoking while drinking. Overeating, overexertion, undersleeping. But above all, how much you drank.

133

Your psychology has something to do with it, too. One who thinks martinis will give him a hangover, or that switching from whiskey to wine will do the same, is more vulnerable than one who drinks his gin or switches from his whiskey to wine serenely confident that he will feel well the next day. For some happy reason, there is a tendency for one to receive from one's preferred alcoholic beverage what one expects to get. I have a friend who wrote after a tour of California's vineyards, "I just returned from a five-day assignment in the grape industry—saw gallons of headaches in the making." There was a fellow facing trouble the next time he sipped a few glasses of Cabernet Sauvignon.

The thing that did *not* cause your hangover was mixing your drinks. "Mix whiskey and beer, and it's fatal. Mix gin and whiskey, and it's disaster. Mix white wine and red, and you're doomed. Follow wine with brandy, and you'll pay for it." And so on. Forget it. Drink *too much,* and you've had it. Too much *alcohol,* in whatever combination of forms.

What *is* a hangover? It is emotional anguish and self-flagellation. It is—and is compounded by—fatigue. It is a whopping headache. It is thirst which by the way can make water taste much better than it ever deserves to taste. It is vertigo sometimes to the point of reeling. It is nausea which you can no longer relieve by vomiting (if you had vomited at the right stage last night, you'd feel better today). It is a pounding heart, dusty tongue, upset stomach, nervous jitters, and general pains, shakiness, and chills. It is a rather comprehensive chemical discombobulation. It is an unsymphonic scrambling and disarrangement of one's metabolism. It is hell on wheels. And while it seems everlasting, thank God, it is temporary.

Above all, it is unnecessary. Maybe that is why the sufferer loathes himself so. Almost every drinker occasionally gets one, but it usually could have been avoided. The proper mental attitude, eating while drinking, and diluting drinks will help. It all boils down to *don't drink too much in too short a time.*

Alcohol is a food, but a different kind of food. It contains neither minerals, vitamins, nor proteins. Since it is not digested, the body must decide what to do with alcohol's components before it enters the bloodstream. If one pours in so much so fast that the body disposal units are overwhelmed, there will be a hangover.

We get rid of less than one-fourth of the alcohol by exhalaration and elimination. The rest must be oxidized. The liver is the commanding officer of the oxidization process—and on its own terms. The liver cannot dispose of more than one ounce of alcohol in an hour. By limiting your drinking to one ounce of pure alcohol (no matter in what form or with what companions it is taken) per hour, one can drink all evening long or for days on end and never get a hangover. But most people drink more than this, causing a traffic jam. The alcohol irritates the stomach, intestines, and bowels. It triggers digestive juices which, having nothing to do, cause gastritis. Meanwhile, the flow of oxygen for the demanding nervous system and the brain is interfered with. This is where the staggering about, slurring of speech, dropping of lit cigarettes, erratic driving, and other evidences of drunkenness appear. Also, for some reason the water is shifted about in the body and the cells are denied their normal portion. This is why a hangover makes you feel like you can drink the swimming pool dry.

It may not seem fair, and probably isn't, but the more experienced the drinker (the heavier the drinker, if you prefer), the more resistant he's apt to be to hangovers. The benefits of experience and capacity in drinking were celebrated many centuries before our time. For example, the medieval medical encyclopedia *Regimen Sanitatis Salerni* said: "If the drinking of wine overnight doth hurt one, by reason that he is not accustomed to drinke wine, then he may drinke wine againe in the morning, to accustom him, and so the drinking of wine shall less hurt him."

Drs. Wilfred W. Westerfeld and Martin P. Schulman of Syracuse reported to the Council on Foods and Nutrition of the American Medical Association that, "A tolerance to alcohol de-

---

HANGOVER: ALCOHOLISM, JUNIOR GRADE

The hangover is a miniscule spurt of alcoholism that comes and goes—and, among other things, leaves a warning signal.

Alcohol does not *in itself* cause malnutrition, which is the cause of cirrhosis, kidney trouble, and neuritis.

The person who drinks and eats regularly—and together—will not fall prey to these troubles, doctors agree. He will not suffer hangovers, either.

---

velops after its continued use, but it is lost after a number of months of abstinence"—just one of the penalties of abstinence, we suppose.

"During the tolerance phase, larger doses of alcohol are required to produce the same pharmacological effect." The doctors pointed out that habituation to alcohol does not effect nor delay the mechanics and disposition of alcohol after it is consumed. "It is quite clear that the phenomenon of tolerance cannot be attributed to a faster removal of alcohol from the system."

The kernel is that "habituated animals and humans sober up faster, even though the level of blood alcohol falls at a normal rate. The phenomenon of tolerance is an adaptation of the central nervous system to alcohol rather than an alteration in the metabolism of alcohol. It is, therefore, theoretically possible to alleviate the intoxication symptoms without altering the metabolism of the alcohol." Which suggests, perhaps, a correlation to the fact that if we have two National Football League quarterbacks of equal ability but one has performed for three years and the other for ten, the latter is most likely to win the Super Bowl.

What is the cure for a hangover? Robert Benchley answered that one in words that defy dispute in the realms of science, legislation, or human speculation: "There is no cure for the hangover save death."

The only *alternative* cure takes longer—the passage of time. Almost every sufferer from hangover who has ever lived has evolved (and tested) one or more anodynes. But this realm of science has yet to register the big breakthrough.

Eddie Condon, the jazz musician, offered an appealing one. "You take the juice of two quarts of whiskey." The only trouble with this approach is that it doesn't cure the hangover, but only postpones it. "The hair of the dog that bit you" assuredly affords temporary relief—but who needs an encore?

There are modifications of this remedy that do have some temporary merit. A bloody mary, a barnyard oyster (raw eggs in your beer), a ramos fizz can restore some measure of health, or seem to. Back in 1940, an angel of mercy named Shipley wrote in the *Medical Record:* "Champagne, the aristocrat of all wines, and sparkling burgundy must not be overlooked. . . . When one is low in spirits and 'especially the morning after the night before,' a glass of champagne will clear the cobwebs from the brain, steady the nerves, settle the stomach and remove that dark brown taste so familiar to those who overeat and drink at the festive board."

Such nonalcoholic stopgaps as clam juice laced with Worcestershire sauce, black coffee, hot baths, hot packs, saunas, long walks, and long swims may provide miniscule comforts and help pass the time (the big problem). Aspirin helps a little, but never enough. Rest and sleep is really the best because that enables time to pass least obtrusively and it fights fatigue.

That distinguished nineteenth-century medical and chemical virtuoso, J. L. W. Thudicum, was also celebrated as a student and writer on the subject of wine. In his work, appropriately entitled *The Aesthetical Use of Wine,* he set down words that merit immortality among the hordes who suffer from hangovers: "Of all alcoholic drinks, however, true wine . . . offers the least opportunity or inducement to abuse. Natural wine may be drunk, but it never produces delirium tremens, never produces those permanent lesions of tissues which are consequences of excess in the use of spirits and beer."

Whiskey hangovers, gin hangovers, rum hangovers exist in abundance. Wine hangovers, including champagne hangovers, also exist. But hard liquor hangovers one glides into rather effortlessly. One must work at it somewhat frenetically to earn a wine hangover. In fact, if one eats while imbibing good wine and doesn't conclude the feast with distilled spirits, a hangover's just about out of the question.

As with most ailments of mankind, the prevention of hangovers is much more rewarding than their cure. And perhaps the best prevention known to man, if one is to drink alcohol, is to drink solely wine. It is much less likely to strike back with a hangover because it has a lower alcohol content than the hard stuff, making it much easier to regulate, and it is usually taken with food. Some stubborn souls insist that wine is more likely to give them a hangover, or gives them a worse hangover, or once gave them a hangover—and they remembered it so long that they will no longer drink wine, or not very much wine. This is really too bad because they are missing so much and so many benefits, and they are getting so many more severe hangovers than they would if they drank more wine and less of the other alcoholic beverages.

"Use and damage, blessing and curse live closely together with wine," commented Dr. F. Maret, discussing this problem.

The toxic effects of fermented beverages (wine and beer) are relatively negligible. "Much more interesting are the higher alcohols and their esters, which are more poisonous. Especially because of their good fat solubility they get into the central nervous system and develop their toxic effect. The higher alcohols are oxidized much more slowly and therefore their narcotic effect remains longer. The surfaces of the ganglion cells of the brain occupied by these alcohols let less oxygen through; they cause headaches and vomiting.

"The bad tolerance and often unpleasant aftereffects of heavy wines and highly aromatic spirits are explained by their high content of complicatedly put together aroma matters."

Dr. Maret acknowledged that in many respects the toxological effect of higher alcohols and their oxidation products is still not clear, but alcohol content in "clean, correctly made table wines is small and cannot cause damage to health."

Indeed, to the degree that wine drinking precludes hangovers—an overwhelming degree when wine is consumed exclusively and with food—it makes both a delicious and a welcome contribution to the health and good feelings of the alcohol aficionado.

16

࿇࿇࿇࿇࿇࿇

Wine and the Head

The impact of wine on the state of mind as an agent for happiness and relaxation is treated in Chapter 18, "Wine and the Nervous System."

Wine and Headaches

Dioscorides recommended wine for headaches: "Both ye green and ye dry [wine] with Acetum [vinegar] and Rosaceum [oil of roses] are a perfusion for ye headache. . . ." He also recommended a related grape cure: "The leaves and the tendrils of ye wine-bearing vine, beaten small and laid on with polenta [pearl barley], do assuage headaches. . . ."

Warren R. Dawson's *Magician and Leech* set forth this fifteenth-century remedy: "For the headache that cometh of cold. Seethe betony in wine and wash thine head therein. And it is good for cold of the stomach and fumes that rise up into the head."

I have not found wine much mentioned by modern medical authorities for headaches or other ills of the head. Doctors I have known suggest that there is little that one can swallow which will alleviate a headache, save to anesthetize it by drugging. Wine can do that, too. If it doesn't cure a headache it may help you forget the pain until the headache has passed.

Wine and the Ear–Nose–Throat System

Warren Dawson presents an Egyptian prescription that may be a historic first application of eardrops: "Medicament for an ear that is watery: Salt, heat with good wine, you apply it

139

after cleansing it first. You scrape salt, heat with wine, and apply it for four days." From the same source comes a prudent word of advice to physicians: "The pain will stop immediately. But do not administer this remedy to a man until you have received your fee."

In early Roman times, Celsus cited Erasistratus with this formula for relief from an ulcerated ear: pepper, cucumber, myrrh, copper ore, and copper scales mixed with wine. He also mentioned the recipe of Crato: cinnamon, lycium, spikenard, myrrh, honey, and wine. When ears emitted a discharge and became swollen they were to be washed with a syringe of wine, after which sour wine with a little tutty was to be injected. If there were ear adhesions and thick matter, "it is best to use honey and sufficient wine to dilute the myrrh."

When there are maggots in the ear, if not too far in, they can be drawn out by ear scoop; but if they are lodged deep within "they must be killed by medication. Wine to the rescue again, this time boiled down with horehound. Then the worms, dying in the first part of the ear, can easily be drawn out—or flushed out with the wine and horehound.

For swollen but not ulcerated tonsils Celsus advised "that root which they call sweet, crushed and boiled in raisin wine or honey wine." He directed the tonsils to be anointed with boiled-down juice of sweet pomegranates, saffron, myrrh, shredded alum, mild wine, and honey. Warm fig and honey wine was a popular gargle of the time.

The ancient Chinese had a prescription for dislodging a bone in the throat: eagle excrement washed down with wine. Hardly a wine taster's delight.

Mansur the Great, the tenth-century Persian pharmacologist, suggested that if one gargled or washed the mouth with "wine in which leaves have been boiled, he alleviates all complaints of catarrh which exist in the throat, neck, and chest."

Otolaryngologist Kenneth G. Cambon of British Columbia, also a winemaker, gave a paper before the Pacific Coast Oto-Opthalmologic Society, treating the application of wine to ear–nose–throat problems.

Several of his patients have volunteered that with the use of wine "their tinnitus [ear ringing] diminished a great deal. This is most unusual in any regimen."

Dr. Cambon also found wine useful in treatment of globus

hysterous (choking sensation felt by hysterical persons). "The 'lump' or tight mass in the throat often becomes most acute at the time of the evening meal, when all the anxieties of the family and of the day come into focus." Hysterical people are generally beyond help by formal medication because drug prescription fortifies their conviction that there is something wrong with them —thus formal medication could make them permanent throat cripples.

"I suggest instead that they develop the habit of having a bottle of red wine with their evening meal, stressing that this should be shared with their family. The formality of having the wine produces a gracious atmosphere conducive to relaxation and enjoyment of the meal."

CLARET VERSUS CARROTS

How deafness upset a doctor's prescription of wine was triumphantly related by Mrs. Martha Allan, Superintendent of the Department of Medical Temperance of the W.C.T.U. in her book, *Alcohol: A Dangerous and Unnecessary Medicine* (1900):

A somewhat distracted mother brought her daughter to the doctor. The daughter was suffering from general lowness. She was pale and listless and did not care about eating or doing anything.

The doctor prescribed for her a glass of claret three times a day with meals. The mother was somewhat deaf, but apparently heard all he said and determined to carry out the prescription to the very letter.

In ten days they were back again and the girl was rosy cheeked, smiling, and the picture of health.

The doctor congratulated himself on his diagnosis of the case. "I am glad to see your daughter is so much better," he said.

"Yes," exclaimed the excited and grateful mother. "She has had just what you ordered. She has eaten carrots three times a day since we were here."

Victims of epistaxis (nosebleed) benefit from wine because it relieves anxiety, depresses blood pressure, and acts as a mild sedative. "Patients with recurrent bouts are advised on having a nosebleed to sit down and hold their nose tightly long enough to sip slowly on a glass of dry red wine." Dr. Cambon admits his predilection for red wine many arise from the fact that it is the only type he produces.

Wine and the Eyes

Eye disorders won some esoteric enological attention from Celsus. For ophthalmia (inflammation of the eyeball) he recommended, "There should be smeared over the eyeball, of saffron as much as can be taken up in three fingers, of myrrh in amount the size of a bean, of poppy-tears the size of a lentil: these are pounded up in raisin wine, and applied on a probe to the eyeball."

For proptosis (protrusion or prolapse of the eyeball) he would administer a salve of Indian nard, poppy-tears, saffron, and fresh rose leaves mixed in wine. For carbuncles on the eyelid "the most suitable poultice is one of linseed boiled in honeyed wine, or if that is not at hand, flour boiled in the same."

His prescription for a black eye: The best salt from Ammon, or some other salt, is pounded, and oil gradually added. Then this is mixed with barley meal which has been boiled in honey wine. Scabby conditions in the eye's corners were relieved by application of bread soaked in wine.

King Edward II's physician, John of Gaddesden, the original "doctor of physic" in Chaucer's poem, listed wine of fennel and parsley as a cure for blindness. Fennel was one of the nine sacred herbs powerful against the nine venoms, or causes of disease, in the ancient Saxon tradition.

Wine and the Hair

Many a farfetched combination has been offered to cure baldness, but one of the most astounding came in the London pharmacopoeia of 1677. It was a combination of steel wine (sic), Peruvian bark, crabs' eyes, human urine, and *Aqua Vitae Hibernorum sive Usquebagh* (Irish whiskey).

Wine and hair health have little enough in common in our

WINE HELPS FIGHT GLAUCOMA

Glaucoma is an eye disease which results in abnormally high pressure within the eyeball. Increased ocular tension causes the eyeball to distend and harden, ultimately leading to blindness. Acute glaucoma can be arrested by surgery. Chronic glaucoma can be mitigated by continuous use of medications, including wine [or other alcoholic beverages].

The alcohol in wine reduces the pressure of the intra-ocular fluid, apparently by suppressing the hormone which interferes with the normal processes that rid the body tissues of unnecessary fluids. Following consumption of the amount of alcohol capable of inducing a reaction [that in one pint of table wine] in intraocular pressure falls during the first hour and then returns toward the preingestion level within four or five hours. Consequently, a glaucoma victim who finds himself without his medication can safely take an alcoholic beverage and thereby avert a possible tragedy.

Wine can also be used to reduce the pressure within the eyeball immediately prior to surgery by those patients unable to tolerate the pressure-reducing drugs normally used for this purpose. On the other hand, if the subject is a victim of glaucoma, alcoholic beverages should not be taken before an eye examination testing the fluid pressure within the eye, because the results would then be lower than they would normally be.

SALVATORE PABLO LUCIA

day and age, but sixth-century Byzantine pharmacologist Alexander of Tralles suggested nutgalls in red wine for gray hair, and for dandruff recommended rubbing the scalp with wine and salves before washing with salt water.

Wine and the Mouth

The French army surgeon Guy de Chauliac (1300–1368) urged rinsing the mouth with wine to prevent dental decay. Dawson's medieval leech book prescribed this for toothache:

"Take figs and cumin and stamp it well together, and boil them well in vinegar or red wine; and make a plaster and lay it to the cheek outside."

"The dental decay frequently found in persons dying from alcoholism was assumed for years to result from alcohol's action in the mouth," wrote Dr. Ferdinand C. Helwig in *Liquor: The Servant of Man*. "It is now known to be caused by bad dietary habits, bad oral hygiene, and syphilis. Liquor, in fact, is possibly a more efficient mouth antiseptic than many proprietary mixtures sold for this purpose. There are no changes attributable to alcohol to be found in the mucous membranes of the mouth, throat, or esophagus."

I can recommend from firsthand experience, proven out a number of times, the consumption of a little wine—a bottle or more in fact—before you go to the dentist's. It won't do a damn thing for your teeth, but you'll appreciate your dentist a great deal more.

17

❦❦❦❦❦❦❦❦

Wine and the Heart's Highway System

Heart disease is the big killer of our time. In the United States more than a million a year die from a form of it, accounting for more than 50 percent of all deaths. Science advances but heart disease not only rages unchecked—it increases. Seemingly, the reason is that the heart is the number one anatomical victim of our twentieth-century life-style.

Accentuating this theme, Lawrence E. Lamb, the world-famed heart specialist, noted that while in 1900 the top three causes of all deaths in the United States were tuberculosis, pneumonia, and diarrhea-enteritis, in 1968 two circulatory ailments (heart disease and cerebral hemorrhage) joined cancer at the head of the list. During this time the heart disease death rate has almost tripled, from 137 to 373 per 100,000. Heart attacks among twenty-five- to forty-four-year-old men rose 14 percent between 1950 and 1967.

Calling for preventive measures to be given priority over cures (what is the cure for sudden death from heart attack?), Dr. Lamb attributes this plague to present-day living patterns. He particularly marked obesity as a major modern threat to the heart.

There are many respected experts who indict increased stress as the major cause leading to the increase in heart disease. Others blame a combination of rich diet and reduced exercise, which creates obesity and the related tissue clogging by fatty foods.

As we have discussed elsewhere, wine can help with the tensions and overweight problems of our uptight age. All of this gives added impact to the opinions of many physicians who have either subtly suggested or bluntly stated that wine is the heart's best friend—either to help prevent heart trouble or to liven the convalescence. An American Heart Association publication, authored by Drs. Marvin, Wright, Page, Jones, and Rutstein, points out that "Besides being a dilator of the arteries [alcohol] can serve as a valuable medicine. Moreover, in many patients, it does much to relax nervous tensions, lessen fatigue, and make life pleasanter."

Wine's help for the beleaguered heart is a tradition that goes clear back to ancient China, as revealed by Franz Hübotter in a study of Chinese and Tibetan pharmacology. "Effective in heart attack with swelling of extremities, unpleasant coldness of the heart, mental confusion: A solution consisting of twelve herbs including such as Angelica polymorpha, zingiber, cinnamon, as well as ground oyster shells; all of the components are to be dissolved in warm wine; the patient is to drink this three times a day for twenty days."

If controlled-sample laboratory evidence is lacking to prove the efficacy of wine as an enemy of heart disease, empirical evidence and testimonials exist in abundance. Here are a few:

A. Trousseau of the Paris medical faculty concocted a "most powerful hydragogue" of white wine, juniper berries, squill, digitalis and potassium acetate, "which I have used for a number of years, and my colleagues have accepted the formula, is easily tolerated and apparently cures symptoms of heart disease in a great number of cases."

Jean Martin Charcot, the great French neurologist and physician to the Salpêtrière, found wine, sometimes with a few drops of Cognac added, a good ingredient in diets for aneurism of the aorta and in advanced stages of endocarditis.

Ivan Gregorivich Koutateladze conducted experiments in 1916 at Novorossiisk University at Odessa, testing wine's historic reputation as a cardiac restorative and vasodilator. Experimenting with the isolated heart of a cat, he compared the effect of wine with a straight alcohol solution of the same strength. The alcohol at first depressed the heart action, while the wine produced stimulation. When the stimulating effect of the alcohol came through later, the wine generated even more pronounced activity.

Searching among the components of wine for the substance inducing the activity, Koutateladze isolated a brownish, bittersweet residue—a product of fermentation not found in the original grape. He classified this substance as an amine and compared its action with that of digitalin. Then he reported his work at a medical meeting in Odessa in 1916. Published in a Russian medical journal, this work was lost at the time in the upheaval of the Communist revolution.

Almost half a century later Osmo Vartiainen at the University of Helsinki discovered that a grape brandy increased coronary blood flow in an isolated rabbit heart by 10 to 25 percent, whereas straight alcohol had only a very slight effect. This confirmed Koutateladze's finding that nonalcoholic substances in wines produce distinctly stimulating cardiovascular effects.

Sort of a roundabout avenue by which wine might help the heart was suggested by a Chicago physician's recommendation of a simple, inexpensive preventive for heart attacks: sex.

Dr. Eugene Scheimann affirmed in *Forum,* "Not only is sex positively good for weak hearts, but too little sex can actually predispose men to have heart trouble. Sexual activity is good for the heart, can enhance the health, and can increase longevity." However, dissent came from another Chicago heart specialist,

---

HOW TO SURVIVE A HEART ATTACK

Regarding a control group observed for history of coronary trouble, a scientist noted:

In those patients who survived attack (82 percent) 71 percent have been using alcohol in moderation anywhere from one to ten years since the attack. In this group all claim beneficial effects, with less anxiety.

While I cannot relate any beneficial effects of alcohol directly to improved coronary blood flow, there is evidence in the literature that in moderation alcohol may diminish the work load of the heart by reducing the pressure in the small peripheral arteries.

More important, alcohol in moderation may relieve anxiety through cerebral action. This anxiety frequently contributes to the onset of heart pain.

EDWARD P. LUONGO

Dr. Jeremiah Stamler: "If he has data to support this, then he must know something that the rest of us in the scientific community don't. For normal, healthy men, sex is very good. But patients with severe heart disease do have to reduce their activity. And sex is activity."

That decision is up to you—and you have our heartfelt good wishes.

Wine and Cholesterol

Cholesterol ranks with pollution as a major mania of our day. Well it may, for it is pollution-by-fat of that basic irrigation fluid—human blood. Also, like pollution, cholesterol evokes a different theory for its control from every professional and amateur expert of our day. No wonder Dr. Milton Silverman told an international medical congress in Bordeaux, "In my country illness due to cholesterol ranks second in importance only to Communism."

Both the medical and nutritional professions are split as to how damaging cholesterol is, what causes it, and how to fight it. If this controversy has breached your fortress, you dare not dismiss it lightly because the people who brand it a killer might be right. Should you fall prey to the fear of cholesterol, many of life's prime delights are now forbidden: eggs and omelets; milk and all its products; avocados; many of the tastiest meats; the best of the great sauces and gravies; sausages and spice; the gaudiest and most tempting desserts—and much more.

You don't *have* to give these things up. After all, you don't expect to live forever. But you are now in the front-line trenches of those most likely to dig their graves with their own teeth.

Interestingly, it was an accident of war that elevated cholesterol into a major menace. When the Germans overran Holland in World War II, they carted off the rich dairy products as spoils of war. The deprived Dutch suddenly developed a dramatic drop in heart trouble. Investigation showed that they had benefited from this war-imposed restriction.

In 1970, the Framington heart disease study in Massachusetts, based on a ten-year experiment with 912 persons, concluded that "If there really is any association between diet intake and serum cholesterol level . . . it is probably a weak one." *Medical World* magazine reacted with this understatement: "The find-

CHOLESTEROL: KILLER OR KIDDER

Cholesterol, like so many other areas of the war against heart disease, is a damned-if-you-do and damned-if-you-don't enigma of perplexity and frustration. One expert says eggs will doom you, another says you must eat them for the body to utilize certain cholesterol-dissolving chemicals. One expert says shellfish is terrible, another says it is good, and another says it is tolerable. One expert says diet is the villain and another says too high-paced a life-style is the trouble. One expert says alcohol will do you harm, another says it will do you good, another says it doesn't matter at all. And your doctor assures you that nobody really knows.

Just listen to this, from one of the nation's most famed, best-selling nutritionist authors, Adelle Davis: "Diets low in cholesterol have also achieved exactly the opposite from what was hoped. Such diets throw the liver into a frenzy of cholesterol-producing activity, causing the amount in the blood to increase." Also, "Volunteers recovering from heart attacks have consumed daily for varying periods ten eggs, sixteen egg yolks, the fat from thirty-two eggs, and even nine to sixty grams of pure cholesterol; their blood cholesterols have not increased provided the eggs were cooked without saturated or hydrogenated fat."

---

ings "may prove shocking to many doctors and certainly to the public." Los Angeles *Times* columnist Jack Smith was more anguished: "I may have denied myself a hearty breakfast every morning for the past ten years for nought."

Thanking medical research "for our precious antibiotics and vaccines," Smith affirmed, "I hope I'm still around when they find out once and for all whether cholesterol is good for your heart or not, and how to raise or lower your level. I also hope they come to some final conclusion on the efficacy of jogging and steam baths. A man could drop dead waiting."

In our frustration, it sometimes seems, we might as well do and eat as we please. What profit is it to surrender a whole world of cherished pleasures only to find that one's cholesterol is going up, and then to read Dr. Super Reputation in the morning paper speculate that the cholesterol-is-a-menace syndrome is a myth, anyhow?

You do have one consolation, if cholesterol is your nemesis. There is a wine school of thought, which numbers as many experts backed with plausible reasons for their findings as does any competing school of thought that derogates the role of wine.

This first group stoutly contends that wine is a prime ally in helping to break up the coagulation of cholesterol, that wine favors the decomposition of fat substances in the blood, and that wine can lower the cholesterol level in the blood, or at least work against a cholesterol concentration.

In 1957, Agnes Fay Morgan and colleagues at the University of California demonstrated that wine protects against excessive amounts of exogenous cholesterol. Young rats and hamsters were fed normal and cholesterol-rich diets with water, with a solution of water plus 15 percent alcohol, and with white and red wines brought to 15 percent alcoholic strength. With the total fluid intake held constant, the wine-fed animals were found to have significantly lower liver fat levels and as much as 50 percent lower cholesterol levels in the blood, livers, and adrenals.

Wine and Arteriosclerosis

Hardening of the arteries, the universal and seemingly inevitable disease of old age, is the eventual outcome of too much cholesterol.

In the 1870s prevailing authorities were convinced that arteriosclerosis was caused by alcohol, and for years this was accepted. However, Dr. Ferdinand C. Helwig comments, "All present-day clinical, experimental, and pathological evidence is against this opinion. Overfeeding, obesity, heredity, and old age are the causative factors in rising arterial hardness," he wrote.

Dr. Helwig continued:

Time after time from wide postmortem material appears the comment that blood vessels of the alcoholics not only show no earlier hardening but on the contrary are consistently in an excellent condition in proportion to age.

It is therefore the present opinion of many authorities that instead of causing arteriosclerosis alcohol can act to retard it. C_2H_5OH, beverage alcohol, dissolves all fats. This does not mean that they are removed from the body, they are only changed in form. Alcohol's action on animal fat . . . does not make you thinner. In the case of cholesterol fat, however, this alteration seems to free it from the walls of the blood vessels, so that it can pass on and be utilized for normal metabolism processes rather than stored up to cause trouble.

Noting that cholesterol is richly present in the fat of milk, which is a great deterrent of alcohol absorption, and even seems to cause the disappearance of some of the alcohol, Dr. Helwig theorized, "There is authoritative suggestion . . . that the two molecules tend to destroy each other. This is still conjecture. What is not conjecture is that cholesterol deposited in the arteries produces the disease arteriosclerosis, and that in users of alcohol there is not so much cholesterol deposited."

Dr. Heinrich Kliewe mentioned published autopsy reports which said that arteries of old alcoholics were found tender and elastic like those in young people, with either no signs or only slight signs of arteriosclerosis. Schweizer reported that arteriosclerosis in teetotalers over fifty years old was 63 percent stronger than in chronic alcoholics.

Dr. Salvatore Lucia noted, "While more data may be required to justify a conclusion concerning arterial disease in man, a 1961 investigation in Italy lends some clinical support to the

---

DIABETES, CHOLESTEROL, AND ARTERIOSCLEROSIS

Now arteriosclerosis, the disease which, if accompanied by diabetes, makes young men old half a generation too soon.

From the poorly converted fat, down into the intima of the arteries, is laid away the cholesterol which causes it. This we know. And insulin doesn't stop it but will permit the reverse. This too is known.

We do not know precisely what alcohol does to the cholesterol; we only know that in the presence of alcohol much of it seems to disappear as though dissolved; that arteriosclerosis in habitual drinkers is reduced in striking percentage.

FERDINAND C. HELWIG

widely held Italian medical opinion that regular use of wine in the diet may have a preventive effect on arterial degenerative diseases.

"Wine is clearly a most effective adjuvant in the treatment of cardiovascular disorders. With its ability to promote vascular dilation; to assist in the control and utilization of cholesterol; to reduce emotional tension and to assure tranquilization; and, in select instances, to offer regulatory assistance to the heart rate, wine soothes the psyche as it serves the heart."

Wine and Blood Pressure

Another index of the inevitable deterioration of the human physical frame with advancing age is high blood pressure, also called hypertension. Here again medical authorities and writers are cautious, but enough of them have championed wine to provide more than a glimmering of hope that the wine drinker may find in his favorite beverage a tentative ally against high blood pressure.

Called the "hidden killer," because many victims do not know they have the malady and because its origins are still obscure, hypertension afflicts some twenty million Americans and is suspcted of killing five hundred thousand of them a year. Is this monster spawned by social pressures, everyday stresses, job responsibilities, unhappy marriages, constant worry, heredity, high-salt diets, high-fat diets, overweight—or some ungodly combination of these? Science still does not know. The role of alcohol in general and wine in particular is still not specifically understood and is therefore controversial. But many reliable doctors think alcohol helps enough to provide justification for the high-blood-pressure victim to drink some of it for general, if not specific, relief.

H. T. Blumenthal, among other geriatrics specialists, has championed the theory that stress, rather than cholesterol, causes arteriosclerosis. Perhaps both are causatory, Dr. John Staige Davis commented, "Should further research support the stress theory, it would appear that the value of beverage alcohol as an adjunct in the management of the disease would still be considerable because of its relaxing, euphoric effects."

There have been no specific statistical studies dealing with the effect of alcohol on hypertension, wrote Drs. Matthew Ferguson and Sister Michael Marie, "However, if one were to reason a posteriori from what has been already noted, it might be said

ALCOHOL AND HIGH BLOOD PRESSURE

Contrary to the usual impression, alcohol does not raise blood pressure, but lowers it considerably, which effect lasts about three to four hours before it rises to its previous level. There is a momentary rise of blood pressure and then a considerable fall. Half an ounce of whiskey will produce a drop of 60 to 70 mm in the systolic, and 10 to 20 mm in the diastolic pressure, and the patients feel much better on account of the conspicuous effects of the alcohol . . ."

Presumably because of their action in inducing vaso-dilation of the peripheral vessels and promoting relaxation, alcoholic beverages have been widely used in the treatment of high blood pressure.

WILLIAM LINTZ

---

that alcohol has no injurious effects and may be beneficial insofar as it is a sedative."

"Light wine in moderate amounts—up to one bottle per day—exercises an unusually favorable leveling effect on the blood pressure," said Dr. M. Hochrein. He specified this should be a "fully fermented light wine" and not oversulphured.

Wine and Angina Pectoris

Another heart killer, angina pectoris, which means agony of the heart, is defined in Webster as "a peculiarly painful disease, so named from a sense of suffocating contraction within the chest. It is usually associated with organic change in the heart or aorta."

One of America's foremost coronary specialists, Boston's Dr. Paul Dudley White, has flatly stated that alcohol may be of signal benefit in coronary disease. "The most effective drug after the nitrates is alcohol. It was used routinely one hundred years ago before the introduction of the nitrates and even now, when nitrates are not available, an ounce of cognac, whiskey, or rum may give quite rapid relief from angina pectoris, usually in the course of a very few minutes."

To show that his opinions were not idly conceived, Dr.

White critically analyzed 750 cases of angina pectoris. He found only one in this group who drank very heavily, whereas among the heavy drinkers, more commonly in the control group, he found no angina pectoris. Only 8 of the 750 drank a considerable amount. One patient who drank excessively was sixty-five and had averaged more than a quart of strong liquor daily for forty years. He was an excessive eater and had had syphilis for forty-six years. The patient who drank the most survived for a longer time (23½ years) after his first attack of angina pectoris than any other person in the whole series.

It was concluded that although alcohol neither caused nor prevented angina pectoris, excessive drinking was rare in the past history of patients with this disease and that in occasional cases alcohol might prevent or relieve attacks.

Further confirmation came from Dr. Heinrich Kliewe, again bolstering his opinion with that of other authorities. "If there are no medications on hand, Heinecke considers a glass of heavy wine, cognac, or whiskey very useful with an attack of angina pectoris until the blood demand of the heart muscle and blood supply through the coronary vessels become adjusted to each other. Heyden supposes that the improvement for an attack of angina pectoris through alcohol does not depend on the beneficial myocardium or coronary vessel effect but on its calming and psychological influence. Russek, Holzmann, and others also observed that alcohol is quieting for angina pectoris and lessens the severe heart pains."

Wine and Strokes

Dr. William Dock, who himself survived a coronary, wrote: "For the man learning to live with a stroke, and aware of the risk of another stroke, or the man learning to live with heart disease, and the threat of another heart attack, dietary management and a program of rest, exercise, and rehabilitation are far more easily accepted if he has a daily intake of 50 to 80 ml of alcohol. Unlike many new agents for treating anxiety, alcohol rarely causes depression."

Stanford Medical School's Leo A. Sapirstein, admitting the lack of scientific evidence to support the use of wine in heart trouble, urged research on the use and effect of wine in connection with strokes. He said, in a speech to a group of doctors,

"Granted that it would be desirable to have more facts, are we in a position to recommend the liberal use of wine and alcohol for the patient with the incipient or progressing stroke? I am told . . . that many physicians do just that. Perhaps they have learned by some clinical sixth sense what no one seems to have written anywhere."

He concluded in a humorous vein: "If I feel signs of an incipient stroke tomorrow I fully intend to drink all the wine I can get as fast as I can."

Wine as Preventive

Wine's effect as a vasodilator (which means an expediter of blood's passage through the blood vessels) and relaxer seems to have a broad value no matter in which particular direction the enemy strikes. Wine is useful to parry the blow that has been struck—and also has value as a preventive to avert the blow, or to reduce the possibility of successive blows.

Dr. Ferdinand C. Helwig summarized it: "It has long been recognized that alcohol may not only check the agonizing attack, but prescribed as regular therapy, prevent an attack altogether. The patient finds this out and is more confident; he is

---

WINE THE DEFENDER

When the viselike pain of angina pectoris strikes, administration of brandy is an effective, efficient, and pain-banishing coronary dilator. But for the prevention of such attacks, small amounts of wine taken with meals may be preferable, for it helps tranquilize, thus relieving emotional tension, usually an important feature in such attacks, and it dilates peripheral blood vessels, thereby easing the load on the heart. Recent studies have suggested that wine, even taken with diets high in cholesterol and fatty acids, may help to prevent atherosclerosis and coronary heart disease. The tranquilizing action of wine is employed by the clinician to reduce the symptoms of hypertension.

ROBERT C. STEPTO

---

at the same time effortlessly receiving food, and he is helped to rest and sleep, by far the most urgent of his needs in this disease."

It is not an airtight case, but there is impressive medical support for those choosing to believe that wine is indeed one of the heart's best friends.

18

❦❦❦❦❦❦❦

Wine and the
Nervous System

That poignant liquor, which the zealot calls the mother of sins, is pleasant and sweet to me. Give me wine! Wine that shall subdue the strongest, that I may for a time forget the cares and troubles of the world.

ANONYMOUS

Stress is today the big killer of men according to Dr. Hans Selye of the University of Montreal, whose stress theory is touted as one of the twentieth century's milestone medical research achievements.

"A motorcar," Dr. Selye said, "doesn't suddenly cease running because of old age. It stops because of the failure of some part that has worn out. It is the same with people. Under continuous stress—either physical or mental—some vital body part gives way, leading to a variety of illnesses, and eventually to death."

Subjecting rats to a variety of stresses, Dr. Selye always came up with the same answer: *No matter what the nature of the stress, the same type of internal wreckage resulted.*

Let any type of stress threaten and the pituitary and adrenaline glands respond automatically. In what Dr. Selye called the "alarm reaction," blood pressure and sugar rise, stomach acid increases, arteries tighten. As the threat passes the "resistance phase" sets in, and calming hormones flow from those glands. But let this alarm resistance pattern register often enough and the organism reaches a stage of exhaustion. Serious disease or death may follow.

In animals under emotional tension, fats are drawn from the body storing places, injected into the bloodstream, and deposited along artery walls. Presumably the same thing happens in man, setting the stage for heart disease. It would appear that tension even more than a diet of fatty foods may be the chief source of those twin enemies of the heart: cholesterol and high blood pressure.

Other woes from ulcers to back pain and from headaches to the common cold tend to signal a person's reaction to tension as it bears down on the individual's "point of least resistance."

Frustration or tension has long been a problem of man. This ancient enemy has taken on raging proportions with the mounting assault upon our nerves of such mass woes as nuclear extinction, racial pressures, megalopolis living, eternal upward spiraling of prices and taxes, Big Brother government, pollution of land, sea, and air, scandals in public life, exhaustion of natural resources, overpopulation, traffic obfuscation, the money mania, a tyrannical work ethic, crime and violence every day and every night, the revolt of our youth, the drug scourge, and other traumas endemic in our time. Personal problems continue to plague us: illness, cold, heat, fatigue, marital malaise, nagging, boredom, failures, hatred, poisons, worry, trouble on the job, and many others.

Experts have called the late twentieth century an age of depression. A public opinion poll has reported that half our contemporaries say they are depressed much or some of the time. Symptoms include fatigue, insomnia, inability to eat, restlessness, boredom, a feeling of going to pieces, frequent crying spells.

"There is a loss of appetite for food, for sex, for pleasures in life," said Dr. Jan Fawcett, chief of the Depression and Suicide Unit, Illinois State Psychiatric Institute.

"Today's depression is becoming epidemic in our part of the world," said Dr. Harold Visotsky, Northwestern University psychiatry chairman. "We are now entering what may be the decades of depression and apathy. Both the increasing incidence of suicides among youth and the widespread use of mood-elevating drugs . . . indicate that depressions . . . are more common even than our statistics have revealed. We are seeing significant numbers of young people as new cases, depressed for the first time."

Dr. Visotsky deplored the implications of depressions downward shift in age level, fearing that it may signal recurring epidemics in the years ahead. "When a person has responded to stress early in life with a specific type of emotional illness . . . he tends to respond to future stresses, disappointments, and adverse circumstances later in life with the same type of emotional illness."

What is the answer for beleaguered man? What can make his emotions friends instead of enemies? *Relax.* Relax and enjoy it. Relax and you *will* enjoy it. But how to relax? There is no more elusive art. There are increasing pressures in our modern technomaniacal confusion that make it ever more elusive. It is easier discussed than attained. For the individual it boils down to anything that will help one forget, help one escape, for a moment or an hour or however mercifully longer.

Things like hobbies, coffee breaks, siestas, entertainments, games, crossword puzzles, a new hairdo, reading, a hot bath, music, a flirtation, a love affair—anything that takes one's mind off oneself can help.

Science tries to help with chemicals and drugs, which sometimes provide relief but can harm more than they help. Doctors, the scientists trained to save man from himself and his environment, try to help with results often ranging from reassuring to miraculous; but doctors, being human like their charges, can be panicked in a drama so overwhelming.

Hospital magazine as far back as 1907 prescribed: "A glass of wine is the best remedy." Not a bad idea in 1907; not a bad idea now. Wine has done many things for people, but maybe not one so constructive as to help us relax. There are many controversies about wine in the realm of health. But for ages past, wine has been accepted as the champion relaxer, the safest, gentlest, surest, most popular of sedatives—better than all of the sleeping pills or drugs, which can exact such a toll for the relief they give. Wine is a psychosomatic anodyne; it relaxes both body and mind as it helps repel stress.

It is the alcohol in wine that unravels us. "Alcohol is the most readily available tension-reducing agent in our society," wrote Canada's Dr. W. H. Cruickshank. Dr. Peter J. Steincrohn told us, "I find alcohol's chief value is in fighting tension." Wine is the best of all possible alcoholic beverages for that purpose.

Dr. Milton Silverman, noted California authority on wine

and alcoholism, and Dr. Leon Greenberg, of Yale and Rutgers, and director of the Center of Alcohol Studies, conducted a series of tests to measure the impact of alcohol on human beings at Yale's Laboratory of Applied Physiology. Emotional tension was measured by electrical conductivity of the skin giving "what has been termed a man's emotional tension index (ETI)."

Tests were administered with red table wine, 90 proof whiskey, and alcohol and water, each diluted to 12 percent alcohol concentration. Subjects were exposed to various sources of stress, including frustration and sudden noise.

Findings were:

1. A man's ETI can be reduced by a remarkably small quantity of alcohol.
2. The greater the amount of wine administered, the greater the reduction in emotional tension.
3. With alcohol and water and 90 proof whiskey, beyond a certain point, the greater the amount administered, the more stress was increased.

Dr. Silverman evaluated: "Wine has survived over these millenia for one simple reason—that it serves as a defense against stress, that the mildly sedative action of wine can provide some kind of relief for the emotional tension resulting from the stresses of everyday life."

Wine as Soporific

At day's end we all face the great bridge to sleep, and some of us will have trouble crossing it. If, instead of the restoration of sleep, there comes the frustration of insomnia, the problems of the day are compounded and the promise of tomorrow is subverted. One of wine's most generous blessings may be its power to induce sleep. This it does inexorably, but gently.

Wine is my own favorite and most reliable sleeping potion —helping me get to sleep, helping me stay asleep, and often equally important, helping me return to sleep in the middle of the night when I awaken all charged up and ready to go. Long ago, I learned to take a bottle with me while traveling—against those places where the wayfarer cannot get a nip unless he brings his own. Fitful nights after a dry day's end have led me to rank this packing practice with a toothbrush, razor, and change of underwear.

Wine's relaxing qualities compared with those propensities of pills prompted Leon D. Adams to write, "Some noted medical authorities have said that wine could well supplant 90 percent of the drugs used to induce sleep. There is also reason to wonder whether Americans would be gulping sixty-five million aspirin tablets every twenty-four hours [in 1957] to reduce pain if more people used wine."

"Take it easy," may well be the best advice that a doctor or friend can give you. But this is more easily said than done. Men have lost Rafael Sabatini's "gift of laughter and sense that the world was mad." One does not turn off an aroused nervous system as one flips off an electrical switch. How to unwind from the daily grind has been one of man's most ancient searches. It is still one of his most important quests. One of his earliest findings in this long hunting may still qualify for the blue ribbon.

Why fight it?
Drink wine, to relax.
Relax, to have fun.
Have fun, to live longer.

19

❧❧❧❧❧❧❧❧

Wine and Obesity—How to Take Weight Off and Keep It Off

Everybody loves a fat man but himself. He regards himself with a self-loathing based upon his ineluctable accusation that he has done it to himself. He has made himself unsightly and ungainly, and, worse, he has made himself more vulnerable to almost every lethal disease known to man. And he has done it by letting himself go; by surrendering to the twin temptations of gluttony and sloth—gluttony in eating and drinking too much of the wrong things, and sloth by neglecting a daily discipline of physical exertion.

Everybody loves a fat man but few admire him. Everybody loves him not only because he laughs a lot, but because his plight makes his friends feel better. Either the friend is himself too heavy, and misery loves company; or the friend has conquered his own weight problem, and the sight of his fat friend makes him feel triumphant.

Overweight or obesity has become the status symbol disease and visible earmark of the affluent society. In oversupplied America it has become an epidemic. As heart specialist Lawrence E. Lamb noted, "There is a general tendency among American men to become fatter earlier in life. A twenty-nine or thirty-year-old man is likely to be as fat as his parents or grandparents were in their mid-forties. What this means is that as far as obesity is concerned middle age comes in the later twenties instead of the middle forties."

162

The battle is on. Billions are spent on machines, diets, girdles, injections, pills, luxury spas, food fads, and other nostrums. To win this battle with obesity there can be no short-cuts, there can be no miracles, there can be no gimmicks, and there can be no escape hatches. If we eat and drink more than we burn, we get fat. We face a blunt and brutal confrontation—a struggle waged on two fronts.

1. Caloric intake: the total ingested into the body.
2. Elimination: how fast and in what manner the body gets rid of the intake.

The bad news is well known to all of us. Some foods taste so good that it is hard to limit consumption. And, of course, the best-tasting foods would have to be the most fattening. But naturally they taste still better smothered in sauces, gravies, and other concoctions that are the most injurious chemicals available in terms of fat. Then the situation is further compounded by cocktails before dinner.

The damage is not undone, although it is mitigated, if followed by exercise. Exercise calls to mind the immortal formula of Robert Benchley: "I never run if I can walk; I never walk if I can stand; I never stand if I can sit down; I never sit down if I can lie down." Benchley's equation may be terrific for our morale, but it is terrible for our figure. We know all about how unhealthy it is to be fat. Because of this knowledge, we hate ourselves since we would rather eat too much of the wrong things and we would rather exercise too little or not at all. A game of golf or a swim occasionally is OK with most of us, but we don't relish the daily brisk walks and jogging in place and exercycling—and what man has ever been born who in his heart of hearts does not detest that miserable form of self-flagellation called calisthenics?

We've got to reorganize our eating habits and take on some exercise habits. And we're not talking about a ninety- or nine-day wonder. We're talking about finding a spartan regimen and sticking to it permanently. We're talking about a new life-style of eating.

This is where the good news comes in at last—for there is a way to help retrain ourselves to believe that the healthful foods on the new, permanent diet are as delicious as the fattening ones we once enjoyed. The good news is that there is something that is actually fun to do which can help combat obesity on both the

I HAVE NEVER MET A FAT VINTNER

There are fat vintners, I have been told—and I believe it.

But I have never met a fat vintner, and I have met a respectable cross section of vintners in various parts of California, France, and Germany.

Every vintner drinks wine, and most of them drink plenty of it. This may not prove anything, but it *suggests* that drinking wine is compatible with a respectable, even heroic waistline.

In all honesty, the trimness of vintners is not due wholly to the stuff they drink, although I think (and they think) that it helps. They get a great deal of physical exercise in the vineyards and that helps, too. Plenty.

---

fronts of caloric intake and elimination: drink wine with meals.

Naturally, drinking wine cannot do the job alone, but it can be a great help. Let's face it, wine has calories too, and every glass you drink adds to your total. Someone with too much weight and a character of iron can get the reducing job done faster by ruthlessly eliminating *all* alcohol and substituting such things as the virgin mary, which has all the ingredients of a bloody mary *except* vodka. Or you can try a sahara martini— three drops of vinegar in ice water—and take care to keep from vomiting.

But who's in *that* much of a hurry? We have to live while we reduce. There are qualified experts who say that giving up drinking while dieting dooms you to quickly regaining all those pounds when you start drinking again. In order to shave off some unwanted lard and still have some compensations, you might consider wine. I know it can work, because it worked for me after many years of fat, futility, and frustration. I shed thirty pounds in 150 days, and kept it off thereafter on a wine-rich diet.

The fat-fighter must use discrimination in his diet (which means self-discipline or less intake), and he must apply himself to exercise (which means more self-discipline and effort). But

if he does these things, wine can be a mainstay in the battle
against obesity. It helps both to regulate the chemistry and to
fortify the character.

Let us spell out how wine can help:

Wine cuts calories. By drinking wine instead of cocktails
before meals and before bedtime, you can reduce calories. A
cocktail, depending upon its size and ingredients, adds from 150
to 200 or more calories to your problems. By contrast a glass
of table wine adds only 50 to 90-odd, depending on the glass size
and type of wine. A bottle of wine will add from 400 to 800 or
more calories. A bottle of hard liquor will run up from 1,700
calories for 80 proof alcohol to 2,200 calories for 100 proof.
One ounce of 90 proof liquor provides you with 73 calories; one
ounce of table wine from about 20 to 30 calories. This is a matter
of pure arithmetic—but there is more to the game than numbers.

Wine reduces volume velocity. In addition to the calorie
count, there is the volume velocity. Dr. Frederick J. Stare of
Harvard, pointing out that the amount of alcohol in any drink
determines its entire caloric content, said that "A ten-ounce
bottle of beer contains 150 calories, but remember that it's also
two or three times the volume of a drink of hard liquor. Volume
is important, too, when you consider wine. Most wines are 30
to 40 proof, though brands vary in calories, depending on sugar
content. This is why you can drink about twice as much wine as
liquor and keep calories the same."

Actually, if you stick to *table* wine your drink will be 18
to 24 proof, and you can drink about three or three and a half
times as much wine as liquor and still keep calories on a par.
And if you pour your wine over rocks and mix it with an equal
amount of water or mineral water, you can drink even more.
While your pals are lapping up those loaded martinis, manhat-
tans, and daiquiris you will be enjoying the taste and texture of a
good alcoholic concoction, the feeling of reassuring liquid flowing down your throat, and the therapy of good company at only
a fraction of the caloric penalty.

Wine metabolizes more efficiently. Hard liquor is absorbed
instantly by your bloodstream. Your body burns the alcohol
calories, using them for fuel. Other food calories are then not
needed and are stored as fat. Wine adds calories and will fatten
if overingested, but it metabolizes in a different way and, calorie
per calorie, it will deposit less fat. Wine is both food and drink,

and, as food, it goes to the intestinal tract and is digested and then either distributed to provide energy and maintenance, or eliminated.

Wine helps digestion. Taken with the meal, wine helps digest solid foods more efficiently. This is good for general health, acts as a fat-fighting auxiliary, and aids caloric intake and waste elimination.

"Wine in small quantities has a favorable influence upon the actual absorption and use to the body of other foodstuffs, the body getting more energy from its proteins on a diet containing wine than upon one free from wine," reported *The Hospital* magazine in June 1907.

Obesity is not always a result of abundant eating and of excessive nourishment. It also deals with glandular troubles, such as the thyroid, the pituitary, the genital (interior secretion), or the liver (exterior secretion). These glands are to burn or eliminate the waste of the organism. Every time that we can by appropriate therapy excite them to help them in their job, we will be fighing against obesity resulting from the accumulation of waste or the retention of water in the organism.

That is why many doctors permit obese patients to drink white or red wine in normal doses. Wine gives them energy while simultaneously stimulating the above-mentioned glands. It is still better to drink with meals, so it can do this good work while the amount of calories in the wine can be computed and balanced with the total amount of calories allowed in the diet.

Wine encourages slower eating. Psychologist Frank J. Bruno suggested in his book, *Think Yourself Thin,* that one way to break the overeating habit is to slow down the eating (most obese people gobble their food) and think about each bite taken. Is it sweet, sour, hot, cold? Try putting the fork down and counting to twenty before picking it up again.

Wine, which invites sipping and not gulping, adds pleasure and relaxation to the meal. By punctuating the food with frequent enjoyable interludes, it pleasantly slows the process of eating. And you can deliberately cultivate this slowdown by looking at your wineglass, savoring each mouthful, letting it loll lovingly in your mouth before it flows down your throat, and taking your time pouring the new glass. By slowing the obsessive pattern of bolting your food, wine—and the savoring of it—can thus decelerate the weight accumulation in the very act of delighting the eater.

Wine substitutes for fattening foods. Obese people should restrict or shun carbohydrates, sweets and fats. Wine, a food as well as a beverage, can chemically substitute for these forbidden substances—enabling the obese patient to compensate with wine as he reduces intake of these taboos to cut his calories.

Wine fortifies character by making dieting acceptable. The more grievous the fat problem, the more important is a sensible diet. This does not mean one of those best-seller faddist specials which slices off a dozen or so pounds that will be added right back on after the diet ordeal has passed; it does not mean a fast which must end sooner or later; it does not mean any of the self-abusing regimens that can have but fleeting and deleterious effects.

The sensible diet for many of us means changing the eating habits of a lifetime. It means good-bye to such standard delectables as dairy products, animal fats, salt, fried foods, gravies, sauces, sausage, sweets, and related yum-yums which contribute so much joy to the sense of taste and so much lard to the storage cells. For some of us the doctor makes this a crash program. For those more fortunate it can be done gradually—let yourself go astray for an occasional holiday but still firmly make up your mind to stick to the long haul.

Whether you must do it the hard way or can do it the comparatively easier way, you are in for a tedious if not downright frightening and emotionally draining program of self-denial. Most of us are, to some degree, compulsive eaters who find solace and inner satisfaction from eating, or overeating. The problem is to find a substitute that satisfies while it does not fatten. After all, a diet is a damnable thing. It is hard to maintain. Often, it seems impossible; sometimes it *is* impossible. Diet equals discipline. Diet requires constant vigilance. Diet requires a special lash of self-flagellation. We can work like hell to gain a mile, then slip a little and lose two miles. Diet is an antisocial regimen under continuous assault from good friends, good parties, and good restaurants.

The mathematics of caloric accumulation is as inexorable as encroaching age or the coming of winter. What is needed is not new formulas or temporary restraints but new eating habits. And the new habits must be something that you can live with. You are not going to kill, bury, forget, or phase out your appetites. You must train them. "Appetite comes by eating," said

Rabelais. As long ago as 1670, one John Ray warned nibblers and sippers, "Often and little eating makes a man fat."

But three square meals a day make few people fat—if the right ingredients are chewed and the wrong ones are eschewed and if between-meal snacks and second helpings are avoided. Here is where wine may deliver its major contribution. By making you smile it helps make you tough. What you enjoy, you can endure. By acting as substitute for calorific hard liquor, wine can supply the same reward of solace and even élan as surely if more slowly. And by acting in harmony with the meal, wine helps you savor what pleasures remain to you under the terms and limitations of your particular diet—so that your new life-style eventually becomes acceptable, and in time maybe even delightful.

The biggest stumbling block in fighting fat is character. You must repeatedly say no when the urge grows more overwhelming to say yes. You must be *motivated* to keep doing what must be done. Sometimes doctors use pills and chemicals for that, or hideous slenderizers that fill you up physically while leaving you empty psychosomatically. But fortifying your character with pills has shortcomings. It can be dangerous and will certainly be boring. Using wine to fortify your character, as I did, can be fun, reassuring, and effective. Wine drinking made the taste sacrifices acceptable by rendering the diet foods not only adequate, but pleasurable. The prohibited foods were no longer missed because the lean meats, fish, chicken, vegetables, and vinegar-and-oil salads tasted so good with wine that life was not only restored, it was improved.

Wine makes several specific contributions to the reducing program, but the most important is in the psychosomatic area. Dr. William Dock reported: "I think there is no question that in lowering plasma lipids and in reducing obesity wine particularly has a useful place. When we are treating a patient whose lipids are to be lowered, and we add alcohol to his diet, we must subtract what are called empty calories, that is, carbohydrates and animal fat. These are not good for people when we try to reduce their weight, or when we try to reduce their plasma liquids. When you add alcohol to a diet low in calories as well as in animal fats and salt, you make the diet much more acceptable to the patient. He will adhere more to his regimen than he would to a diet without wine."

Experiments with animals have repeatedly demonstrated that groups drinking wine show positive reactions in such factors as growth rate, obesity rate, and longevity, as compared with groups drinking only water or drinking alcohol diluted with water. Tests have also shown a tendency for the animals to regulate their own caloric intake so that any calories absorbed in the form of wine or alcohol are in turn compensated for by reduced food ingestion. This is related to the animal instinct not to overeat, and to seek plants and herbs that are beneficial when specific physical conditions exist.

Dr. Curtis P. Richter conducted an experiment with three groups of twenty-four rats—one group each on alcohol, wine, and beer.

The wine group grew at a rapid rate, and at the end of 269 days showed no nutritional deficiency. All three groups reduced their food intake in direct proportion to the calories obtained from the beverage. They never ingested more than a certain amount of calories.

WINE AND WEIGHT LOSS

Wine should be consumed with the meal rather than before it and considered as a one-for-one replacement of some other food calories.

If wine is being introduced into the diet, very little willpower will be needed to diminish the volume of a meal.

Experiments along these lines have shown that *persons voluntarily and even unwittingly reduce the amount of food they eat when wine is served as part of a meal.* The reduced food intake usually continues as long as wine provides its calories in substitution for other calories.

In whichever manner it is employed, wine is a highly stimulating and a most salutary nutritional element.

In order for wine to be effective, it should be included regularly in the diet, together with other healthful foods, rather than be taken sporadically and without plan.

SALVATORE PABLO LUCIA

"Rats have a striking ability to make beneficial dietary selections. For this reason attention must be paid to any general principles of dietary selection made by these animals."

Wine should be taken instead of rather than in addition to a proper amount of fats and carbohydrates. This works well if a balance is achieved in supplying the body with the required vitamins and nutrients.

U.C.L.A.'s Dr. Louise Vanslager suggested a standard weight-reducing formula: lose weight slowly, don't weigh daily, shun fatty foods, reduce starches, eat plenty of cooked and uncooked vegetables. She stressed a sensible attitude toward desserts, soft drinks, and alcohol. "I always mention to my patients that alcohol is high in calories and, if they are regular drinkers, I urge them to shift from mixed drinks to dry wines."

Actress Natalie Wood was invited to account for her slim figure: Work at it. Eat fresh foods. No candy—fruit instead. Cut down on desserts. No snacks. No junk food. Plenty of exercise. And this capper: "Drinking a glass or two of wine with meals helps to stabilize weight."

Dr. Giorgio Lolli conducted a study of thirty-five obese patients to test his theory that wine could help diet programs by relieving tensions and anxieties that have such a damaging effect on self-control.

Summary findings of the study were:

1. In most of these cases, wine ingestion resulted in a lowered daily caloric intake and a gradual but consistent loss of weight.
2. In twenty-seven patients the best results were obtained when wine was taken with dinner. Wine drinkers lost more weight than people who didn't drink wine in a ratio of two to one.
3. Moderate weight reduction was noted when wine was taken after dinner or before bedtime.
4. With subjects having an urge to eat at night or raid the refrigerator, and who likewise suffered from insomnia, wine after dinner or at bedtime resulted in a decrease in refrigerator raids, a reduction in body weight, and an alleviation of insomnia.

Wine as a reducing agent might not work for everybody. It might not work for you. There's no way around it; wine, too, has calories. But case histories, experiments, and medical opinions offer a formidable body of empirical evidence that wine can help one lose weight if it is made a part of a sensible program. In a civilization in which so few things do offer relief, it might be worth serious thought. It might even be worth a try.

If it does work for you—as it has for so many—you can join the growing numbers who are finding that weight watching and weight reducing can be tolerated and made more pleasant. On several accounts, wine seems to be a civilized, appealing, healthful, happy ingredient to incorporate into dieting.

20

❧❧❧❧❧❧❧

Wine and Pregnancy

Love sometimes leads, whether intentionally or not, directly to pregnancy. We have considered the contributions of wine to love, fruitful or not, but wine has also been prescribed at some times as contraceptive.

Aetius of Amida, considered the first important Christian physician, offered two formulas for contraception: "Cyrenaic juice the size of a chick-pea, drunk with two ladles full of diluted wine, will prevent conception and will induce the flow." Another: "Grind equal parts of Cyrenaic sap, rue leaves, opopanax, and cover with wax. Take an amount equal to the size of a fava bean and swallow with diluted wine."

Getting back to a more fruitful theme, Dr. Morris Chafetz suggested that a little wine or other alcoholic beverage may not only encourage union but even help generate a better product. "Some geneticists imply that being brought up in an alcohol-prone society improves the strain. I do not know any basis for such a conclusion. What I would prefer to believe is that all those people who have not the capacity to let themselves go, or who are not emotionally mature enough to throw themselves completely into a sexual relation, will one day try a small amount of liquor and lose some of those inhibitions."

Lacking this, a cold union can cloud the resulting offspring's life, Dr. Chafetz speculated.

In many marital sexual experiences, the woman, through frigidity, has narcotized herself against the onslaught of her husband, while the man expels his tension to a stranger. It is done; it has little meaning for either. And it will produce meaningless memories. If conception ensues, the pregnancy has not the same beauty and meaning as that born out of a mutual embrace.

172

Indeed, the child may not be the same, for subtle maternal and paternal feelings can later tell him so much about his parents and how they really feel about him. On the other hand, should a moment of sexual beauty feed a marriage and conception ensue, both partners can reminisce happily about their mischievous pleasure, and the newborn child will be viewed with a warmer, more favoring eye."

Aetius offered wine for the nausea and morbid appetites of pregnant women, particularly those unaccustomed to work. The classic sage specifically advised, "They should abstain from sweet foods eaten with bread; they should drink old, tawny, fragrant wine, which is a little tart." Wine should not only be taken internally but "it is advisable to aid the weak stomach with ointment made from wild grapes, blossoms of the wild pomegranate tree, roses, calyx of the pomegranate blossoms, myrtle, leaves of myrrh, and fennel seeds applied with wine in the form of a poultice." Another recommended external application: "Put on the stomach dirty woolen or linen rags soaked with wine and oil . . . or nard flavored wine and [ordinary] wine. These drugs ease the gnawing pains of the stomach." One wonders, when reading such things, how the race—or specifically the mothers of the race—survived to deliver us into our enlightened age.

Consider also the comparatively modern passages from the eminent Dr. Robert Druitt, written more than a century ago: "Then what a boon it would be to the very flower of our female population if the medical profession were courageous enough to set at defiance all the Army of Mrs. Gamps, who infest the lying-in chambers and who insist on cramming young mothers with the heaviest beer or porter, brandied wine, and ardent spirits, on the pretense of keeping up their strength and assisting them to nurse!"

One shudders to learn this from Dr. Druitt: "A poor woman, after the pains of childbirth, was loaded with bedclothes and carefully shut out from fresh air and denied wholesome ablutions, in order, as it was said, to keep out the Demon Cold. She was starved, denied a slice of roast mutton or any solid food, and saturated with gruel and other fearful slops to propitiate the Demon Inflammation. Fruit and vegetables were denied because of the belching Demons Acidity and Wine. Then, when duly softened, sweated, blanched, puffy, nerveless, and breathless, she was exhorted to take stout or ale and port wine to keep up her strength and make milk for the little one." If she were still alive, that is. All of which seems to support those who contend that our forefathers were made of sterner stuff than our pampered generation.

However, Dr. Druitt rode to the rescue with a serious prescription of good table wine for the ladies of the upper class: "But I affirm that, whilst the laboring man's wife, with her active muscular system, can nurse very well on table beer, and wants not a drop of gin, so the lady, with her more active nervous system and delicate organization, can nurse very well on pure, clean claret."

Now we are getting into the kind of wine use our modern generation might more likely consider: "She may drink abundantly of it, and be fresh, young, rosy, and fit for another inning when her duties are over—and with none of the dusky, venous tint of nose and cheeks, none of the misshapen 'figure' for which anatomical corsets and belts are prescribed in vain."

Dr. J. M. Eylaud agreed that "wine drunk in moderate amounts prepares the woman's bone structure and muscles for maternity, pregnancy, and childbearing. During breast feeding, it is not harmful to prescribe wine as a hygienic and nourishing beverage when one considers that the antitoxic power of wine can protect a woman in childbed from infections and other complications."

The use of champagne or chilled brandy to help control nausea and vomiting during pregnancy has often been applied, although such use has never been proved in scientific tests.

Dr. Heinrich Kliewe was cautious in his treatment of wine drinking for mothers or mothers-to-be, but he did venture: "Women who have regularly drunk wine may be allowed a half bottle of a light wine daily. . . . Wine has no influence on the course of pregnancy if drunk in moderate amounts. Because of its rich vitamin and mineral contents, wine should even be recommended for pregnant women who have a higher demand of these matters."

Dr. Robert Stepto is a noted gynecologist and obstetrician and a serious wine lover. His pregnant patients receive a glass of chilled champagne instead of pills for morning sickness. "And it's more effective than tranquilizers," he insists. He considered wine good for relieving menstrual cramps, for preventing morning

YOU DON'T HAVE TO DRINK TO FEEL BETTER

The value of intravenous alcohol infusion for analgesia, sedation, and amnesia during labor and delivery has been discussed. When properly used, alcohol fulfills the therapeutic requirements for this purpose, namely, to keep pain at a minimum, avert fatigue and shock, maintain the patient's ability to cooperate, cause minimal disturbance to the infant (either *in utero* or *postpartum*), and yet provide safe, inexpensive, practical, and uncomplicated therapy.

Infusion of alcohol has additional advantages. The calorie content provides additional energy which the patient in labor may welcome, it reduces the necessity for postpartum catheterization of the urinary bladder, it induces a desirable estate of dehydration, it establishes a route for further intravenous administration of drugs or blood should this become absolutely necessary, and it engenders a general sense of well being, at times approaching mild euphoria.

EDGAR R. PALAREA

---

sickness, and for easing the fears of a woman facing a Caesarean section. While Dr. Stepto never allowed wine or any other liquor for a woman in labor because it might cause vomiting or complicate breathing, six or seven hours after the birth he often poured a glass of wine to ease the new mother's exhaustion.

Whatever the scientific proof or lack of it, many of the nation's outstanding authorities believe that wine has a helpful role to play in the drama of new life entering the world.

21

꩜

Wine and the
Respiratory System

Sit close and draw the table nigher;
It's late and cold; stir up the fire,
Be merry, and drink wine that's old,
A hearty medicine 'gainst a cold.

WILLIAM G. HUTCHISON

An annoyance that some weather without much trouble, the common cold is for me a pet bane and a major discomfort—an outrage to be avoided at all costs, but if inevitable, it is to be battled, uprooted and temporarily assuaged with a beaker of something to drive it out of mind. I hate colds so much that often, when wracked with excruciating back pain or some other complaint, I have managed to console myself that at least it's not a cold.

One of the best defenses against a cold is to protect yourself from anybody else who has one, and the Japanese have the right idea. When one of them catches a cold, he covers the nose and mouth with a face mask to prevent the spread of germs. But a masked Japanese in the cold months need not necessarily be a cold victim. He may be a cautious man assuming an ounce of prevention.

An ancient Chinese remedy to cure a heavy cold called for an owl to be smothered to death, plucked and boiled. The bones were then charred and taken with wine.

There is no proof, says the American Medical Association, that alcohol in any form is either the preventive or the cure for periodic colds. Just the same, I have found—and there are doctors who agree—that wine and brandy are reliable though not infallible deterrents to colds, and reassuring comfort if a cold is

176

caught anyway. In a world lacking any surefire medicine, wine remains as fine a substitute for the ultimate as any I have discovered. My own reason for classifying wine as a preventive of sorts is that since restricting my alcohol intake to wine only I have passed years without catching a cold, and completed two extended international journeys without contracting the usual cold.

For centuries wine has been a universal antibiotic. It may not repel cold germs by its presence in the body, and it may not kill the germs after they've breached the body's fortress, but then again, it may. Alcohol's prowess as a germ killer is too well established to require reinforcement here, but Dr. L. F. Herz had an appropriate word: "In malignant diptheria, streptococcus infections, typhoid fever, and other septic conditions, its action is frequently truly miraculous, and its has undoubtedly saved many lives. In pneumonia, alcohol is frequently essential as it prevents circulatory failure while simultaneously acting as a food." That is to say, if the cold germs escalate their mischief into something more serious, the alcohol may compensatingly escalate its usefulness.

While neither wine nor brandy will exterminate a cold instantly, both excel anything else I have ever found for imparting maximum available comfort during the miserable passage from the first sneeze to the final hacking cough. And they help keep the afflicted one in bed, and asleep while in bed, the best situation to accelerate recovery while protecting both the sufferer and his innocent friends.

Goodman and Gilman concurred in their book, *The Pharmacological Basis of Therapeutics:* "For generations alcoholic beverages have been used to check impending head colds. Perhaps the greatest therapeutical advantage of such therapy is that it makes the patient drowsy and sleepy so that he stays in bed whereas otherwise he would be ambulant to the detriment of himself and his associates." Quoting from an old English book, this authoritative pharamacological encyclopedia prescribed: ". . . at the first inkling of a cold . . . hang one's hat on the bedpost, drink from a bottle of good whiskey until there are two hats and then get into bed and stay there."

Chicago otolaryngologist Noah D. Fabricant explained what happens just before the cold develops: The temperature in the nasal passages is lowered and the blood vessels within the nose become restricted. Defenses against invading cold viruses are weakened as the nose area dries up. This exposes one to acute infection. The first remedy is to try to bring the nasal passages back to normal by raising the temperature of the membranes.

Tests by Dr. Fabricant with twelve men and women suffering incipient colds called for the administration of alcohol every fifteen minutes. Nasal membranes warmed up within half an hour. It was found that expanding of the blood vessels by the alcohol reestablishes circulation in the chilled membranes, increases peripheral cutaneous circulation, and provides the needed warmth, comfort, and protection.

A cold can lead to many things, including fatal illnesses, and wine can alleviate a number of them.

"There may be something to say for the age-old remedy of hot wine to prevent bronchitis and other upper respiratory diseases," observed Dr. Robert Stepto. "Some physicians have reported that the alcohol in such a beverage, which is quickly absorbed, dilates the peripheral blood vessels and causes a general redistribution of blood throughout the body, with prompt induction of sweating. The resultant heat loss usually tends to reduce fever. In addition, it provides a feeling of comfort and relaxation."

Wendelstadt and others demonstrated that alcoholic beverages, including wine and brandies, which contain large amounts of esters, tend to have a more pronounced stimulating effect on the respiratory system than straight alcohol. From Greek and Roman times until early in the twentieth century, wines were popular in treating respiratory disease. Today, the medical blessing on such use is more restricted to either earlier stages or the convalescent phase.

To repel the assault of respiratory diseases against many of the body's organs, and particularly lungs, heart, kidneys, and nervous system, Dr. Boulet, at the National Congress of Medical Friends of Wine at Dijon in 1936, detailed some of the merits of warm red wine perhaps spiced with cinnamon: Decongestive power on mucous membranes, antiseptic power on the whole organism, nutritive power, tonic power, stimulating power, diaphoretical power (to induce perspiration), and internal warming power. Such warm red wines act as preventive of further spread of the illness by shoring up resistance, and as curative by stimulating the body defenses to fight back against the infection.

Champagne is especially helpful for respiratory ailments

because of its carbon dioxide, which is what produces the bubbles. Dr. G. A. Engler explained:

It is a well-established fact that the exhibition of carbonic acid to the human organism produces, when absorbed, an increased breathing volume by stimulating the respiration center. [Because of champagne's] special quality in the natural carbonic acid, which can be absorbed with great ease, it is self-evident that all patients suffering from temporary or permanent impairment of their breathing volume will feel great relief at its administration.

In the convalescent stage of pneumonia, there are considerable parts of the lung not yet cleared, thus impairing the breathing volume felt by the patient in the form of lack of breath and anxiety. This deficit in breathing surface is balanced by increased breathing frequency and this is brought about by the carbonic acid in champagne.

There is hardly any better way to relieve without drugs the physical and mental anguish of the asthmatic than a glass of chilled champagne. The spasm of the small branches of the windpipe is relieved and the mental anxiety calmed. Also the periodic fits of lack of breath in patients with emphysema of the lungs can be quickly cured by the tonic effect of champagne. This appears to be more important if we consider that there are very few, if any, other remedies beside drugs that can actually offer some help in this chronic disturbance, which is caused by an abnormal loss of elasticity of the thorax.

Tuberculosis treatment has advanced so much in twenty years that early remedies and theories have very little applicability. Previous admonitions about the dangers of alcohol for TB patients are now being turned around. Today, doctors believe that wine teases the appetite, facilitates digestion and assimilation, and contributes to nutritive values. It also has a narcotic and sedative property, is a remedy for pain, and cuts down coughing.

Wine is also being recommended for pneumonia victims. Dr. A. L. Soresi reported recovery was speedier and easier for patients receiving it rectally than for those taking it by any other means. This is a pity, since it dispenses with the values of pleasure, psychosomatic uplift, and the boons of selectivity.

An old medical joke has it that a doctor can cure a cold in seven days but left to itself without treatment the cold will hang on for a week. The American sniffling public pours out $550 million every year on various cold medicines promising fast, furious relief. This may not cure colds, but it generates dividends for the stockholders!

It has been noted that "cold" is a misnomer, since the cold has nothing to do with the weather. "Coryza" and "catarrh" are more technical names—the latter meaning "a running down," which is a fair description of your nose when you've been hit.

Call it by what name you will; a cold is hell. And it could lead to worse. Until somebody makes that biggest of breakthroughs, consider wine. It may not cure you, but it will soothe you until time cures you. Perhaps its happiest contribution, many doctors believe, is that while the cold rages, wine can help you to both keep breathing and *want* to keep breathing.

22

❧❧❧❧❧❧❧

Wine and Combat

Eating, loving, and fighting are the three basic human drives. Fighting comes in two forms—war and athletics. Wine embellishes combat just as it embellishes eating and loving.

War has been called the ultimate application of politics. Actually, it combines politics with an athletic contest, minus rules and minus referee. Combat is a combination of strategy plus muscular exertion. And in combat, whether on the battlefield or playing field, it is usually the healthier side, the side in the best condition, that wins. That is why armies and athletic teams build the best retinues of doctors, trainers, and medical auxiliaries they can get.

Wine is traditionally drunk to celebrate victory. But it is thought to be forbidden before a contest, notwithstanding Joe Namath vaunting that he spent the night "with booze and broads" before propelling the New York Jets to an upset triumph in Super Bowl III.

Shall we take another look?

Wine and War

Perhaps the *first* world war was the Trojan War—which gave us the first mass amphibious landings, the first fifth column (Trojan horse), and the first recorded medical annals of military warfare (wine as medicine).

Homer presented wine as an exquisite, hygienic, and strengthening beverage that gave energy and courage to noble heroes and valiant warriors. In a very practical context, Homer's passages about battle wounds and their treatment by wine, and the antibiotic and disinfectant properties of wine, reflected such

181

sophistication that many scholars believe that he was also a practicing physician. Wine is the medicine most frequently identified in *The Iliad* and *The Odyssey*. Wine's virtues transcended the mundane sphere of food, drink, and mere medicine since wine became an inspiration and a godlike stimulus to the supreme effort needed to win in war.

Throughout history, the commanders of great nations were drinkers and lovers of wine (or the prevailing alcoholic beverage of their time and place). There were practical as well as romantic reasons. From the legendary Trojan War to the sophisticated superwarfare of our own times, wine has fought an enemy more terrible than all of the troops and all of the hard weapons and complicated engines either side could muster: man-killing bacteria in the water the soldier drinks or in the wounds he sustains in action.

Cyrus the Great of Persia cherished wine himself and ordered his troops to drink it for their health to avoid infection and illness during his campaign to conquer Babylon. Darius ordered this inscription on his tomb: He could drink much wine and bear it nobly.

Julius Caesar commanded his soldiers to drink wine daily for their health and to avoid intestinal infection during their campaigns—and like all great leaders, he did not hesitate to set a personal example for his men.

For centuries, Greek, Macedonian, Persian, and Roman success on the battlefield was attributed more to their health because of wine than to any such prosaic considerations as superior strategy, greater numbers, impressive resources, or more scien-

---

ALEXANDER THE GRAPE

The Macedon youth
Left behind him this truth,
That nothing is done with much thinking;
He drank and he fought.
Till he had what he sought;
The world was his own by good drinking.

JOHN SUCKLING, 1609–1642

---

tific weaponry. Their great commanders managed to keep the troops healthy in countries where paratyphoid, dysentery, and cholera were endemic. Those were the days before shots with the needle, so those old military giants got the job done with shots of wine.

A thousand years ago, the Vikings (which means "sea warriors") terrorized most of the coastal regions of Europe and established a reputation for both courage and invincibility in war. They left their conquering footprints and their progeny as vital infusions in the formation of Spain, France, Ireland, England, Germany, and Russia (which they called *Garoariki*). Their pattern was to get drunk on mead before combat, giving rise to joy and a peculiar fury in battle that was known as the "berserk's way" (*berserksgangr*).

Attila was credited with being a drunkard. Prowess with the cups has been a historic earmark of martial leadership. Attila was said to have died from drinking too much mead. The formidable Hun had swept everything before him and was on his way to conquering the world. Wine-drinking Aetius, heading an army of Gallo-Romans, Gauls, Goths, and Franks, heavy drinkers all, crushed Attila and his Huns in 451 near Troyes, in France.

Perhaps wine's apogee as a military staple was its role as a weapon of war and an instrument of heroism in saving Germany's beautiful walled city of Rothenberg from destruction during the Thirty Years War. Rothenberg was at the mercy of the victorious Tilly's thirty thousand men when that fieldmarshal, in a moment of mercy, promised to spare the city if one of its aldermen could empty a 3½-liter goblet of wine at one draught. Burgermeister Nusch proved equal to the challenge, and the site of his epic fete is called to this day *Freudengässlein* (Lane of Joy).

In our own time in the little nation of Israel, a wine-loving handful of military precisionists, based in a land smaller than most American states and many American counties, decisively defeated an alliance of teetotaling Arabs numbering half a dozen nations and two hundred million people. It took a week and became history as the Six Day War.

Napoleon Bonaparte was a discriminating wine and brandy drinker and came from a long and unbroken line of hardy wine lovers. Part of his secret on innumerable victorious campaigns was that he knew how to take care of the health of his soldiers.

He assiduously kept them plied and supplied with adequate quantities of wine and brandy.

France's soldiers during the Napoleonic campaigns, as the legions of Cyrus and Caesar before them, escaped epidemics by liberal reliance on the fermented juice of the grape. Practically all the grenadiers of Bonaparte were heavy drinkers, and the world has never saluted braver, stronger, and more successful soldiers.

Wine didn't cut much of a swath in the mid-nineteenth-century United States, probably because the California wineries had not been established in a Golden State still preoccupied with extracting a more indigestible treasure from her soil. But whiskey was the big thing at the time, and it played an unsung role in our Civil War. The North had a big enough preponderance of men, capital, acreage, resources, and industries to smother and overwhelm the South. But the South had the initiative and a monopoly on elitist generals—who may very well have been wine drinkers although that has not been researched yet.

Then there came out of the West a bewhiskered commander named Ulysses S. Grant. When Abraham Lincoln was pressed by complaints that General Grant was an ardent imbiber, the president displayed the leadership that was to win in the end: "Find out what brand of whiskey he drinks; perhaps we can prescribe it for some of my other generals."

During the Crimean War, wine and spirits were shipped to Florence Nightingale at the Scutari Hospital for the use of Britain's wounded. During the Boer War more of the same was shipped to South Africa for hospital use.

During World War I, the wine-drinking soldiers of France suffered less from influenza than the American soldiers. But American soldiers in France enjoyed better health than their compatriots at home, notwithstanding the hardships of war: bad lodging, exposure, poor food, sometimes no food at all for days, the mud, the water, and the trenches. Frenchmen like to tell how the American boys, when they had the chance, loved to patronize the places where they could buy good French wine, champagne, and cognac.

Major Albert G. Love commented:

The total admission rate [for sickness] for the enlisted men in the United States was more than twice as high as that of Europe

. . . the total number of cases being 2,390,878 versus 873,816. That two million men could be transported to a foreign country and approximately one million of them engage in active field operations versus a military enemy, with very inadequate facilities for all of them, and that even in the presence of a world-wide pandemic, less than three men out of five should require actual hospital treatment during the period of a year is certainly satisfactory evidence of preventive medicine.

In spite of the terrible hardships of war, in spite of being in a strange climate, and in spite of living often in muddy trenches and being almost constantly exposed to very heavy rains, the death rate from disease among American soldiers was much lower in France than in the United States (13.04 in France, 16.10 in the United States). Therefore, instead of slaying them [as Prohibitionists claimed] alcohol seemed to add vigor and resistance to disease to the American troops."

Marshal Ferdinand Foch was at an age past that of retirement for most men when he commanded the Allied armies that won World War I. He was born in wine country in France, came from a long line of wine drinkers, and carried on the tradition himself. His comrade, Marshall Joseph Joffre, was born in a section of France where no one would even think of taking a meal without wine. He, also, was beyond normal retirement age when directing France at the first Battle of the Marne.

Perhaps the most dramatic military confrontation between teetotaler and wine lover was to come in the mid-twentieth-century. In 1940, Adolf Hitler was in the saddle—one of the few famous leaders known to history who wouldn't touch a drop. The modern Attila was sweeping everything before him and toppling a new country every weekend.

Eventually Stalin was to say in words immortal: "It will take three things to beat Hitler—time, money and blood. The English will provide the time. The Americans will provide the money. The Russians will provide the blood."

But from 1940 to 1941 until the invasion of Russia there was precious little money and blood, there were no belligerent allies, and there was damned little time. It seemed there was only the doughty bulldog, Churchill, and words. Words aplenty. Immortal, heroic words. Alone, unaided, with hardly a pat on the back he performed the historic tour de force of modern times. What sustained Churchill as he defied the whirlwind? As famous

PASS THE BRANDY, PLEASE

One full moonlit night in 1943, a British warplane was streaking over Mesopotamia. Aboard was a precious burden, Prime Minister Winston Churchill. With him, as always, was his personal physician.

Temporary health problems led the doctor to attempt to reduce Sir Winston's brandy intake. The doctor came up through the belly of the plane to present the minister with a most unpalatable medical concoction.

"Ugh," snorted the old warrior.

"Sorry, sir, it's a must."

"Make a deal with you," parried Sir Winston. "I'll take this vile stuff if you go back and fetch me a double brandy to wash it down."

While the doctor was back getting his patient's beloved brandy, Mr. Churchill opened a sliding window and poured the offending chemical onto the unprotesting Mesopotamian sands.

The doctor returned, bottle in hand.

"OK. I've done my bit. Pass the brandy, please," said Sir Winston Churchill.

---

as his indomitable challenge, "I have nothing to offer but blood, toil, tears, and sweat," was his penchant for alcohol—more than a bottle of brandy a day and floods of wine with his meals, with whiskey and cigars in abundance.

Had every man a capacity for alcohol remotely like Churchill's, there would be no alcoholism. Had Churchill a susceptibility to alcoholism, the history of the twentieth century would have been incredibly different. He summarized it modestly. "I took far more out of alcohol than alcohol ever took out of me."

Leo Rosten paid him the summary tribute:

He looked like a Toby Jug, a character out of Dickens, but he was born to command, to fight, to inspire, to prevail. He lived with much unquenchable gusto, sipping massive quantities of champagne, brandy, whiskey, and wine; fondling long cigars all day long; working in bed until noon, lunching at two; taking a siesta—one hour, two hours, unclothed, in bed—then working again, and again after dinner until 3:00 or 4:00 A.M. or dawn.

Dr. J. M. Eylaud wrote that wine is necessary to man, both on a physical and a mental level, hence it is required in the soldier's diet:

1. "Wine helps the soldier, psychologically putting him in a good mood, to overcome the bitterness of defeat while at the same time to enjoy victory." That is, whether things are up or down, wine helps the soldier's morale.
2. "Wine is, by its consumption, necessary to the balance of the national economy." Now the cat is, indeed, out of the bag. Warfare itself, may be necessary to the national economy. Or, if not necessary, helpful. Now, how did the United States withdraw from the seemingly endless tailspin of the Great Depression? World War II. How did Germany do the same? World War II. How did we avoid a post–World War II economic cataclysm? The Cold War?

Perhaps this is getting too sociopolitical. But it was so—*engaging!*—to read this climactic argument for wine drinking in a French book called *Vin et Sante.* Anyway, it provides a ray of hope. If the California wine industry becomes big and important enough, might wine rise to become a staple of the American armed forces? Could be. If so, I for one did my hitch in the army several decades too soon!

I was heartened to learn that nowadays the German army puts the troops into the vineyards to pick grapes if the weather suddenly turns bad and threatens the crop. Nothing so constructive has been done by any army since Caesar divided Gaul into three parts and introduced vineyards into each. Since wine has sustained armies for so long, it is only fair that an army should sustain wine.

Wine and Athletics

Whether bullfighting is a battle or a ballet or a marriage of the two, it is the deadliest confrontation of the entertainment world because traditionally only one protagonist will emerge from the ring alive—if either does. In this ritual it is not so much a question of whether the hero wins, but whether he lives. Barnaby Conrad, the American aficionado, told me that the triumphant matador usually drinks a great deal of wine—by many standards perhaps too much—on Sunday night when he is withdrawing from his dance of death. The cape caballero will often take a brandy to bolster himself for the showdown before entering the ring.

On Saturday night, the eve of Sunday's "death in the afternoon" drama, the torero will have table wine with his meal, generally about eight ounces. Before dinner he is apt to drink manzanilla, "the treacherous blond," a crisp, dry, fortified sherry. After dinner, usually a brandy. The idea on Saturday night is to drink enough wine to insure the deepest, most restful sleep possible. Manolete was the only whiskey lover of Spain's great bullfighters. And what happened to him? He was gored to death in the bull ring.

Barnaby Conrad noted that most of the bullfighters try not to drink too much during the season—except possibly on the night after the fight when they unabashedly seek release and celebration in both wine and brandy drinking. "However, in season most of them have wine with every meal; and out of season perhaps more wine."

Dr. Gerard Debuigne, a specialist on physical education and sport, bluntly dismissed alcohols and aperitifs from the athlete's regimen, especially during training—but wine is something else again: "To condemn wine without appeal is to fall into the snare of a ridiculous and regrettable exaggeration, for it is to deprive a man [who more than any other needs to be on his best physical and mental form] of a precious food, which stimulates cell functioning and whose happy action on the psyche is undeniable."

Stressing that an athlete's condition depends closely on his diet, Dr. Debuigne wrote, "For this reason, it is useful for sportsmen to know which wines are to be recommended to them and which not." He recommends Beaujolais (a light Burgundy) or light Bordeaux. Red wine "is a powerful aid to the digestion of proteins," which are richly present in the athlete's diet. Some wines are to be saved until the deeds are done, however. Dr. Debuigne suggests that the "full-bodied Burgundies" and "generous Cotes-du-Rhone" be forgotten during training.

He also keeps the cork on white wine as "not recommended to athletes. It has the reputation of going straight to the legs and 'cutting the ground from underneath your feet,' and this is well known among mountain guides, who categorically forbid it. . . . However, the sportsman can keep it for the evening meal and for washing down his off-season meals, outside periods of training and competition." But the athlete still has an "entire range of light, attractive red and rosé wines to choose from. He needs no commiseration."

The doctor assails various lesser thirst quenchers. Fruit juices are not always well tolerated. They hardly make "good gastronomic partners with a well-cooked meal. Beer dulls the mind, burdens the stomach, and produces unwelcome belching and flatulence." Cider irritates. Coffee and tea lead to insomnia and excitability, and "athletes are already quite nervous enough." Milk, usually badly tolerated by most adults, is a food not a drink.

"Particularly during training, and when the sport in question involves considerable muscular effort, the athlete is advised to adopt a diet very rich in proteins. Wine, it will be remembered, is a powerful aid to the digestion of these substances. Its vitamins help to counter muscular and nervous fatigue and keep the athlete in good shape."

Dr. Debuigne cites the mineral salts in wine to prevent deficiencies that will upset the athlete's balance; the iron, to enrich and aerate the blood; and the sulphur, to eliminate toxins.

"The tonic and calming properties of wine are most beneficial to the general morale of the athlete, whose strict discipline, often fanatically intensive training, and obsession with optimum performances often result in a delicate and even precarious mental state. When he is exerting considerable muscular effort, his pulmonary activity speeds up and he can eliminate alcohol more easily than persons leading a sedentary life."

Concluded Dr. Debuigne: "In these conditions, it is in the athlete's interest to drink a reasonable amount of wine."

Dr. Mathieu, Olympic medical adviser, recommends that "if the quantity of wine does not exceed half a liter a meal, or one liter a day, alcohol is entirely burned up by the organism and wine then becomes an excellent nutritional drink."

Pointing out that athletic endeavor consists of bringing the body and mind to a peak of exertion in competition with others doing the same thing, Dr. Jean-Max Eylaud stated that wine is more important during the training period than during the competition itself.

Dr. Eylaud mentioned the Olympic champion Paavo Nurmi and the tennis master Rene Borotra as consistent wine drinkers. But he feels that wine is the only form of alcohol that should be drunk by athletes. "It would be different if we had to speak about distilled alcoholic beverages, or liquors or drugs that are presently being taken, alas, by certain athletes before they perform."

Noting that cigarettes and alcohol are traditionally taboo for athletes, Dr. Morris Chafetz wrote, "But why beer, or wine, or spirits in small amounts cannot be served at the training table is beyond my understanding. All day long, the athlete in training must drive himself under physically and emotionally tense conditions. Then comes the evening meal, a little relaxation, and an early bedtime. Why not some wine with the evening meal, or a highball before retiring? The relaxation and appetite stimulation which liquor can supply would be invaluable."

The Russians are coming on strong in both sports and the military field. "For their Olympic athletes, cases of Russian wine (not at all bad) are made available at the competition," Dr. Chafetz wrote. "Perhaps recent Soviet Olympic victories have been achieved not alone by subsidization 'above board,' but by liquor for relaxation on the dining board. In my opinion it makes good sense. Furthermore, athletes are excellent ego-ideals for our youngsters and could effectively illustrate in practice that a little liquor can do some good—not necessarily some harm."

Liquor is not given before or during arduous muscular efforts or at the time delicate coordination is required. But neither are steak and potatoes. There are times for both.

A bit of wine for the French soldier's meal; a spot of rum daily for every sailor of the Queen's navy during all those years when Britannia ruled the waves; wine as a necessity under orders for the conquering legions of Caesar and Cyrus; wine as a staple for Napoleon's army—there must be something to it.

There are sages who claim a bottle of good table wine never hurt anybody. Certainly a glass or two to help a high-strung athlete or soldier enjoy and digest his meal, and get a better night's sleep, plus perhaps a bit more after the big event to help restore mental and physical equilibrium, would seem to be not only the right of a champion but the course of downright common sense.

23

Wine and Genius

Never did a great man hate good wine.

FRANÇOIS RABELAIS

Whether genius is the ultimate of mental health, or the disease of the gods, or a tortured state of madness, we know genius has blessed mankind by the works of its possessors. It seems to be a characteristic, almost universal, appetite of genius-driven men to drink alcohol—particularly wine.

Wine is a brain food, or perhaps we should say the brain balm, so universally adored by the great and the near-great possibly because it has helped restore and bring the best out of so many of the foremost poets, musicians, statesmen, philosophers, artists, writers, commanders, and other establishmentarians (including doctors) down through the ages. Wine unwinds and softens the genius, and yet stimulates him. It enables him to tolerate himself better and to live with his inner demons. And so wine has blessed the race by acting as a chemical midwife to the genius as he labors to bring forth the gifts within him.

An old Japanese proverb says "Metal is tested by fire, men by wine." Another ancient aphorism tells us, "Wine is wont to show the mind of man." Plato wrote, "When a man drinks . . . he begins to be better pleased with himself, and the more he drinks, the more he is filled full of brave hopes and conceits of his power." According to Emerson, "On turnpikes of wonder . . . [wine] leads the mind forth, straight, sidewise, and upward, west, southward, and north."

Dr. Charles Mercier spoke definitively about the relationship of wine and genius before the Midland Medical Society, as quoted in *Lancet* in 1912:

192

In further corroboration of my thesis that the effect of moderate doses of alcohol is to stimulate the mental faculties of those who possess mental faculties and stimulate those faculties which some think the highest, such as imagination, fancy, picturesque imagery—the artistic faculties as we call them—I point to the fact that there has never been one distinguished originator in any branch of art who did not take alcohol at least in moderation, and many have taken it, alas! in excess.

Alcohol has the power to unlock the store of energy that exists in the brain and to render available for immediate expenditure energy that without its use would remain in store, unavailable for our immediate needs.

Denouncing all those who attempt to prove that alcohol is a poison, Dr. Mercier proceeded to emphasize that the benefits from proper use of alcohol far outweigh the evils arising from its abuse. "They forget what they often owe themselves to the moderate use of stimulants, and what the world, what their own country owes to alcohol. They forget that from Chaucer, the son of a royal butler, to Ruskin, the son and grandson of wine merchants, every poet, dramatist, artist, and writer of genius, every great thinker has been a wine drinker; that every ruler, every prime minister, every brainworker who has ever merited his country's and perchance humanity's gratitude, all have used and some have abused that most noble gift of a divine Providence: wine."

Further discussing wine's contributions to creativity, Professor Puntoni wrote, "The moderate use of wine does not decrease the swiftness of the mental processes." Wine "increases the possibility of controlling certain reflections, increases confidence and trust, diminishes suspicion, multiplies the activity of associating ideas, and generally makes possible more social relations."

In short, wine helps set the stage for the generation of ideas and intellectual works. Dr. Charles Fiessinger described wine's capability of psychic liberation: "Wine maintains in balance visions of the mind and games of the heart, allows one to give sensibility to the sensations and to extract from their fire the sparks that attract the flame of judgment and of will."

Wine as the stuff of genius goes back more than a few centuries. In *Alcohol and Civilization,* Dr. Provost Saunders commented on ancient Greek wine-drinking parties: "Here arose

ALCOHOL: THE ICHOR OF GENIUS

Alcohol has the very remarkable property of deadening to a certain extent the passive or receptive faculties of the brain while exciting and stimulating at the same time its active or creative powers and the inner self or personal psychological ego of man.

Alcohol cannot supply brainpower where there is none or make a selfish man unselfish or a fool clever. It will, however, bring into play, stimulate into action, and intensify the temperament and qualities, good, bad, or indifferent.

Alcohol will help the poet, the artist, the orator to forget the petty cares and troubles which may harass him; it will deaden the sense of self-consciousness and diffidence which drove him to sterile inaction, and, at the same time, it will stimulate his genius to greater activity.

Alcohol urges the gifted to remember and use their gifts and hides from the giftless the injustice of fate.

ANDRÉ SIMON

the refinements of civilization, the symposial songs and the literary tradition of poetry as stated by Cratinus and echoed by Horace that the best poets have sought and found inspiration in drink. Here, under the mellow influence of wine, came social and intellectual entertainment to inspire Plato, Xenophon, and Plutarch to label famous dialogues symposia."

Bacchylides expounded on the subject half a millennium before Christ: "Wine excites the brain and influences the thoughts of men to their finest flights." The wine drinker "throws down the walls of cities and feels the urge to become a ruler of men. In his innermost consciousness he builds houses of gold and ivory. Ships come to him from Egypt filled to the brim with golden corn. He has wealth beyond the dreams of avarice. It is thus that the spirit of one drinking wine is uplifted."

Demonax, the Cretan philosopher who was said to resemble Socrates in his mode of thinking and Diogenes in his way of life, was asked if it was allowable for wise men to drink wine. Demonax replied, "Surely you cannot think that nature made grapes only for fools."

TESTIMONIALS TO WINE AND GENIUS

The witty bard finds a swift steed in wine,
While water drinkers can write nothing fine.

CRATINUS

Wine brings to light the hidden secrets of the soul,
gives being to our hope, bids the coward fight,
drives dull care away, and teaches new means for
the accomplishments of our wishes.

HORACE

Sober, I can write nothing; when I'm drinking
A fifteen-poet fire aids my thinking.

MARTIAL

If you drink nothing but water,
    You'll never write anything wise;
For wine is the horse of Parnassus
    That hurries the bard to the skies.

LORD BYRON

My books are water: those of the great
geniuses are wine. Everybody drinks water.

MARK TWAIN

Gold, music, wine, tobacco, and good cheer
Make poets soar aloft and sing out clear.

JOHN DAY

The most renowned composer of the modern world did not
hesitate to pay his obeisance to wine and other alcoholic beverages, which he engulfed in oceanic quantities. When asked
whether he had ever tried drugs, Igor Stravinsky replied, "I am

an unquenchable user of very ordinary drugs, procured in the forms I favor, chiefly from Scotland and France." At his table, in the presence of food and wine, ideas were discussed and shaped, minds were opened and persuaded, reports and rumors were deliberately launched, and 'sponsors were enticed to contribute their money.

A commentator on Stravinsky writes: "Until the last few days of his life Stravinsky's enormous capacity for alcohol remained unimpaired. His wife Vera once wrote to a cousin commenting on the huge gusto with which the great composer 'slurped and sloshed' while enjoying his dinner drinking. 'All this must seem like the description of an outer barbarian,' but she justified them as 'the colorful idiosyncrasies of genius—a case of *genie oblige.*' "

One of Stravinsky's best friends was the great English poet W. H. Auden, and the seal of their friendship was their mutual capacity and adoration for alcohol. At a celebrated dinner the two enjoyed in 1952, with Stravinsky's wife, Vera, a packing case of Pommard was set on the floor at the host's feet and five bottles were consumed while Auden's display of intellectual power increased in brilliance and lucidity.

Stravinsky's climactic salute to the poet's liver power: "Livers learn, of course, and Wystan's is undoubtedly the most intelligent liver in town."

Donald W. Goodwin, Washington University professor of psychiatry, said that writing is an obsessional job and restricting obsessions to that part of the day spent working is difficult to do, which causes writers to have a higher rate of alcoholism than any other group. He said of the six Americans who have won the Nobel Prize for literature, four were alcoholics according to their biographers: William Faulkner, Sinclair Lewis, Eugene O'Neil, and Ernest Hemingway. A fifth, John Steinbeck, was described as a heavy drinker.

Dr. Goodwin offered these reasons for the alcoholic proclivities of writers: writing is a form of exhibitionism, and alcohol lowers inhibitions; writing requires an interest in people, and alcohol makes people more sociable; writing involves fantasy, and alcohol promotes it; writing requires self-confidence, and alcohol bolsters it; writing is lonely work, and alcohol assuages loneliness; writing requires intense concentration, and alcohol relaxes; writing requires an endless number of small decisions, and alcohol emancipates from the tyranny of self and memory.

Critic Leslie Fiedler agreed, saying that great writers need a flaw, a charismatic weakness. "You're a rummy, but no more than most good writers are," Ernest Hemingway told F. Scott Fitzgerald, who himself called alcohol the 'writer's vice.' "

"If one runs over the list of the greatest English, American, and German poets, one will find that most of them, not to say all of them, used intoxicating beverages," Dr. Celestin Cambiaire wrote. "Among French, Spanish, Italian, Roman, and Greek poets of great fame not even one can be found who was a total abstainer. It is well known that creative power when put into action demands a great display of mental and cerebral energy. After the creation of a masterpiece the author feels much tired and depressed. Alcohol is one of the best and most wholesome remedies for removing from the human system the poison generated by fatigue."

This writer went on to say,

> Many a great poet wrote fine verse after a few drinks. Whenever you go to a theater and listen to a beautiful opera, remember well that all the great masters who composed operas . . . were wine, beer, and liquor drinkers. Whenever you read beautiful poetry, remember that no Prohibition man ever composed a poetic masterpiece. Albert Einstein liked wine and had a well-stocked wine cellar. The fact is that all the great men with creative genius such as Homer, Plato, Virgil, Cicero, Napoleon, Goethe, Dante, Lope de Vega, Cervantes, Descartes, and many others used wine or other alcoholic beverages.
>
> Victor Hugo, one of the greatest geniuses of the world, was fond of wine and kept his mental powers to his last day. He died at eighty-three.

Dr. Cambiaire's list of wine users also included George Washington, Christopher Columbus, and "all the great discoverers," Horace, Shakespeare, Michelangelo, Corneille, Racine, Molière' Balzac, Martin Luther, de Maupassant, and practically "all of the greatest geniuses of the world."

Quoting several passages from the Bible in which Jesus extols wine, Dr. Cambiaire wrote, "Pasteur is one of the few men who have greatly helped mankind in every part of the world and for all times. His discoveries have saved the lives of millions of people of all nations. Thus we have Jesus, the greatest healer of souls, and Pasteur, the greatest healer of bodies, endorsing and recommending the use of wine.

"After having done long and careful research work, Pasteur stated: Wine is the healthiest and most hygienic beverage of all. His *Studies on Wine* (1866) is one of the best books ever done on wine. He knew what he was talking about. The whole medical world follows the path blazed by Pasteur. Experience has proved that all the important statements of this great benefactor of mankind were correct."

Dr. Heinrich Kliewe suggested that most men control their drinking and use it deliberately to fuel their inner fires: "They do not drink wine to satisfy an addiction, but they stay inside the limits of the drinking habits of their respective cultures."

How do you account for it? It's a mystery, but venturesome thinkers have tried to cast enlightenment upon it. "No culture on earth has denied that reasonable wine consumption gives a great susceptibility for the artistically stimulating, the esthetically beautiful, and the mentally valuable," said Dr. F. Maret.

Those who are not moving on the paths of greatness can take joy, too. It is well established that a comfortable majority of the human race have found alcohol good in one way or another for many thousands of years. Think of it this way: If you are a genius, you drink wine to console yourself for the burden you carry. If you are not, you drink wine to console yourself for the aura you lack.

24

❧❧❧❧❧❧❧❧

Red versus White Wine

"Wine is very good for your health,
providing it is a Bordeaux red wine."

Any authority from the
BORDEAUX REGION OF FRANCE

"Wine is very good for your health,
providing it is a Mosel white wine."

Any authority from the
MOSEL REGION OF GERMANY

"The best glass of white wine is the first and
the best glass of red wine is the last."

PROVERB

Half the fun in wine drinking is talking about it, and half the talking fun often narrows down to whether red or white wine is better. Both have their ardent champions, but among vintners and in the medical literature I have read, the overwhelming vote is for red wine.

R. B. Read, the San Francisco gourmet, challenged, "I say you have to do your own lovemaking," but he still voted in favor of red:

Except in Germany, where no true reds whatever are produced, it is everywhere harder to produce a decent white than a decent red. Whites are also less able to survive shipment; many can be drunk only locally, and many more should be.

The therapeutic and digestive qualities attributed to wine are very real, incidentally, but apply only to reds [for the record, I disagree]; many internists regard whites as actually harmful to the system.

A great wine is one which carries the attributes of a good wine to a height of nobility, and which has great lasting powers. Only a handful of whites meet these criteria, and for all practical purposes reds alone figure in talk of great wines.

Dr. H. Sambale, winemaster of the state wineries of Trier, couldn't agree less. "Mosel wines are often under 10 percent alcohol by volume, one reason they're better for your health. In Germany the alcohol volume is not the thing; the thing is the quality and the taste, the inviolability of the quality, and the naturalness without any fortification or other destruction of the 'naturality.' Here when you drink a bottle of wine you are getting quality and purity. It shows while you drink it and reflects in the way you feel the morning after."

He further branded as a myth the convention that white wine must be drunk while it's young and will not age gracefully; this depends not on the color red or white but upon the chemical content of the wine. Then he poured for me a 1929 and a 1949 Ockfener Bockstein of unparalleled magnificence to prove his point.

The Swiss Medical Association conducted a three-month experiment with six hundred people, testing red versus white wine. Group one drank a liter of red wine daily, matched by group two drinking a liter of white. Members of both groups were found to be in better health than at the start of the experiment—as you would expect.

The next two groups drank two liters a day. Group three, the red wine division, was also found to be in better condition after three months, but group four, after two liters of white daily, relapsed to slightly poorer health.

Group five's redoubtable experimenters took on three liters of red wine a day with no damage to their health, but those in group six, after ninety days of three liters daily of white wine, were in considerably worse health than at the outset. The most common complaint was liver injuries.

After the chauvinism I found in Europe's winelands, I was wide-eyed to read that Dr. Heinrich Kliewe championed red wine, notwithstanding the fact that his native Germany produces some of the world's most illustrious white wines and no noteworthy reds at all. Kliewe even had a chapter entitled "Biological Effects of Red Wine," in *Wein und Gesundheit,* without a balancing chapter on whites.

He noted that red wines seem to be richer in vitamins, especially vitamins C, H, B$_6$, and B$_{12}$, although white wine influences internal absorption of vitamin A.

Reds are OK in some cases for ulcer, prostrate and multiple sclerosis patients but whites are forbidden. Dr. Kliewe recommended red wine for blood building and anemia, described hot red wine to warm up winter sports enthusiasts after a day in the snows, and permitted a glass of red wine with main meals for athletes.

Dr. Kliewe also recommended red wine for elderly people. He said that red wine "contains almost all minerals and trace elements which are found in two multivitamin preparations of the pharmaceutical industry." In old people, in whom a decrease in cell energy, stomach acidity, and intestinal enzyme activity occur, along with intestinal permeability changes and more difficulty in chewing, "deficiency symptoms ensue which can be partly alleviated by drinking red wine." For heart and circulation patients, red wines are preferred. They usually have "a delicate bouquet, a soft taste, a lower extract content, less alcohol and acids." Red wine "is more relaxing than stimulating and therefore eases quantity control. Generally speaking, it is the wine for the sick which is also appreciated by many aging people."

White wines are better as a diuretic and for chronic stomach affections. They are stronger antibiotics, and they are of more benefit in respiratory ailments.

H. F. Stoll preferred white wines for old people. "Because of their fresh acid and low alcoholic content, they are easily digested and are particularly suited to people along in years." Good reds, owing to their "moderate proportion of tannin, relative richness in iron, phosphates, and phosphoric acid, are powerfully tonic and recuperative without being exciting or fatiguing for the stomach."

White wine is preferred in chronic affections of the stomach, when urinary functions need stimulating and for those whose nervous system is very sensitive, according to A. Durso-Pennisi. Professor Suckadorf claimed, "A quart of red wine a day diminishes considerably the number of fecal bacterias, while white wine diminishes in minor quantity."

The red versus white wine debate undoubtedly goes back to the beginnings of wine. Athenaeus wrote in classical times, "White wine is weak and thin. The dark-colored wine is the strongest, and it remains in the system of the drinkers longer." Avicenna, the Arabian physician and philosopher, wrote: "White light wine is best for those who are in a heated state, for it does not cause headache. The wine which is best for elderly persons is old, red, with warming effect, and diuretic. New and white sweet wine should be avoided, unless a bath is taken after a meal at which such wine is taken, and unless there is thirst."

Dr. Tobias Venner analyzed properties of white wine in detail in *Straight Road to a Long Life:*

> White wines and Rhenish wines do least of all wines heat and nourish the body, they consist of a thin and penetrating substance, wherefore they are quickly concocted, and very speedily distributed to all parts of the body, and theretofore they lesse annoy the head, than any other wine. They cut and attenuate grosse humors, provoke urine, and cleanse the bloud of the veines. They moysten the body, and cause sleepe, mitigate the paines of the head, proceding from a great heat of the stomacke.
>
> They are most accommodating for those that are young, for hot constitutions, for hot countries, and for the hot times of the year, and for those that would be leane and slender. They are less hurtfull for such as a feverous, than other wines are; but being mixed with water, they are very profitable for all hot distemperatures.

Dr. Alexander Henderson especially recommended Rhine and Mosel wines: "In certain species of fever accompanied by a low pulse and great nervous exhaustion, they have been found to possess considerable efficacy, and may certainly be given with more safety than most other kinds; as the proportion of alcohol in them is small, and its effects are moderated by the presence of free acids. They are also said to be of service in diminishing obesity."

Preference for red or white (or rosé) wines more often hinges on personal, geographical, climactic, chauvinistic, frivolous, quizzical, and/or empirical reasons than chemical, tested, proven, or scientific ones. That's what causes such great debate.

My wife is the family shopper and dotes upon department stores, discount houses, bazaars, boutiques, supermarkets, roadside stands, and damn near any place that resounds with the clanging of cash registers. I hate all kinds of shopping, except

PRICE IS A MATTER OF RELATIVITY

Karl Wente told me why Wente Brothers winery at Livermore for years specialized in their great white wines. "Grandpa used to haul barrels of wine into San Francisco. He could sell reds at four cents the barrel and whites at twenty-one cents the barrel."

Reason enough for them to specialize in whites—and for you and me to calculate that maybe we were born fifty years too late.

---

one: comparative shopping for wine in a restaurant, wine shop, supermarket, or any kind of winery tasting room.

Mas, my Japanese wine man, can tell from tasting a wine whether I will like it. If he thinks I will he sends up a bottle for sampling. If I like it (and I invariably do), I order a case or two or three, or maybe Mas's entire supply of that particular wine, and store it away in the wine cellar.

In Germany, all wine lists start with the lower-priced wines and lead up to the most expensive one at the bottom of the list. This is always Trockenbeerenauslese, which is wine fermented from a selected picking of dried, shriveled grapes. My wife and I never tried it, because we didn't want to spend from fifty to eighty dollars or more for one bottle when we could get such splendid wines for two, three, and five dollars a bottle or go overboard for a fourteen-dollar bottle. However, for my birthday my wife went to Mas to get a bottle of Trockenbeerenauslese.

"Mrs. Baus, I hate to turn down your money but I can't sell it to you."

"Why not, Mas?"

"Because Mr. Baus would not like it. It's much too sweet."

Mas was right. So instead of getting one bottle of supersweet white wine which I would not have relished, anyway, I received a case of excellent mixed reds and whites—for the same price. Incidentally, when buying your wines, why not order by the case and earn the usual 10 percent discount?

All wines cost too much, their prices are constantly going up, and they may continue to rise. But they will never go up high enough to stop my buying. And if you look hard enough you may be surprised at how well you can manage. I have never found a more fun way to increase my capital. For some reason, a good wine, like everything else, tastes better if you think it's a bargain.

If I am in a restaurant and the best wine on a limited wine list—or the best comparative bargain available—is a white, I'll let that dictate my choice of food and order chicken or fish; and if the best is a red I'll order steak or veal or lamb and fall to. Although I prefer white wine with Chinese food, one Chinese restaurant offers Cabernet Sauvignon at the same price as green Hungarian. The red Cabernet should cost up to twice as much and green Hungarian is too sweet for me. So it's red wine with Chinese food at that retreat, even though (blasphemy!) they *insist* on serving it chilled and in an ice bucket.

The vast majority of people I know are impartial; they like white wine at one time and red wine at another time, depending on the weather, the menu, and what is available. One commentator says red wine is weaker or stronger alcoholically; another says white wine is. They usually have the same alcoholic content —although you can get German whites at under 10 percent and even under 9 percent and there's a Yugoslavian red that has 15 percent. It depends on the particular wine. Most California reds and whites are 12 percent or thereabouts, and most French reds and whites have a similar alcoholic index.

George Christy, the bon vivant commentator on things enological and gustatory, wrote, "The best rule, of course, is the old one: reds have an affinity with meats and game; whites go well with seafood, fish, white meats. But, as every wine lover knows, this is a general guide that is meaningless once you begin to appreciate the nuances of wines. A white wine—say, a Semillon—can be an intriguing companion to a lamb curry. And a champagne can be superb with an entrecote. Once you have begun to explore this captivating California world of wines, don't be afraid to veer from the basic guide."

The French are the world's number one wine people on almost all counts, but a Sofres-organization opinion poll, published by the Gault-Millau food guide, astounded me with the intelligence that many Frenchmen in a restaurant like to ask the advice of the waiter on what to eat, and three out of four like to ask the owner to suggest which wine they should try. Now millions of Frenchmen can't be wrong (about wine, at least), and if they can ask, so can you. They may ask for sophisticated reasons, while you may ask for reasons of bafflement, but no matter. You might even learn something.

My idea of a great evening is to start with white wine, sometimes over rocks, before dinner, flowing into red wine with the meal. However, if the dish is fish or fowl or other white meat, it is white wine all the way but a different and more lofty white with the food.

Bordeaux's vintner-fermenter-shipper-author Edouard Kressmann suggested that beginners explore the less complex taste of whites before experiencing the reds, just as an individual working out his evening may start with white wine before switching to red. "Whites have to be served cold, a detail women like," he said. (I rather like it too.) "No matter how mellow and smooth the red wine, its dryness is hard for the beginner to understand."

One of the best, most profitable, most rewarding, and above all most reliable investments you can contemplate is that of storing red wine—which appreciates in value more inexorably and more rapidly than most other equities you can name. A prime virtue of such an investment is that you can drink the capital appreciation without getting stuck for a capital gains tax. The drawback, of course is that you eventually will drink the profits. Console yourself with the wisdom of H. Gregory Thomas, wine connoisseur and president of Chanel, who reminds us: "A bottle of wine has no value until it is opened and drunk." And what profit could you possibly savor more?

In my notes is a report by the Rev. Dr. J. P. Daraio analyzing testimonials from a medical school in Salerno.

On one line is reported that "white and sweet wines are most nutritious."

On the next line another reference is quoted: "Red wine has an alimentary value superior to white wine."

You can't lose.

25

✦❧❦❧❦❧❦❧✦

How to Wine Your Way
to Good Health

Consider the man who became so upset upon reading that good
eating caused heart disease, good drinking caused liver disease,
good smoking caused lung cancer—that he gave up reading.

We have considered wine as both a daily delight and a preventive
medicine to keep you well. We have considered it as therapy to
make you well. We have considered it as a psychosomatic aid
to make you think you're well (which is more than half the battle) or to make you *want* to recover if you're not well.

Now, how do you go about making wine a part of your way
of life? No one can do this for you, but a few simple, straight-
forward ideas from one who has worked at it to his own reward
and satisfaction may be to the point.

You want to please yourself as you please others. You want
to reasonably indulge yourself without trespassing on the lives of
others. You want to embellish your waking hours without doing
violence to either physical or financial health—two reserves that
you must learn to shepherd as you spend. You want to do this
with savoir faire.

Here are my ten rules for good health—and if they provide
a few guidelines for your happiness, I'm glad.

Drink No Longer Booze

This may be a stringent measure for some of you out there,
and I shall not press the point. To each his own. Early in life I
learned that alcohol is a big help providing that one keeps it in

its proper place—a challenging problem in self-management. I spent several decades helping myself to my great share of the stuff in every guise from beer to Demerara rum.

Then a few years ago, for reasons explained throughout this book, I decided to stop drinking hard liquor and stick exclusively to wine. One game does not make a season nor one man a system, but for me it has worked. The alcoholic proportion is less, but it is there and it does its work. Wine caresses; liquor clobbers. Wine does as much for you, but not as much to you. If wine is slower than liquor, I found it as sure, and it lasts longer, prolonging as it intensifies the most delightful part of the day.

There are exceptions to all rules to make them endurable. For me, one exception is an occasional after-dinner brandy. Brandy is, after all, wine's first cousin, also produced from the grape. Sometimes I will substitute a crisp, cold beer with a tangy Mexican meal, especially if it's Mexican beer. Here is one of gastronomy's most rewarding diversions, abundantly available in California and the Southwest and beginning to emerge in some of our big cosmopolitan Eastern cities. Another exception (and a favorite one) is an occasional margarita without salt (*strictly* forbidden me, but *so* good on the rim of the margarita glass). The margarita, a Mexican masterpiece, is the ultimate in cocktails—*if* properly made. Combine four parts of tequila, three parts of fresh lime or lemon juice, one part of cointreau or triple sec. Add crushed ice to match the liquid by volume and grind it up in a powerful blender. Serve in large, chilled glasses with salted rims.

I fondly remember the party at a beachfront hotel in Mazatlán, where our cruise featured "all the margaritas you can drink." And they meant *all*. The silly little shot-glass-sized thimbles featured at some of the snooty enchilada houses I have encountered were unheard of at this party. The margaritas came in generous goblets, promptly refilled from bottomless pitchers every time they became half emptied. So I decided, "Why fight it?" and drank them down as if they were wine. I call them "Mexican wine," anyway.

Mazatlán isn't the only place where wine is hard to come by. Try the majority of American hotel and restaurant bars or almost any neighborhood tavern. For that matter, try the homes of many of your best friends—either you arrange for the wine in advance or you drink tonic over ice. And at almost all organized cocktail parties, forget it. The booze is for stand-up drinking and the wine is for the dinner tables (if you're lucky), and never the twain shall meet.

For example, the Beverly Wilshire Hotel is one of California's epicurean temples. But at a top-level affair which was later to feature unlimited superior wine at the dinner table, the cocktail party was rocking along nicely until I came and asked for a glass of wine.

"Port, sherry, or vermouth?" the waiter politely asked.

"Never touch the stuff. Make it Chablis, Riesling, or Pinot Blanc, well chilled, please."

He was stunned and silent. I had accomplished the equivalent of requesting a Rolls-Royce at a Volkswagen convention.

The maître d' sensed the impasse and miraculously materialized. "Is there anything at all we can do, sir?" he purred in his best troubleshooting manner.

"Look, here in your new hotel annex we are surrounded by a Burgundy Room, a Chateau Room, a Bordeaux Room and a Champagne Room. I can't believe that in this environment a glass of table wine is unobtainable before dinner . . ."

"What would you prefer, sir?"

I nimbly named Pinot Chardonnay.

The master whispered into the ear of his minion, who swiftly vanished and in little more time than it took to pull a cork, reappeared with a bottle of California's finest. He poured it into a splendid large glass for one happy patron.

I was a bit dismayed when the time came for a third glass to find that I had picked up unknown company and the bottle was empty. But my happy ubiquitous maître d' immediately emerged to the rescue, whispered again, and a fresh bottle arrived before I could say "Pinot Chardonnay."

Such good fortune is rare in the modern United States and many ships at sea. Wine is for dinner and booze is for predinner, and you live with it. That's the way it is and that's the way it has been, and things are not about to change.

Except that I am working on it.

Do Your Own Thing

If wine is to become an alcoholic staple of your diet, how do you handle it? Will you take exclusively the great reds of Burgundy or Bordeaux, the great whites of Germany or Burgundy, the great vintages of California, or the cheapest bulk wines available at your local wine shop or supermarket—or some happy combination?

One thing for sure: you do not have to be a big spender or a wine snob to enjoy wine for your health. The wine snob may intimidate some people, even to the point of making them afraid to serve wine or to order and pour it in his presence; he is not only an insufferable bore but if he is a wine snob all the time instead of just when he's showing off, he is depriving himself of some of the real joys and genuine bargains of wine drinking.

To me, all table wine is good wine, but some is better than others. Wine is like sex: when it's great it's out of this world; when it's not great it's pretty good, anyway. The best wine is the wine you are drinking at the moment, and it is better still after you've finished the first half bottle or so, just as the best restaurant in the world is the one you are enjoying yourself in *right now*.

The important thing is that *wine will do it for you*—not *which* wine, just *wine*.

"There are far better ways of getting into semianesthesia than by wine. But there is certainly no pleasanter way," said Dr. Mark Lewis Gerstle. He argued that there is a jargon about wine, just as there is one about art or music. "There are people who know a great deal about it, and I am sure there is a great exhibitionism, the need to be the expert and to be the hypercritical person. It's like the cliché, 'I don't know anything about art, but I know what I like.'

"Now, about wine, I think you can almost say to those naïve people like me, 'I like wine because I like it. It tastes good.' But no, that isn't quite good enough. You don't belong. You have to say, 'It's noble,' or 'It's sincere,' or 'It's not important but give it a little more time.' You can't just say, 'It's damn good and I like it.' "

Why the hell can't you? Whether a lord or a peasant, if you like it, that's good enough.

One can plunge into the adventure and delectation of drinking wine with many of the emotional rewards but none of the legal and personal complications or hangups of a like indulgence in sex—for there are no reasons to be surreptitious, nor other persons to hurt, nor valid social objections, nor personal guilt feelings and hang-ups which can add so many knives to the love game.

To be sure, wine by the cask and the jug can let you down, and my friends who shake their finger are right to say, "You can't really mean that *all* wine is good . . ." Still, anyone who plays the field in any game knows there must be downs as well as ups, but by way of compensation he knows what the downs contribute to heighten the ups. Play every game at Las Vegas and you must lose some, which only makes the winners more rewarding.

Some of the modest and inexpensive California wines you get for a few dollars a gallon at your favorite wine shop or supermarket can be as good or better than some high-class vintages from abroad; they're almost bound to surpass the cheaper "bargain" imports, and they can furnish an excellent springboard for an evening's drinking—leading up to deeper delight in some superior and more expensive offerings.

For those who know what they like, the best advice about wine must still be that offered by Rabelais: *"Fays ce que vouldras"*—fifteenth-century French for "Do your own thing."

Personally I love my "vin du pays" (wine of the country) when traveling or "vin ordinaire" (ordinary table wine) obtained by the gallon at my local outlets or by the liter at choice restaurants and taverns at home and abroad. I delight in decanting a gallon into five regular wine bottles. These are lovingly laid away in my wine cellar. From these, I frequently pour white wine at the cocktail hour.

One of my favorites is an excellent California red Burgundy, which I decant and pour for red meat and other appropriate dinners. The *vin ordinaire* adapts for lunch and for picnics, pleases for cocktails, and serves for a regular dinner at home with just the family. For more special occasions, we'll break out some of the French, German, or California vintage wines.

Henry Wadsworth Longfellow advised:

> When you ask one friend to dine,
> Give him your best wine!
> When you ask two,
> The second best will do.

On some special occasions—either just the two of us, or for another couple, and sometimes for big parties—if the mood seizes, we'll roll out our best wine. But it's always to celebrate, and never to downgrade the "second best." André Simon set the rhythm: "Drink good wines habitually and fine wines occasionally."

"You can never reach perfection, but you must always approach it," says an old German proverb. Some wines come closer to it than others; with the simpler ones you just approach it more gradually. The thing to do is to drink and enjoy the wine you like. If you like only vintage wines, fill your wine cellar, help yourself, and more power to you. If you like the cheapest and most ordinary wine (*vin ordinaire*), go to it and do your stuff. Do not let wine snobs, officious waiters, helpful friends, or anybody else keep you from doing it the way you want to. If you don't like the wine you find, look until you find the wine you like.

I rather like the bad wine, one gets so bored with the good.

DISRAELI'S MR. MOUNTCHESNEY

Never Drink Before Noon

Coffee until noon, wine until midnight. No alcohol in the morning, not even to rectify the ravages of the night before. I have friends who go on the wagon for all of January or all of Lent or for some other period to dry out, or lose weight, or just to prove they are still boss. For some, this may not be a bad idea since it is really a variation of never drinking in the morning.

Again, there are exceptions.

Sometimes on my wife's birthday or on a wedding anniversary or on some other very big occasion, I'll open a morning bottle of champagne.

The great Los Angeles earthquake of February 1971, caught me in my studio laboring over a million-word crossword puzzle dictionary. My coffee cup rattled on its saucer as shelves and books fell down around me, power lines crackled like guns at a shootout, the house and neighborhood were plunged into predawn darkness, and my frightened and beloved mate sprang out of her deep sleep somewhat earlier and much more spryly than usual. You can bet your favorite vintage that a big bottle of champagne was withdrawn from our refrigerator before sunup *that* morning—after all, there was now no way to keep the coffee hot . . .

My wife and I once spent two weeks on a houseboat on the River Thames. When my spouse, striving to rectify my shortcomings as a navigator-pilot, failed to dislodge the boathook from a ledge at the Marlowe Lock, she was catapulted overboard for a morning swim in what had to be the coldest waters that side of Greenland. After briskly drying her off I administered a double Cognac, though it was a good two hours before noon. It was better, and quicker, than a sauna.

Never Drink Before Working

I like to get my work done, whatever it may be, in the morning and then have a few glasses or a bottle of wine for lunch. The morning is my best time for working, anyway. But if I am unable to schedule all the day's work in the morning, or for any other reason there is important work to do in the afternoon, my program is to omit wine for lunch, or only drink a glass or two at most. Wine is wonderful but it doesn't mix with work. If there is too much work and too little time in the morning, I often stretch the work session until one or two or later to get it done before the relaxation of a good lunch with wine.

H. L. Mencken loved both labor and liquor, but separately: "If I've got a job of work to do at or lasting until ten at night I wouldn't take a drink up to that time."

If your work is the lonely, creative kind you will learn whether you do it better with a quantity of coffee or a belt of alcohol. There are those who benefit from a glass or more in the composition process—work that out for yourself. I know writers who, in the volcanic eruption of the first draft, will not touch a drop, but they like to adjust themselves with a glass or several before and during the more philosophical drill of the later drafts, which require a thousand decisions: a word change here, a new sentence there, a deletion elsewhere.

If yours is the social type of work—a meeting, speech, conference, trial work in court—where you need your wits at attention for the effective counterattack or the instant critical decision, alcohol, for all its merits, is much better afterward than before.

Churchill, on a lecture tour of the United States during Prohibition, was said to have a contract requiring a bottle of champagne before every speech. I admire him for it. For my part, a speech or meeting, even late in the evening, comes off much better with no more than a light snack until the work's all over with. Then a recess to a favorite restaurant, a bottle of wine, and a hearty meal. I can relax when my work is done.

Never begin work after drinking is the corollary to this prescription. There is a time to work and a time to play. You'll live longer and much more happily if you grind out your work, however demanding it may be, then turn it off for the rest of the day and relax with some good drinking and eating.

The punch-drunk syndrome of taking your work home with you and returning to it after dinner revs up your motor again— and it is apt to keep running long after you hit the pillow, which makes sleep difficult if not impossible. This is a pattern for stress and strain that destroys the relaxing value of your evening food and drink—unless you down enough just before bedtime to get unwound again.

You face the same set of circumstances with lunchtime drinking. Unless the amount consumed is miniscule, an unlikely event, you impair your work efficiency for the afternoon. If you are semiretired, or a writer or professional person able to concentrate all your productive time during the morning and then take the afternoon off, it's easier. In any case, the best solution is to relax and drink with lunch, then take a good siesta before starting again.

If there is one most precious lesson we can learn south of the border and in Spain, France, and Italy, it is their siesta after lunch. A little wine with lunch encourages a siesta; a bit more *commands* a siesta. Natives in those lands close the doors from noon to three or four. They take a little wine with a little lunch, and they retire for a nap. This is much easier on the vital organs than the American custom of jumping up from the lunch table. And it's much too good, too smart, and too wise *not* to do whenever you can. In our country you can't always take a siesta because it just isn't done. Often you can't find a bed, and you haven't got three hours off, as in those friendly, sunny countries, to go home and plump yourself into your own bed. But if you have an office you can install a couch. Or recline in your chair. Or stretch out on the seat of your car. Or plop on the floor. Things may be improving at home, however. Under strict doctor's orders, Presidents Eisenhower, Kennedy, Johnson, and Nixon had a siesta fixed into their daily schedules. Why shouldn't what is obligatory for presidents spread down to everyone else?

The formula we suggest: you take your wine with lunch. You relax. You lie down and sleep for ten to twenty minutes, or an hour or two or more. You awaken and arise renewed. You're starting a new day. You have ended up with two days instead of just one. Thus, you double the number of your days—if you do it regularly you could say you double your life span . . . and you are stretching out your lifetime in more ways than one.

Drink Wine with Love

Before, during, and after drinking wine you can love it and revel in it. The preliminary is shopping at wine shops and liquor stores to build up your supply, and evaluating menus to measure the right bottle for your dinner table. You can stage comparative tastings with several different bottles of competing wine to determine from experience which you like best and will buy and store in quantity.

On a restaurant wine list you can have fun bargain hunting. In one restaurant the European wines may be overpriced compared with Californian, so you buy domestic. In another, California wines may be overpriced compared with European, so you buy imported. In one restaurant the house wine is a bargain, in another it's grand larceny. In one restaurant the mountain Chablis and the vintage Pinot Chardonnay may be priced the same, so with glee you order the Pinot Chardonnay, and at least two bottles if you're lucky enough to feel so inclined.

In one pretentious restaurant near my desert home I found a "big carafe" of the house wine to be the same price as a bottle of prestige, name-brand wine, but ordered it anyway as an experiment. Then I found the "big carafe" in this restaurant to be the same size as a modest syrup pitcher, and the "small carafe" to rival the size of a thimble. So I took two steps. One, I sent the "big carafe" back to the kitchen and demanded instead a fifth of the other wine. Two, I avoided that resturant thereafter like a leper colony and warned at least a hundred of my best friends about its larceny at the wine barrel.

In the actual drinking, wine is better sipped than gulped. Before dinner or during hot weather, wine can be diluted with mineral water or poured over ice cubes or both, if it's *vin ordinaire*. This makes it cooler, less caloric, and less alcoholic. Some of the best and most knowledgeable people do it. But the great wine with dinner should always be taken straight from the bottle. Now you are coming into a feast for each of the five senses individually, and for all of them in concert.

You hear the cork pop and you hear the precious fluid gurgling from the bottle into the embracing glass. You smell the bouquet in the bottle, the cork, and while you drink, the wine. You see the aesthetic beauty of the wine—in the bottle, in the pouring, in the rolling around the glass, in the light. You feel the tangy cold of the white or rosé, you feel the rich warmth of the noble red. And then you taste. All the rest was a buildup to that end. You virtually inhale it, drawing the air over it as it caresses your palate, as you roll it around your mouth and let it flow down your throat. And so you get the smell-taste and the taste-smell and enjoy the ultimate recognition of the flavor-texture and texture-flavor of the magical nectar. Food and drink both should be selected and admired for flavor and texture alike —it tastes better if it feels good and it feels better if it tastes good. The senses are allies; please one, please all.

And treat yourself to big, generous, rich wineglasses. They make the wine sound better, smell better, feel better, look better, and taste better. If your hostess serves wine in some atrocious, inadequate glassware, bite your lip and pray for better times. But do not commit the same crime in your home. And if any of your favorite restaurants are behind the times glasswise, help educate them. They'll thank you for it even as their other patrons thank them for it. At least, most of the time.

Hungry and thirsty following an afternoon exploring the magnificent flora, fauna, and rock panorama of Joshua Tree National Monument, four of us repaired to a high desert roadhouse miles from anywhere that did not sell wine but permitted patrons to bring their own. Our table was nicely set up, except that their wineglasses were filled with water and the glasses set out for wine were thick-lipped, flat-bodied sherbert glasses. Since it was Saturday night the owner was more than preoccupied and a bit abrupt-mannered, so I helped the cause by moving our wineglasses to an adjoining unoccupied table and retrieving in their stead four empty wineglasses for our serious drinking.

As I started pouring the first round of wine, the owner flipped up and started filling these glasses with more water, even adding water on top of the wine I had already poured.

"In our restaurant you simply must do it our way," he snapped rather testily. "And these are *water* glasses *here*. We have your wineglasses set up."

Our party reacted with unanimity and speed. We arose and

departed. "Is there anything wrong?" the owner asked us on our way out.

"As long as you have wineglasses available, we refuse to drink wine out of sherbert glasses," I replied, and we trooped out into the night. We drove twenty miles to a favorite little Mexican restaurant where the moist, meaty burritos were a dish to remember. And we happily drank our wine out of their regular water glasses, there being no stemware of any description on those otherwise hospitable premises.

After dinner you can still have fun loving your wine. It is cigar time and you can dip your cigar in your wine. I have done it for years, and there is not a trace of cigar taste. Try it yourself, anytime, and see.

There is a Chinese legend about the ultimate in loving wine. The Chinese think their way of drinking more civilized than any foreign way. They do not gulp wine to quench thirst but sip to savor every mouthful. They have a saying, "Do not waste one drop of this precious wine! Remember the labor the farmer put into growing the crop they take it from."

But one legendary wine lover went overboard. Having for years enjoyed every atom of his wine with his tongue, mouth, nose, and throat, he decided one day to go all the way. He would give his whole body a treat. He ordered a large tub filled with wine and after drinking several potfuls he stripped and stepped into the fragrant vat.

"Now, for the first time, I have given all parts of my body an equal chance to taste and enjoy this wine," he enthused—and remained immersed for hours.

Never Drink Alone

"Let us then look to our kitchens and stock our cellars, call friends and family to the dinner table, salute each other with beaded bubbles blinking at the brim and purple-stained mouth. Pull the cork, act now, don't hesitate. We've nothing to lose but boredom and despair!" sang Dr. Angelo Pelligrini.

Above all, drink together with your wife, together with your friends, together with somebody. Drinking with someone else is twice the fun, and drinking with other people seems to geometrically multiply the fun.

There are many things wine does for happiness—it gratifies every one of the senses to name five examples—but what greater

In water you may see your own face,
In wine you may see the face of another.

GERMAN PROVERB

thing than to bring us together, to shatter the hard barriers that make each man separate, to bring one human being closer to another?

Drinking alone is dangerous. It can be a direct highway to alcoholism. Drinking alone is also dismal. Wine drinking is a *social* pleasure, a bond of togetherness. This is what you were looking forward to during the working hours, when you were getting wound up like a steel watch. Now, for your spirit's sake and your health's sake, you should unwind. It is the best thing you can do. It is great before eating, even better with eating. Never, never do it alone.

Never, that is, except on those rare occasions when for some unavoidable exigency, you are caught. You have to eat alone. Careful planners do not allow this to happen often, but it happens to everybody sometimes. You may be traveling, or your wife or girl friend is traveling. Then a glass or two of wine is permitted. It is good for your digestion—but only to embellish the physical act of eating, not the several social glasses that are good with companionship.

I have found that wine's social graces make me a successful proselytizer for wine rather than mixed drinks at the cocktail hour. Friends arrive and I will ask, "What will you have to drink?"

"What are you drinking?" they invariably ask.

Lack of imagination or lack of taste? Not really. The camaraderie of drinking together intensifies with drinking the same thing.

"I only drink wine, but I still keep martinis premixed in the freezer—or name anything you like."

You wouldn't imagine how many of my inveterate hard-liquor-drinking buddies react, *"Wine!* What fun, I'll join you."

Or, after drinking their first cocktail, with envious glances at my glistening, long-stemmed glass, they'll say, "Well, now, that wine of yours looks so tempting, do you mind if I join you and switch to wine?"

A few years ago my dearest friends were almost exclusively, like me, cocktail people before dinner. A number of them have now switched to become wine people before dinner, in my house at least.

Consider the point of view of Charles Frankel, a Columbia University professor and onetime assistant secretary of state: "Wines are so much better than whiskey. Whiskey is a conversation killer, while wines encourage fascinating talk."

Henry Sambrook Leigh once drooled in print over the "rapturous, wild, and ineffable pleasure of drinking at somebody else's expense." So true—but not a bit more rewarding than the big, expansive, generous pleasure of pouring your own vital juices for someone else's delight.

Incidentally, speaking of expense, don't get the idea that you are necessarily economizing if you convert to wine. In my early wine-only days I congratulated myself on saving money as well as my liver and calories, until I recovered and started to count. Several people swallowing several bottles of vintage wine at three to five dollars or more add up much faster than a few shots of liquor from one bottle costing four to seven dollars.

Here is where *vin ordinaire* can come to the fiscal rescue and help your budget. That sturdy staple of social joy comes at two to five dollars a *gallon*. And that gallon decanted into five fifth bottles checks out at a comparative forty cents to a dollar a bottle. If you can save money while making your friends happy with a good country wine at one-tenth to one-quarter the cost of the more pretentious beverages, it can easily become a favorite pet economy. And it can help underwrite bringing out the special bottle on the big occasion.

The icing on the social cake is, of course, conversation. Nothing gets that game under way better than free-flowing wine. And what is there better to talk about than that same wine? Before drinking, while drinking, after drinking, around the campfire, or the hearth fire, the coffee table or the dinner table, your favorite restaurant or picnic spot—half the fun of drinking wine is to talk about it and build up your own lore about it.

Balance Your Budget

It has been said that whoever earns a dollar and spends 99 cents will be happy and is on the road to wealth. Whoever earns a dollar and spends 101 cents will be miserable and is on the road to bankruptcy.

This goes as much for your drinking and eating habits as for your financial ones. It is a matter of common sense. Extremism in any direction leads to dismay and disarray, to ulcers and obesity, to unhappiness and, ultimately, to disaster and death. The latter you will reach anyway, but much more happily with an orderly journey. Why rush it? Why not enjoy the whole trip?

It is said the human is the only beast to dig his grave with his knife and fork. But he need not. He can mimic the animals and reduce his food and drink intake proportional to the amount of calories involved, ingesting only as many calories a day as the body can burn. Animals have repeatedly shown some instinctive capacity to calculate their calories. The parallel human instinct seems to be eating another helping if it is good enough or the hostess is persuasive enough.

But humans can balance the budget in other ways. After a big meal, the prudent man can balance his budget by reducing accordingly. One can travel in Europe eating those sumptuous meals with carbohydrates and sauces and goodies and creams, if one will balance this with days of eating roast chicken and vegetable salad until equilibrium has been restored. When you put too many calories in the bank there are only two ways out: a few light meals to offset the heavy ones, or enough exercise to burn off the calories—or both!

You don't have to be a nut about exercise and kill yourself with trying to be an all-American for a day. One can get a little exercise a lot of times a day. A bicycle ride or two, a walk or two, a swim or two. Walk around the office or the house or the block from time to time for silly little reasons or no reason at all except to breathe, stretch, and stimulate the heart. Walk up the stairs instead of taking the elevator. Get in a walk between dinner and bed. Dogs can earn their keep by making you do it. Even, heaven forbid, try a bit of calisthenics. Jogging in place one or two hundred times may be the most acceptable variation.

As for the amount of wine to drink, we'll repeat that moderation has its rewards. Too much can make you fat as well as drunk. What is too much? We repeat again—too much depends on the individual and every man must decide for himself.

"Really, it profits a man very little to set his goal to live a hundred years if he has never known the soft glow of drunken-

WHAT IS TOO MUCH?

George III once said to Sir John Irwin, a notorious bon vivant, "They tell me, Sir John, you love a glass of wine."

Bowing deeply, Sir John responded to his monarch, "Those, sire, do me a great injustice. They should have said a bottle."

Dr. Ivan Popov, a European doctor who is making news with his rejuvenation theories, explained his own sixty cigarettes and quart of red wine each day, even though he'd been forbidden such indulgence after a coronary several years before: "If any restriction imposes stress, it's no good for the heart. If any abuse gives you sound pleasure, then it's not an abuse . . ."

---

ness, the luxury of an after-dinner cigarette, the sweet guilt of illicit love, only to be struck down at forty on the freeway," said Dr. Richard Bates. "Live a little while you're still young enough to enjoy it, and yet practice moderation in all things, including moderation."

Overindulgence is a question of quantity times speed. Someone who drinks only an ounce per hour could do it for a week without becoming drunk. Slow down and enjoy it more; and realize that you are enjoying it.

Never Drink Without Eating

You can increase your tolerance for wine by nibbling while you drink. Tolerance is the amount you can consume without harming yourself.

Drinking does not make alcoholics. Drinking on an empty stomach does make alcoholics. Drunkards first, then alcoholics, then cirrhotics.

Even when drinking light wine as an aperitif it pays off to eat a little while sipping. A dip, a piece of cheese, a raw vegetable, whatever is at hand. Eating while drinking is the most healthful way you can safeguard both your liver and your dignity.

Perversely, the Old World's wine wonderlands of Burgundy and Bordeaux and the New World's wine wonderlands of California's Napa, Sonoma, Livermore, and Santa Clara valleys do a fantastic job of encouraging us to drink wine but damned little to suggest eating while drinking. These regions markedly and woefully lack restaurants providing victuals to match their wines —probably because the natives have been too busy making the premiere ingredient of outstanding restaurants elsewhere. However, these wine-country restaurant shortages are easier to forgive with Paris and San Francisco so near.

Never Eat Without Drinking

Exception: breakfast.

Wine with dinner or lunch can be a daily symphony. It makes everything taste better. It expedites and uplifts the conversation. It slows down the eating. It abets the digestion. It obviates laxatives. It fights obesity on all these counts.

Eating is a fun time of day—to many it is the *most* fun time of day. That is, for example, why the true food fancier so deplores the American theater hour of eight-thirty. Just at the right time to force you to rush through dinner for a pleasure that can't compare with it. Barbarous. In more enlightened parts of the world, the theater starts at six or six-thirty or seven, preceded by maybe a drink and a nibble and followed by dinner. That places things in their proper perspective. The new Broadway hour of seven-thirty is at least getting closer. Dinner is king, and after the preliminaries are out of the way it can be done properly, deliberately, with gusto, and without interruption.

One living the biblical threescore and ten has, as an adult, about fifty years of lunches and dinners, which is about eighteen thousand lunches and about eighteen thousand dinners. If a good meal is twice the fun with a little wine, isn't it lamentable to do something that many times with only half the fun?

Chinese food is especially appealing to me. It has wondrous texture; it fits blood pressure and cholesterol diets if you stay away from the fried entrees; it is magnificently varied. But the Chinese have all kinds of hang-ups about grape wine because of their centuries-old rice wine tradition.

When I moved to Palm Springs I had to develop a new list

of Chinese restaurants to replace those I lost. I heard raves about one desert Chinese inn and phoned for a reservation.

"Do you serve wine?" I asked.

"No, thank you."

"But may I bring my own and pour it at the table?"

"No, please."

"But why not?"

"It would set a bad example for the children." In all the times I have been there since, I have not yet seen a patron under thirty in the house. But I let it pass and found other restaurants. Several months later I tried again.

"Do you serve wine?" I repeated.

"No, thank you."

"But may I bring my own and pour it at the table?"

"No, please."

This time I was strategically prepared.

"But that gives me a terrible problem," I protested.

"How is that?"

"My doctor wants me to drink wine with my meals."

"Why not have all you want before you come here?"

"But my doctor is funny . . ."

"How is that?"

"My doctor *insists* that I drink wine *with my meals,* for my health. You wouldn't want to make me ill and make my doctor unhappy . . ."

"Well, now, you bring your wine. But be discreet and don't tell anybody. I'll bring you glasses . . ."

We took two bottles of well-chilled white wine. The "glasses" were paper cups. But wine in paper cups still has it all over tea, not to mention water.

And after all the other patrons had left, the proprietress, with whom I had enjoyed the preliminary dialogue, came to our table to chat. So did her husband, by then freed of his duties as chef. They pulled up chairs. We offered each of them a glass of wine. They accepted—glass after glass. The conversation waxed spiritedly as the four of us convivially polished off both bottles of wine.

If you like to order wine with Chinese food, you have a whole chain of experiences in store. You will get red wine chilled and white wine at room temperature. You will get the finest Cabernet Sauvignon for very little money. You will find only sweetish green Hungarian and mountain Chablis among white wines and they will cost the same amount.

In one Chinese restaurant my waiter recommended "Oriental wine." Since rice wine is not my bag, I ordered it with trepidation. It came in an odd-shaped bottle and looked like good, familiar white wine. Its taste was reassuring. Examination of the label, which said "Oriental wine" in both English and Chinese, also revealed in the fine print that it was bottled in France. I found it to be a respectable white Burgundy coming in a bottle size called "pot," halfway between a fifth and a tenth in volume.

On a thirty-thousand-mile journey across the Pacific and around the Orient, including seven weeks on a Chinese passenger-freighter liner, I acquired some frightening insights into the ritual of wine drinking in the mysterious East.

The Orientals do not drink grape wine; they just tax it. In many restaurants out there you can't get wine at all and must make do with beer. That may be just as well, for their beer is good and costs about half what it does in the United States, while the native wine is invariably bad and the overtaxed imported wine costs three to four or more times as much as it does in the United States.

Near the end of our trip, my wife and I were ensconced in Bangkok's most esteemed Chinese restaurant. I discovered that it actually had a wine list which contained a French rosé about four dollars a bottle less expensive than the going price in those parts for wine of comparable quality.

I shook my head at our good fortune when this precious stuff was served crisply cold, even dripping with beads of sweat —an unheard of amenity in most Chinese restaurants anywhere, let alone their native Far East.

After triumphantly downing my second glass I couldn't believe my eyes when they saw a busboy bringing up an unsolicited ice bucket. I had learned long since the folly of asking for such embellishmnets in the Orient. He plunked the bucket on our table and inserted the bottle of wine.

With a feeling akin to sheer bliss I twirled the bottle a couple of times and poured a fresh glass. As the contents passed my lips I shrieked, dipped my hand in the ice bucket, then jumped to my feet and roared, "My God, it's filled with boiling hot water!"

Fortunately, that was the last stop of our Asiatic adventure and we were soon to reenter the United States—which may be replete with woes, at least in election years—but where an ice bucket is an ice bucket, when you can get one.

Every lover of the good life should have a favorite restaurant or several where he is always welcomed and always understood, always mollycoddled and always saluted. I have a little Mandarin restaurant staked out in my old Los Angeles Silverlake neighborhood called The Shanghai. This was my retreat, my rendezvous, my private club. Here I came, when living in Los Angeles, once or twice a week for those old familiar favorites I loved so well and could find no place else. And since moving to Palm Springs, I hardly ever go to Los Angeles even for a day without planning at least one meal there.

But it took training. I had to learn what to order. The staff had to learn that I wanted the big bamboo chopsticks instead of the runty splinters; and I wanted the cloth napkins instead of those disintegrating paper things. And the wine—every Chinese dining experience can be a new adventure in wine "orientation."

In the early years, The Shanghai was limited to one brand, which we shall call XYZ. Now this is an excellent and famous wine, but there are some I like better. Frequently and unavailingly I remonstrated that they should offer a choice of some other brands. Finally, at a time when Mrs. Dorothy Chu, the creative owner, was traveling in China, her maître d' asked me to write a note about it.

A few days later I returned to my office from lunch to learn, "A man from XYZ was here to see you."

"Fine. He'll come back," I assured my secretary.

Two days later he did. He was waiting in my office when I came in. On my desk was a gift package of six bottles of XYZ's finest.

"Now will you quit writing letters?" he grinned.

It took months of effort to indoctrinate my Shanghai friends to the Occidental mysteries of the ice bucket. We worked out the ritual with every kind of contraption from dishpan to flowerpots. But one night every waiter in the place gathered around my table giggling gleefully and glowingly as the maître d' presented me with a silvery ice bucket on a tripod stand. "All for you personally, Mr. Baus."

Now they are as well trained as a Prussian regiment, and every time I enter that cherished institution of higher Chinese gastronomy the maître d' grins, "Chenin Blance, of course."

"Of course."

Then the waiter comes up and repeats beamingly, "Chenin Blanc, of course." And in *my* ice bucket, of course.

Whereupon there is again under way another happy marriage of wine and food—the best from two worlds.

Enjoy

Many of the favorite pastimes and hobbies of our time are throwbacks to activities once necessary to life. Our ancestors hunted and fished or they starved; they rode horseback and later bicycles or they stayed home; they sailed or they remained landbound.

Similarly, wine was once a necessity of life instead of polluted water and as a medicine for many purposes in the absence of today's more potent compounds. Nowadays, it is a great pleasure and hobby for people from every walk of life. What our ancestors had to do to solve life's problems, many of us play with today because they're too much fun to miss.

Anything worth doing is worth enjoying. Doing it, you live twice as much if you enjoy it.

There are a lot of distinctions between man and other animals, not all of them happy for man: man can talk, he can write, he can use money, he can bend the elements to his will, plus a hundred others. But the important distinctions, and the ones that justify man's rejoicing that he is a man, are three: man laughs, man makes love for pleasure, and man drinks alcoholic beverages.

Pity a man who does not laugh, for you know he is a man who does not love and does not drink wine.

Sir Alexander Fleming invented penicillin, that landmark of medical advancement which has routed so many of the enemies of mankind. But Sir Alexander kept everything in its true perspective: "Penicillin cures, but wine makes people happy."

What could better be said, and felt, and deliberately sought as we raise our first glass with our friends than: *To health—and happiness. To happiness—and health.*

Bibliography

Adams, Leon D. *The Commonsense Book of Drinking.* New York: David McKay, 1958.

————. *The Commonsense Book of Wine.* New York: David McKay, 1960.

Amerine, Maynard A. "Wine." *Scientific American,* August 1964.

Amerine, M. A. and Joslyn, M. A. *Table Wines: The Technology of Their Production.* Berkeley: University of California Press, 1970.

Amerine, M. A., and Singleton, V. L. *Wine.* Berkeley: University of California Press, 1967.

Anderson, Judith. "A Natural Tranquilizer." *San Francisco Chronicle,* January 4, 1972.

Baccigaluppi, Harry. "Why the Vintners Sponsor Medical Research." *Bulletin of the Society of Medical Friends of Wine,* February 1963.

Barthe, Edouard. "The Food and Medicinal Qualities of Wine." Translated by H. F. Stoll, Jr. *California Grape Grower,* September 1934.

"Beer for the Aged." *Time,* June 29, 1970.

Berland, Theodore. "The Oldest Medicine—Wine." *Science Digest,* August 1968.

Block, Marvin A. "When Does Social Drinking Become Over-Drinking?" *Reader's Digest,* September 1964.

Brandt, Johanna. *The Grape Cure.* 18th ed. New York: Harmony Center, 1953.

Cambiaire, Celestin Pierre. *The Black Horse of the Apocalypse: Wine, Alcohol and Civilization.* Paris: Librairie Universitaire, 1932.

Carbone, John C. "The Wine-Cirrhosis Myth." *Bulletin of The Society of Medical Friends of Wine,* February 1961.

Chafetz, Morris E. *Liquor: The Servant of Man.* Boston: Little, Brown, 1965.

Childs, Alfred W. "Recommending How to Use Wine." *Bulletin of The Society of Medical Friends of Wine,* September 1971.

Chroman, Nathan. "Wine: What Doctor Ordered?" *Los Angeles Times,* May 4, 1972.

de Groot, Roy Andries. "Do People Snigger When You Order the Wine?" *Esquire,* May 1970.

Engler, G. A. "Health Values of Champagne." *Wines and Vines,* November 1941.

Eylaud, Jean-Max. *Vin et sante: vertus hygieniques et therapeutiques du vin* (Wine and Health: Hygienic and Therapeutic Values of Wine). Soissons: La diffusion nouvelle du livre, 1960.

Ferguson, Matthew, and Sister Michael Marie. "Alcohol in Clinical Medicine." *GP,* January 1960.

Fishbein, Morris. "A Doctor Looks at Wine." *Bulletin of The Society of Medical Friends of Wine,* February 1960.

Franz, Arnulf. "Wine Kills Disease-Causing Bacteria." *Wines and Vines,* January 1937.

Goldberg, Leonard. "Wine and Drinking Patterns." *Bulletin of The Society of Medical Friends of Wine,* February 1962.

Goodman, Louis S., and Gilman, Alfred. *The Pharmacological Basis of Therapeutics.* 4th ed. New York: Macmillan, 1970.

Great Book of Wine, The. New York: World Publishing Co., 1970.

Hall, Wesley W. "A Physician's Thoughts on Wine." *Bulletin of The Society of Medical Friends of Wine,* September 1971.

Healy, Maurice. *Stay Me with Flagons.* London: Michael Joseph, 1940.

Hyams, Edward. *Dionysus: A Social History of Wine.* New York: Macmillan, 1965.

Johnson, Hugh. *The World Atlas of Wine.* New York: Simon and Schuster, 1971.

————. *Wine.* New York: Simon and Schuster, 1969.

————. "Wine as an Apéritif." *House and Garden,* September 1968.

Joslyn, Maynard. "Potential Medical Aspects of Wine Research." *Bulletin of The Society of Medical Friends of Wine,* February 1960.

Klatskin, Gerald. "Effect of Alcohol on the Liver." *Journal of the American Medical Association,* August 1, 1959.

Kliewe, Heinrich. *Wein und Gesundheit* (Wine and Health). Neustadt an der Weinstrasse: Verlag D. Maininger, 1971.

Kressman, Edouard. *The Wonder of Wine.* New York: Hastings House, 1968.

Lake, Max. *Vine and Scalpel.* Brisbane, Australia: Jacaranda Press, 1967.

Leake, Chauncey D. "Current Research on Medical Aspects of Wine." *Bulletin of The Society of Medical Friends of Wine,* September 1967.

————. "Refreshing With Wine." *Nursing Homes,* March 1967.

Leake, Chauncey D., and Silverman, Milton. *Alcoholic Beverages in Clinical Medicine*. Chicago: Year Book Medical Publishers, 1966.

———. "The Clinical Use of Wine in Geriatrics." *Geriatrics,* February 1967.

Lichine, Alexis. *Encyclopedia of Wines and Spirits*. New York: Alfred A. Knopf, 1968.

Lolli, Giorgio, and others. "Wine in the Diets of Diabetic Patients." *Quarterly Journal of Studies on Alcohol,* September 1963.

Lucia, Salvatore P. *A History of Wine as Therapy*. Philadelphia: J. B. Lippincott, 1963.

———. *Alcohol and Civilization*. New York: McGraw-Hill, 1963.

———. *Wine and Health*. Menlo Park, Calif.: Pacific Coast Publishers, 1969.

———. *Wine and Your Well-Being*. New York: Popular Library, 1971.

Marchant, Pierre. "Strictly for Serious Wine Drinkers." *Réalités,* October 1971.

Mendelsohn, Oscar A. *The Dictionary of Drink and Drinking*. New York: Hawthorn Books, 1965.

Morgan, Agnes Faye. "Wine in the Normal Diet." *Bulletin of The Society of Medical Friends of Wine,* September 1962.

Nussbaum, Leon. "Is Wine Good Therapy for Heart Disease?" *Journal of the American Medical Association,* October 13, 1963.

Powers, John J. "The Antibiotic Values of Wine Anthocyanins." *Bulletin of The Society of Medical Friends of Wine,* September 1972.

Primer, Charity. "The Red-White Wine Controversy." *California Living,* March 28, 1971.

Richter, Curtis P. "Alcohol, Beer and Wine as Foods." *Quarterly Journal of Studies on Alcohol,* December 1963.

Roueche, Berton. *Alcohol*. New York: Grove Press, 1960.

Sapirstein, Leo A. "The Potential Value of Wine and Alcohol in the Treatment of Incipient and Progressing Strokes in Man." *Bulletin of The Society of Medical Friends of Wine,* February 1966.

Schoonmaker, Frank. *Encyclopedia of Wine*. New York: Hastings House, 1969.

Schwerin, Ron. "On the Drinking Habits of the Very Young." *Esquire,* March 1970.

Silverman, Milton. "The Contribution of Wine to the Prevention of Alcoholism." *Wines and Vines,* January 1961.

Simon, André L. *Wines of the World*. New York: McGraw-Hill, 1969.

Simon, André L., and Hallnoter, S. F. *The Great Wines of Germany*. New York: McGraw-Hill, 1963.

Smith, Walton Hall, and Helwig, Ferdinand C. *Liquor: The Servant of Man.* Garden City, New York: Garden City Publishing Co., 1939.

Stepto, Robert C. "Clinical Uses of Wine." *The New Physician,* January 1968.

————. "Wine, the Healthful Holiday Spirit." *Chicago Medicine,* December 9, 1967.

Stoll, H. F. *Wine Wise.* San Francisco: Crocker, 1933.

"Table Wines." *Consumer Reports,* October 1971.

Torbert, Harold C. *The Complete Wine and Food Cookbook.* Los Angeles: Nash Publishing, 1970.

Waugh, Alec. *In Praise of Wine and Certain Noble Spirits.* New York: William Sloane Associates, 1959.

Westerfield, Wilfred W., and Schuman, Martin P. "Metabolism and Caloric Value of Alcohol." *Journal of the American Medical Association,* May 9, 1959.

"White Table Wines." *Consumer Reports,* November 1971.

"Wine: The Boom That Cheers." *Newsweek,* October 26, 1970.

Younger, William. *Gods, Men and Wine.* New York: World Publishing Co., 1966.